One Journey, Different Pathways
A Scotsman's Life Story

Sean Anthony McFadyen

One Journey, Different Pathways
A Scotsman's Life Story
by Sean Anthony McFadyen

Printed in the United States of America

ISBN 9781613791387

www.xulonpress.com

CONTENTS

INTRODUCTION

Life is one exciting ride and challenging journey! Knowing what lies ahead of us and the end result is the great desideratum, but if it is the opposite, we could panic. One thing we ought to know is that, there will be choices we will make all throughout. And the consequences of our choices could very well determine the complexity or simplicity of our lives.

I've had a burning desire to write this book for so long, but like most excuses in life, it ate me up and said to myself, "Na", a Scottish lingo for NO. Until I realized, the "Na" can be "Aye", which means, YES. Weekends, holidays or even beachside writing is all that I imagined to start this book. But here I am, lying in my room on a rainy and windy ambiance of a little town called Greenock. It is 1:40 a.m. and all I can hear is the raindrops on the bedroom window.

My desire is that, whatever shared in this book will somehow inspire you to face everyday challenges, deal with circumstances, overcome obstacles, face barriers, conquer fears, motivate yourself and others with great faith, strength and hope. Join me as we share this exciting journey together! Open your heart and mind and let your life, dreams, visions, and your desires be challenged and changed. Experience a life changing journey as it travels different pathways leading to a life full of promised hope. A Scotsman's life journey begins.

Chapter 1

DETACHMENT

January 9th, the year 1969 and the scene were at the Rankin Memorial Hospital in my home town of Greenock. This is on the West Coast of Scotland where it is known for its fierce winds and wet days. It is 3 minutes past 3 in the morning and here comes kicking and screaming into this world the cutest, most joyful and excited baby boy called Sean Anthony! (Yes, it's me!) Little Sean was so excited to get into this world that he forced the issue of being born by coming out 6 weeks earlier than scheduled. Yes, I was 6 weeks pre-mature.

This charming little miracle was already causing trouble and he wasn't even born into the world yet! Sean was lying on a nerve in his mother's womb which was causing his mother, Mary, so much pain, and at the same time was causing complications on her health. Due to these conditions, my mother was losing blood every month along with parts of the after birth. So inevitably, I had to come out. Being only 4 pounds due to being pre-mature, I spent the first two weeks of my new life cuddled up inside an incubator. To add on to this, because of the antibodies in my blood, I went through a complete blood transfusion. Here I was, so excited to get into the world and probably in my own wee innocent mind thinking "if I knew this was what it's going to be like, then, I should have stayed where I was".

Growing up as a baby toddler was so eventful; I just couldn't get enough of life. I was into everything, I touched everything, I lifted up what I could, and broke what I could. It was so much fun. The best thing about it was the attention I got, it was brilliant! I was a star. As soon as I moved, touched something, or made a sound, I was looked at by all who were with me (yeah probably saying to each other, "oh no, what will he do now?"). I was enjoying the continuous attention and was amazed why I was the main focus. As I see it now, I am sure the attention I was getting may not have always been because I was cute or innocent, probably quite the opposite. Surely it would have been because they were watching or worrying about what I was going to do, or going to break. If I could only see the expressions on their faces.

I know I was a handful for Mum, like most kids. I believe I was always up to mischief, never staying in one place and being content, always on the move. Mum was amazed at how much energy I had, she said, "I would wake up very early in the morning and sleep very late at night". So I can imagine how tired she must have been.

One thing Mum noticed about me was I loved the sunshine. So she would put me outside in the garden at every opportunity that the sun came out (which wasn't many times). She said it was the only time that I would be still and quiet, it's like I found a special way to find moments of tranquility. So obviously this was a great reprieve for my Mum, I am sure she was hoping the sun came out every day. Troublesome baby could have been everybody's description about me; from out of Mum's womb until I set my foot on the children school, I was literally screaming in fear and shocked seeing lots of kids waiting around with their Dads and Mums. I cannot let go off my Mum, I wanted to go back home and screaming to highest level of my tone. And I was not caring if the other Lads were laughing at me. But now I realized when that incident echoes to my memory when they said, "Stop crying like a baby"! And obviously, that didn't happen just once, it repeated until I found once again that momentum of detachment from Mum and established my trust to the other kids and of course toys that I finally liked going to school! My energy and excitement was all used up at school, that I would come home so tired to even put the food in my mouth then sleep. That gave a big relief to Mum…, for a while because days, months and years are so fast, and the heat is on and I was just starting when I reached seven years old. At this stage of my life, things were starting to heat up. I would start to find lots of ways to annoy and disturb my family. Having an older brother and sister, "This was great", I told myself. Being 'The Wean', as they call a baby in Scotland, was an open door for me to do what I wanted and get away with it. Now I see the resemblance of my school-age to my nephews, Dylan who is 9 years old and Cameron 6 years old. When I visited Scotland during the winter time, I've seen their actions, energy, naughtiness and the things they do, and I found myself smiling thinking that I was exactly doing things like that. I really can't say that when I play with them I wanted attention, but it's just my nature that I wanted to play, all the time.

And in saying this, I remember every detail of Mum's visit to my school, not to see me, but my teachers wants to speak with her due to my playfulness. The teachers started to realize that they had a trouble-maker in their class. I was just so playful and always wanted to enjoy every minute of the day and I would do whatever it takes to get my way. Being very forward in my actions and words never won me favor with my teachers. I would be in trouble quite often and that would always be embarrassing for my parents. I believe I earned the nickname 'Trouble'. The more attention I was getting from the teachers, the more visits my Mum had to make to school. I guess my Mum started to realize she had to get me interested in a subject, topic or hobby of such to keep me amused. So here comes the turnaround, the fabulous sport of Soccer (football as other nations call it)! St. Andrews Primary School was so close to the house, and most of the kids in the area were part of that school. And it had a huge playground for me, that I just don't run in a four corners of our house and classroom to drain my energy but a massive land to run my wee legs off, chasing after a ball, having fun with the other kids and enjoy every minute of it. This was a whole new adventure for me, chasing a ball, running faster than the other boys and the ultimate goal was to put that ball into the large white net. For me, Mum, my family and teachers at school, this was a win-win situation. I was enjoying playing with other lads, running off a lot of my energy, getting out the house, stopping me tearing the house apart, and giving my Mum her much needed rest time. The main objective is being achieved (to play) and at the same time, I love Soccer.

As I look back at those early soccer days, I truly remember running around a soccer pitch in the very cold weather, where the rain was falling down so hard that it would create pools of water on the ground and the ball would actually stop in these pools of water making it more difficult for us to play. Our wee bodies were soaked through; water dripping down our faces, nose running and eyes could hardly see anything. But all we had in our mind is to 'score a goal', put that ball in the net so our team would win. To me, this is what motivated and allowed me to focus on the task ahead and to gain the prize of winning. For some bizarre reason the cold weather was not a hindrance for me. All I saw were bodies running fast, and a large net to put the ball into and hearing everyone cheer for you. It amazes me to think of those times, being a young boy and putting up with harsh weather conditions, and bearing the coldness in achieving something that makes you happy, or just something to be part of that will keep you persistent to the goal. I believe, the determination, mentality, focus and attitude I had when I was a young boy, is the same attitude I have today to allow me achieve my goals and dreams as guided. Somewhere, somehow, lessons in life are learned from the bottom. At the age of eight, I was coached how to kick the ball (and oh, if that fails, ouch to the player) using the different parts of your foot and with various body movements. In doing this, it would allow you to accurately pass the ball to your focus point. Trying to understand all these different aspects of kicking a ball is interesting and the outcome was very challenging and fun. Sometimes I would get frustrated, get annoyed and not listen; after all, I just wanted to put the ball in the net, 'how hard could that be?' We would attend training sessions two nights per week so that we can be coached on passing a ball, taking free kicks, dribbling the ball around obstacles, taking penalty 'spot' kicks, then running up and down the field to build our stamina, strength and speed. And then we just love the end result of it. We never really understood or appreciated the training sessions or how this would play a major part in us either winning or losing the game against our opponents. We just wanted to get on that field and get a hold of that ball, and then we could show everybody what we could do. Well, we got our chance to show what we could do and I tell you the truth, it wasn't very nice to watch. We were just running around like crazy, all of us chasing that wee ball, all wanting to score into the net so we can be a hero. Although our manager and supporters (of which are usually our parents) must have been looking quite miserable at our performance, they must surely have been laughing their heads off at all of us running around in circles after that ball. It obviously was going to be a very long and tiring process for us to learn what we were supposed to do, and how we were to achieve it, but we had all the time in the world; we were only kids.

One of the examples of learning is; David Beckham's passion for soccer. He didn't just wake up and was instantly magnificent. David started out like every other kid in every sport, and he started with a desire, to be a soccer star. He still had to go through the preparation stages of being coached, he still had to attend weekly practice sessions; he had to be taught the theory and knowledge to understand why things happen or may not. The how, what, where and when are pretty much the ingredients on how to utilize the main goal of scoring. Same thing with the famous basketball player, Kobe Bryant, who didn't just walk onto a basketball court and immediately be known as a star. He went through a similar process, disciplines and lots of hard works to get where he is today just like every other sports athlete. This is the small sacrifices we must go through in order to progress to the next stage of becoming a better athlete no matter what sports we are in. We won't get better or progress any further if we don't put time, effort, practice and prepare in learning and gaining more experiences. As we mature, we will certainly see a difference on our overall performance. Even at young age, when I was learning the basics of soccer, I never thought at that time, how beneficial it would be for me in the years to come. I was taught, coached, tried and tested on the field that brought momentum peace to my family and people around me, but it also brought much beneficial lessons for me to be a consistent, mature, stronger and successful player (although never be like David). Each individual has a part to play, that even we were educated about the soccer techniques as a team; a player has a special role to contribute for a better end result. In other words, kicking the ball to the opponent's net; get all your team activated leads to a score. And that's when everybody grasped the meaning of teamwork, where you include others in what you do, teach them what you know and learn every single thing you can from everybody for a visible growth of maturity and humility. After going through such a positive and very effective area of my young life, the negative side can't be boxed in. I was not always the good, wee cute innocent child that others may have perceived. There were times where I never had things I wanted and no matter what, I go out my way to have it. This often resulted in doing things the wrong way in order to get what I want, the one I crave, (at that time of my age)......CHOCOLATES!

Being me, who was very much into eating candy and sweet stuffs, like chocolates, I started craving for more, more and more chocolate every single day. I would get some chocolates here and there from my parents and even from my brother and sister. Christmas is the best time for us because we would always get stocking fillers which were usually just full of candies and chocolate bars, or even better, we would get what we call, 'A Selection Box', full of all our favorites (Mars, Snickers, M & M, Crunchies, Bounty or Milky Ways, to mention a few). These were crazy times because I, my brother and sister would always fight over each other's chocolates, accusing each other of getting more. But unfortunately because of my greed and selfishness, especially for chocolates, I would go one step further. I would wait till my brother or sister were out, or down stairs and I would go up to their rooms and search for their 'selection boxes' and steal their chocolates. I thought it was fun as it was only sweets, little did I know, it would lead up to something more. It was funny, I used to eat their Chocó bars and put the wrappers back in the boxes as if nothing was touched. I thought it was a foul proof plan. Until it all went wrong once they opened the boxes and found empty wrappers, heehaw! My thoughts brought me back to my soccer days, I knew then that exerting all my energy has a price to pay (come on, my legs are still good!), and yes, it is the energy booster, Chocolates! It was a crazy craving; oftentimes lead me to question myself, "How do I get the chocolates?" Too many times my wee sticky fingers were used in ways they shouldn't, be used for the wrong purpose. This was especially true when going to school in the mornings. All I saw in front of my wee lit up eyes was, sweets, sweets, and more sweets. We used to go past the local confectionery or candy store (of which in most cases are positioned there for school kids to buy) in which was loaded out with all sorts of candies, chocolates and sweets that we always wanted. Because we were normally with parents or someone was dropping us off in the morning, we never really got anything. The fun begins once school's finished. After school, we would try to wait for whoever will pick us up to get us at the convenient store. This was a perfect spot for parents because it was a safe place for us to wait, as there were also other kids and adults around. This scenario is best for everybody; our parents knew we are in a safe place; teachers could leave because we were off the school grounds, and the happiest person on those moments is the grocery store man. But for me, a different perspective was twirling on my mind. Chocolates cost money! Well, I didn't have any money and was looking at the displayed candies and chocolates, thinking they want me to eat them. It was a situation, where I want to have them but I can't, I don't have money and my Mum will definitely not buy it because it makes me hyper-active. But it's seems like, a wee voice in my mind saying that it's ok to get some, free of charge. So after days and weeks, of being in that situation, wanting something but no means to pay it, I finally gave in to the temptation of taking the candy without asking anyone or paying for it. Yes, I would start stealing candy from the store. I would look around to make sure no one was watching me, considering there were so many kids in the store, it should be easy. So when I thought everything was clear I would pick up a piece of candy and put it in my pocket very discreetly. Wow! I did it! I can't tell exactly what my feelings were; all I know is that, I got a wee sweet! I was thinking I was so cool, getting candy and not having to pay for it. I felt as if I was a king, just picking something that I want without a cost added to it. Well that was the beginning! I was soon carrying this action of stealing; at every opportunity I could, that it became a regular activity for me. However, taking one piece of candy was like too easy, I wanted more but it may have shown in my pocket, so I changed my tactics instead. For more sweeties, I used my school bag. Here I am becoming a very sneaky thief. What I didn't realize was I was feeding greed, a desire that could eventually get me into big trouble. At the same time I never thought of how it affected the shop owner, a loss of sales, or if it would have any impact on his business. After all it was only once a day and only a few pieces of candies, but then came Saturday. This was my favorite Saturday, a swimming day. We used to go to the local swimming baths every Saturday morning, but before we go, I would pay a visit to my favorite 'grocery store'. Yep, you guessed it! My habit would continue even out of school days.

The situation was different on a Saturday, as I never had a school bag to hide the candies. All I had was a white plastic bag that was holding my towel and swimming trunks. That didn't stop me! I would look around and check where the owner was. This was early morning, the store was quiet and the owner was always at the back preparing his meat section. I couldn't believe how easy this was, I was just filling my plastic bag with whatever I wanted. But I knew there was a large mirror where he may have seen me standing at the candy area, so I thought I would buy something really cheap to pretend, nothing happened. This seemed to work all the time and I never get caught because we moved house (just for the record, my parents never knew this...until they read this book). Again, I never ever thought about the consequences if I ever get caught or even thought about the effect to the shop owners. A lesson that can be learned from this, (in which I have not acknowledged before) is, my selfish actions created a negative effect on myself and on others. While the owner of the shop was losing out on sales revenue, I would have been in serious trouble, putting my family in such a mess called, embarrassment! Although this should have been my thoughts, it never was. I was a kid, and loved the excitement of doing something knowing it was wrong but at the same time it was all about me, what I want and what I need to do to get it. I was a young boy who wanted to try things, especially in a mischievous way.

I remember I had to wear spectacles due to having one eye that seemed to wander now and again. Normally, it happens when I get tired, that my eye would suddenly be so close to the other eye (wondering if eyes also greet each other!). I believe it's called, 'Lazy Eye' or 'Amblyopic', (not really suitable for a boy who was never lazy, to do troubles). Anyways, because of this wandering eye, my parents decided that I should start wearing glasses. Knowing that our family was not financially well off, I had to get the glasses offered by our local council (authorities) at no cost. This was a great help to my parents as it was not easy raising three kids in those days and even up to this day I guess. As a result, I went for my eye examination and I was presented with these glasses, of which were called 'National Health' glasses. They have no brand names unlike Oakley, Ray-ban & Armani or other popular brands. Nope! These were the basic of basics. I must admit, this was one of the most embarrassing moments of my life, and the hopeless case was, the glasses never even came with a choice of colors. I got what was provided. So here I am, waiting in anticipation to open the glass case and see what was inside. And guess what? I opened the case, and a huge frame, blue color (yes, blue!) eyeglasses that without a doubt can cover my whole face is staring at me. I really cried and told my Mum I am not wearing those things. And I said, "It's ugly, and everybody will laugh at me in school." So without hesitation I went into ('cream puff' a huff,) a bad mood. I repeatedly told my Mum that there's no way I will wear those specs, and many times too that she responded, "Oh yes, you are". So, being the cheeky, stubborn wee actor, I would stand there and argue with her, thinking I will win the fight. But I was wrong. Never satisfied, I tried blackmailing Mum with this statement, "If you make me wear those ugly glasses, I'm not going to school". My Mum will give in to this, I thought. She played along with my threat and said, "Okay then son, you don't need to go to school, you can stay in the house and help me clean up, do the washing, vacuum the floors, clean the windows, then you can put your pajamas on after dinner and then go straight to your bed". In short, she didn't give in to my thinking. So that shocked me. There was no way I wanted to get involved in all that cleaning stuff, and not having the chance to get out to play. So I obviously disagreed with that idea and started telling my mum (not asking her) that I am going out to play. My mum laughed and said, "That's what you think young boy. You're going nowhere but to your room." So after crying for about an hour, hoping my Mum will have pity on me, (I normally get my own way with this…but not this time), I gave in. I agreed to wear the glasses to school. Man, this was one of the most depressing times of my life. I was so unhappy having to put these big blue 'Elton John' (a very popular musician) specs on my face! Anyway, here I go, put them on and headed to school, holding my head down towards the ground so that no one will recognize me and hopefully gets no verbal abuse. Yeah right! (I would have been better standing on top of the school roof and shout, "Hey everyone, look at my new specs."). Everyone noticed them right away and then all the 'Names' started, "hey wee specks", "heehaw four eyes". Some kids would say, "Hey Squint Eastwood" (Since I was definitely not Mr. Clint, the famous western actor).

So after going through the first day of humiliation, on the way home, I saw the ground drain near our house which the rain water flows into and disappears underground, there came up the great idea. "Hmmm, I'll just throw them down the drain and that will be the end of these laughs", I murmured. I was still thinking how I will hide my specs because they are so huge, but, let me do my plan first. So I did it and ran into the house and told my mum I lost them. She looked and me and probably thinking, 'he broke them, lost them intentionally, or sold them'!! Anyway, to my surprise, my Mum said, "It's ok son, maybe someone will hand them into the school, we will wait and see". Wow! My plan worked. I was amazed, I got away with it. Yippee! I don't have to get laughed at again and I can still go out to play after school. (Man if you could only see the smile on my face at that point).

Being a kid was great! You get away with doing so many things. I loved being young and spoiled, so much spoiled to my horror, that after four to six weeks and due to my parents love and care for me they decided to apply for a new pair of eyeglasses. With much dismay, I was sitting in front of my Mum and there she presents to me another pair of specs. Well, I wanted to just crawl under the carpet and hide. The smile was just wiped off my face. Man my wee world just fell apart right there and then. My mum explained, "Son, we thought you would have been upset because no one found your glasses, so we ordered a new pair for you. It will help your eyes in the long run." (Yeh right Mum!). I was a hard-headed boy, but what to do? Same 'names', same kids, same school where I was laughed at, but different eyewear...this time, a black, huge double-glazing glass in my wee 'squinty eyes'. So I needed a plan that will work like how I did before. If I keep throwing the eyeglasses down the drainage, what I was thinking was, my parents will be fed up and give up! So plan number two in action! Here I come back from school, find the road drain, and threw my glasses down it. Yep! All smiles as I ran into the house and shouted, "Mum, Dad, I lost my glasses, they're gone". So when asked what happened, I had a wee story ready for them. So here I go. "Well Mum, Dad, I was just walking up the hill towards the house and I was just looking on the ground, and I thought I saw a coin (money) lying beside the drain. So I went closer and then knelt down over the drain to pick the coin up and then my glasses suddenly fell off my face. I did try to catch them Mum, but I was too slow, they fell down and now they're gone." I know what was going on their minds, their wee thoughts would have been, ("How does he managed to come up with these stories? He must be reading books to get these ideas or something, because this is a great story!") So I was thinking, 'ha ha, beat that, my wee specs are gone and you can't do anything about it'. How could I be wrong on my thoughts? I was shocked and amazed, my Dad turns to me and said, "Ok son, it is ok. Just show me where you lost them". I said, "Dad, they're gone, there down the drain; you can't get them!" With eager anger in his voice, he said, "Show me son." "Ok," I replied.

We went out and there both of us standing at the drain, I said, "Down there dad, they fell down there." "Alright son, just you stand back, I will try to get them." I am thinking, 'Yeah right, who do you think you are, 'Superman?' There's no way you can lift up that drain.' My eyes nearly popped out, as I try watching Andy 'Superman' Mc Fadyen, bending over and lifting up the metal drain and putting it to the side. After being gob-smacked by that heroic effort, I am still thinking, 'yeah you got it opened, but the specs are away at the bottom and they will be under the water'. He won't see them. "Hey son, look, your glasses is lying at the bottom."(I looked at my Dad to see if he transformed into Superman). I said, "Dad, how can you see them with all the water?" "No son, there is no water; it hasn't been raining the last few days, so I think I can get them," he informed me. Oh no, my wee plan is failing and it's making me scared, so I quickly responded, I said, "Dad, don't go down there it may be dangerous, you might get hurt, (being the wee considerate and compassionate child I was,:)) just leave them, they're broken anyway." My Dad carried on, and man, the sweat was pouring down my back thinking 'what if he gets them and they're ok'. So here he comes, pops his head up out the drain then pushes himself out the hole with a pair of black superman specs, saying, "Look son, I got them, and they're not broken, they look fine." Well at that point I wanted to throw myself down that drain. My dad saw that I was not jumping up and down with excitement after retrieving my glasses, so he said, "Why are you not happy, I found them son." So I started to cry and told him I didn't want to wear them. That changed his face. "Why not son?" he asked. So I told him how I was being laughed at in school, other boys is calling me names that it is hurting and embarrassing for me. So he then got thinking! Then he asked me, "Son, did the glasses really fall off your face and go down the drain, or did you throw them down?" So of course I am going to say they fell down, and cry, hoping for the sympathy vote from him. But it never seemed to fly with him, as he kept asking me and saying, "Now, don't tell lies, you know what happens to boys who tell lies, Santa Claus don't give them presents".

Man, I cried even more (not as part of my plan), but I know I'm now in big trouble and was terrified of the consequences. Believe me; I was so afraid of my Dad. He only needed to look at you and you would pee on your pants. So he just asked me, "tell me the truth son and we will forget about it." Well, after hearing that I thought, this is my chance to get out without being punished, (get out of jail free card). So I took the courage, I stood up and I told him that I threw them down the drain so I wouldn't have to wear them to school and get laughed at. Man, it worked! Dad let me off with no punishment. What a feeling of freedom from pain. Yippee!

My brother Drew and sister Pauline couldn't believe it! They were saying, "Only you would get away with that, if that was us, we would be grounded for a month, you're so spoiled!" I was laughing. I was so happy thinking I was the right wee con artist, thinking I could get away with anything. I was on top of every plan, of every move, but not until I push it a little further. After my Dad's letting me off the hook and warning me not to do it again, and not tell lies, I was not contented of being quiet and a good boy in a corner. I sought after more adventure and disobedience. So I repeatedly threw the eyeglasses down the drain a few more times and always getting away without a punishment until dad had enough. He put a stop to it, and started punishing me by grounding me inside the house and not letting me out to play after school. Well that drove me crazy. I hated staying in the house. I needed to get out and play. I had so much energy to be locked in the house, I needed the outside environment! I would stand by the window and cry so I can play. I would watch my friends playing and it would hurt me so bad not being out there with them. But that was my punishment, that was how my parents would get me to behave...to be grounded. The days of being grounded would start from one night to eventually seven nights. And, believe me, in a house for seven nights without playtime? I was banging my head off the walls. So through a short span of time I would give in and be obedient and wear the glasses (sometimes) but stopped throwing them down the drain. But a rule was established by my parents, that, whenever I get naughty, cause trouble, get into mischief, then there will be punishment that they can apply that will surely make me think twice about committing the same action again, and it worked. I regretted doing things wrong because of the valuable time I lost being grounded and not spending it outside with my friends.

Chapter 2

A HANDFUL

Too many lonely nights that tears flowed down my cheeks, hoping for comforting words and sympathy cuddles, a feeling, similar when you win the favor of your parents, and get your own way. But unlike the previous years, it's not easy to get everything you want now and expect parents to tolerate it with a cuddle. I now realized that the cute little face and teardrop eyes were only getting me so far, so my plans weren't really being fruitful anymore. Being halfway through my elementary years, I was obviously growing up, but maturity seems to fall behind. The once adorable, innocent, young and cute baby boy was starting a new adventure. I needed more actions in my nights out with friends, considering I was ten years old. Of course we would take part in the children games with all the other kids. We would play 'rounder's', a game similar to baseball in the United States. We make our 1st, 2nd, 3rd, and 4th inning, (target points), where you hit the ball and run to the first post. If you hit a good shot, then you keep running to try to make the home run. The only difference for us in Scotland was that instead of using normal baseball bat, we would use a 'tennis racquet'. Maybe that is why British are no good at baseball and America is super champs. As a matter of fact, we're not much better at tennis either. Anyway, we had lots of fun. Yes, we played our favorite game, 'soccer' or known as football. We would play soccer anywhere we could, on the street, in a playground, car park, behind or in front of people's houses, in a field; anywhere we could kick a ball. We would play for hours, and hours. Most times, one of my parents would have to come looking for us, late at night. And of course, I would get a lecture for not coming in on time.

My parents were so strict, so protective of us. Man, they wanted me to be in the house by 6 pm, which was rubbish, because we barely started that time. The times I come home late was building up (10mins, 15mins, 20 minutes), which for me is brilliant as it gives me ample playtimes. So in the long run, I was allowed to play out until seven pm and the best time I can negotiate with my parents is up to nine o'clock in the evening. Another wee devious plan started to kick into action. But again, my brother Drew and sister Pauline always got annoyed with me because I was a brat and always address the situation with Mum and Dad, as they were never allowed to stay out at that time, (well, if you are the cutest, what can I say). The best time was during the summer months of June, July, and August. These were the months (but very seldom) to have a nice sunny weather. Also, we break off school for the holidays in June. We all enjoyed not going to school for seven weeks, and I can tell you, it was pure brilliant! We had done so many things during those seven weeks. We would go play crazy golf (a children's mini golf course) with many different hills and obstacles to get over and go through, which makes it difficult to put the golf ball in the holes. It was very funny playing it because; the course was so hard and challenging. I know I used to lose my temper when I missed the holes and my friends got it in. I am sure these were the early signs of becoming a very competitive young man, that everything I played I wanted to win. Also at the same time, not realizing I would become a very bad loser. I used to hit the ground with the golf stick and sometimes throw it away in anger. Could you imagine that this innocent young cutie had a temper of a mad man? Yep! That was me! The worst part about it was not just when I play crazy golf, but everything I played (all sports, all games, all gestures) I always wanted to win; always wanted things to go my way; as I planned.

So we continued through those summer nights playing our games of soccer, tennis, rounders and swimming. Yeah, we even went to the swimming baths (as we call it). There was a huge indoor pool which also included a children's pool and cafeteria (that was cool dude!) and the large pool, where I was not allowed until I get a badge. We always played around the kid's pool as we couldn't really swim well and we were scared to jump in the big pool. We used to run and jump in the kid's area and splash all the water at whoever was in the pool. And yes, we ran towards where people were, so we can intentionally splash them with water (it was so funny). We got use of listening to other parents shouting at us because we were splashing their kids and their kids would start crying. That would make our day when we upset other kids and see them cry. We really would be little terrors to other kids. After a while, I started lessons to learn swimming of which was taught to us by our teacher in school. It was so funny paddling around with the rubber arm bands and practically going nowhere. I believe it was called, doing the 'doggy paddle'. If you can imagine how dogs get their way across water with their wee front legs paddling and slashing away? Well I was the same; wasting a lot of breath and energy and getting nowhere. But we had a goal! Our teacher was training us towards receiving a certificate if we swam across the breadth of the pool. Man, when I look at it now, it seems like it's nothing to swim across the pool from one side to the other to receive a certificate.

But when you are small, skinny child at age nine! It is a terrifying experience! I clearly remember jumping on one side and looking at my teacher calling my name and encouraging me to paddle and kick my legs and I was thinking, I am going nowhere here. It was like, I was swimming against waves, and I wasn't moving. The worst part about this test was it is a timed activity, in other words you had only a certain time to get across to the other side of the pool. Well of course, swimming was not one of my strongest points at this age, so I failed quite a few times, and after swallowing about a bucket of water I gave up. I got out of the water and as usual went into a wee bad temper, took off my rubber rings and threw them on the ground and sat in a corner, sulking, just wanting to punch the ones who passed. Well, teachers being teachers, I was soon put in my place. I was shouted at for having such bad behavior and also not showing good conduct towards the other kids in the class. Anyway, after consistent training and perseverance on my part, I managed to pass the test. Then the rubber band came off and I thought I was 'Duncan Goodyear', a famous British swimmer or like 'Michael Phelps', the superman of swimming from America. I just ran and jumped in the shallow end of the big pool which was around 4 feet in depth, and I didn't even touch the bottom (oh, what I have just done?). Did I get the fright of my life? I was paddling like crazy, like there was no tomorrow trying to get my head out of the water and stay afloat. Once my head was out of the water I grabbed onto the ledge inside the pool and would not let go. I cried and cried and would not release my grasp of that ledge. When the teacher came over, he was telling me that it's ok, it happens to all of us. I wasn't even listening; I was on another planet at that time. I was holding on for my life. After staying like that for around ten to fifteen minutes, my teacher managed to persuade me to let go. He came in and guided my hands off and let me get my confidence built back up again. Once that was achieved he would tell me, "Now Sean, I am going to let you try on your own, if that's ok" "Yeah right! What was he thinking", I murmured to myself. Of course I said, "No sir, please don't let go". Again he replied, "It will be ok, are you ready Sean?" "No sir," I sobbed, "No sir."

So what did my teacher do? He let my hands go. Well, I cried and cried and never felt so alone and forgotten, I was scared stiff, I panicked and just reached over to the ledge again and I stayed there. Inside, he must have wanted to laugh his head off, but he again assisted me and held my hands until I was comfortable, half away across, he just let go. I knew what he did and just accepted it. But my eyes never blinked, they were completely focused on every move I have learned in swimming and lo and behold, I made it across. Whew! My teacher was amazing. His name was Mr. Jimmy Stinson; he was a great Physical Ed teacher. He persisted in training and teaching us kids to succeed like what I did in swimming. I managed to swim across on my own and got my ASA (Athletic Swimming Association) badge. This badge was very important, as it allowed your access to the large pool. It had to be sown onto your swimming trunks to let other pool attendants know that you are qualified to be in that pool. Until this day, I might not be a very good or strong swimmer; I still thank Mr. Stinson for his perseverance in teaching the kids (and not walking away and giving up on us) to try our best towards excellence and overcoming fears. Thank you, Sir.

When I look at those times when I was in a secure place with teachers or older people, I believe that would have been my Mum and Dads' comforting thoughts that I was being looked after. I am sure my parents would have loved me to stay in school day and night. Even in school I could be a little trouble maker. I remember the most embarrassing moment I ever went through. I was still in elementary around fifth grade and I was in class and as usual, went into my usual daydreaming mode. I always tried to get a seat in class at the window so I can just stare out and see what is going on. My mom kept telling me I was a nosy wee boy that I always wanted to know everything that was going on; always sticking my nose where it didn't belong. When I looked out the window, I always saw myself out there doing something, being out in open mingling with others, wanting to achieve all things I see. And I really don't like when my daydreaming would be broken by my teacher calling my name. On this, the other kids would laugh at me because I was getting into trouble for not paying attention. So many times this would happen and the teacher would tell me that if I continued to do this, she would put me at the front of the class and sit me on a corner chair facing the wall.

Being hard on rules, I didn't believe her; so as always, I put people to the test. I called her bluff and yep, she kept the rules. I was taken by the ear and put on a chair in the corner facing a wall. Well, I was really shocked that she did this and I was so embarrassed to all my classmates. Being wee naughty, I got used to the laughs and remarks being made at me after a while. So I tried turning it back on the teacher. I would slowly turn my head around to see what the teacher was doing. Once I monitored her actions, and when she faced the class giving those instructions, etc., I would turn to class and wave at them, just to get their attention. Obviously, they would be terrified to look at me as it may get them in trouble if they were caught. Knowing this, I would always try to distract them so the teacher would get annoyed with them, and give them trouble too. Once I got attention from a couple of them, I would get brave and start making wee funny faces to make them laugh. In doing this I needed to keep an eye on the teacher as well so I don't get caught. This was great fun to me, so after continuous weeks and months of me being put in the corner, I would always try to distract the other kids; it was working well due to the fact that the teacher couldn't see me as there was a large 'writing board' that she would use for the studies and it was covering me.

So this was my camouflage in not getting caught. I formed an alliance with a couple of kids, so that when I was joking, they would give me a signal if the teacher would be turning around. They would bang a desk or cough or make silly noise to let me be aware. So over the months, we were having fun in that class. We never really learned much, but had a great time. As young ones, we think we know everything to outsmart our elders or peers. I guess that is why they call teachers, 'Teachers', because they know what to teach and how to teach it. But I didn't care about that, nope! I was much more confident now that I have attention of a few in the class and think I am some sort of hero. I continued to pursue my wee comedy acts in the class. Like all things in life, if you continue down a path of disobedience or lawlessness there will eventually be consequences.

My time came! My teacher was not stupid not to know what I was doing all those times. She knew I would kid on I was facing the wall when she has to check on me and do my 'actions' if her eyes are out of my gaze. And this time, she worked her way across the blackboard to the end that I couldn't see her. What she did, she quickly popped her head round and caught me! She screamed my name and I almost had a kitten. I jumped off my chair with a cold sweat feeling; the laughter suddenly dropped from my wee cute face and there was now a look of fear. The teacher grabbed me by the neck and marched me right down to the principal's office and made me sit there until he was ready to see me. "Oh man", I thought, "the world had come to an end". The longer I waited, the more frightened I became. I was shaking in my shoes; I was scared stiff wondering what was going to happen to me. This was it; the time of punishment had come. Judgment day was upon me. Then it happened, the door opened and I was led into the principal's room. I was never so terrified to face someone as I was at that moment.

I was thinking the worse. Will he shout at me, will he suspend me, will he tell my parents, will I get detention, will I get homework to do? Here I am, face to face with the head master of the school. And when I was looking at him, as if, I never saw an angry man.

I saw a calm little bald headed man who smiled at me and said, "So you are Sean". "Yes sir", I replied. He said, "I have heard a few stories about you Sean, and what I expected to see was a big angry lad with a very bad attitude. But for someone who can disrupt a class like you, so small and innocent looking; I am shocked and confused!" And he continued, "Would you like to tell me what is going on in the classroom?" I said, "No sir." So after a few minutes he asked the ultimate question, "Would you like me to call your parents and see what they have to say?" Oh man, my heart started pumping hard, and I was thinking if they hear about this, then I am dead, I will be grounded for a month. So immediately I said, "No sir, please don't tell them!" So obviously this was his ace card against me! So he said, "That means I won't see you in this office again"? "No sir," I replied. And because it was recess, I took off from his office as fast as I could to the playground. All the class was asking what happened. "Did you get the strap?" they asked. The 'strap' was the kind of punishment in my days. It was a leather belt with one solid end and on the other end be three or four single straps.

The teacher holds the single ends and then whacks the solid end in your hand that is stretched out in front of them. I still carried out some little distractions in class, but mostly I went back into my daydreaming mode. However, there was one time when I was really laughed at. As always, I would do things to distract the teacher and the class, in order to get out. I would always say I needed the toilet, so I kept asking to go to the restroom. The teachers always say, "Ok. Quickly, and hurry back." But as it was becoming a routine, they suddenly caught my wee game. So then, the teachers started refusing my request, and obviously I did nothing to object, as I knew I was just messing around. Well, one normal day, I needed to go pee for the second time after intervals. But the teacher refused because she thought I was fooling around again. But this time I really needed to go, so I kept raising my hand and asking. Every time I was refused, my pee is building up and I needed to hold my pee-pee in. Then I said, "Miss, I really need to go or I will pee my pants." So she obviously thought I was playing and still said no. I pleaded and pleaded to be let out and I was denied. So I told her that I am going to pee my pants in which she didn't believe me. So I did it! I just let it out and a large wet area appeared on the floor and everyone was laughing and I told her that I done it.

Well, she raced towards me so angry and took me by the hand and put me inside the cupboard store room and left me until class was over. Wow, I was in so much trouble! My teacher was angry, and she then made me pay for what I did in her class. So as my pants were all wet, she made me take them off, I had no idea what I would wear for the rest of the day. She had other plans. She made me wear red stockings and pulled my shirt over them to cover my bottom half. Here I am, ready to walk out to the school, wearing those stockings and no pants. I was completely and utterly embarrassed. I was the laughing stock of the school. Man, I was so angry and upset with the teacher. So then she told me she was taking me home and I wasn't to return to school for that day. I knew I would be in big trouble with my parents, another issue to ground me.

So here I am, going to be punished by my parents and I am a complete laughing stock of the school and it's all because I was not allowed to go to the restroom (that I deserve). Once I got my head around the situation, I got thinking! "Since I will be punished anyway, then what can I do to get back at my teacher for humiliating me in front of the school?" I whispered to myself, "Teacher, here I come", it's payback time! Revenge is sweet! I knew the teacher could drive right to my parent's front house door, but then, I knew my aunt stays across from us and it usually means, if you walk from their house to our house, you have to cross over a piece of grass ground. So this in my wee brain, and considering it was raining; the verdict: grass ground will be wet and muddy (you got it right!), I decided to have the teacher stop at my aunt's house and explained, there is only one way across to my house and that's by crossing the grass area. Yippee! My plan is in place. So we are walking over the muddy, wet grass and our feet are sinking in the ground, I saw the teacher, so angry looking and was complaining that her shoes and pants were getting dirty.

Man, this was great! I was so happy holding her and jumping up and down so that I can splash her more with the mud and water. She was so furious and wanted to strangle me if she could. Well, I was so pleased with myself in achieving my wee plan. As we got to the house, my Mum opened the door and was astonished and angry to see me in those red stockings and she asked the teacher for an explanation. My teacher was so serious explaining what I have done and the reason of her punishment to me. She was so proud in her stories, thinking I would be punished severely by my parents. I was just standing there with a huge smile on my face knowing I just got revenge in a sweet way. My mum looked at me, looked at my stocking then at my teachers' shoes and pants. My Mum knew at once that I dragged my teacher through all that muddy ground. And to my surprise, Mum laughed in front of the teacher. My teacher could not believe what she was witnessing. My mum finished the conversation with the teacher and she said that she will address this situation with me inside the house. So my teacher went away. I went inside the house and my family started to laugh their heads off because they knew I made my teacher walk through that mud ground just to get back at her. I was so relieved my Mum was on my side. This always seemed to be the case; I was noticing that no matter what I've done, my Mum would always take my side. I guess that's what happens when you're the baby of the family. I certainly wasn't complaining.

There were many moments like these scenarios I have mentioned, where I just did the wrong things to people. I remember when my Mum used to take me to the town center and used the local bus service of which I loved, I got to run up and down the aisle of the bus just annoying everybody. Being nosy, I would ask people where are they going and why. My mum was so embarrassed and always had to come and pull me away from them and try and make me sit down. She knew I was not going to keep still, I always heard people saying to my Mum, "Mary, why don't you leave Sean at home, he is a handful". And my Mum would always say, "He won't stay in the house, he wants to go out." Remember, I was the small, innocent little boy (according to the headmaster of the school). You're right! So I was picking up on these conversations that my

Mum was having on the bus and starting my little game plan. My mum would always let me go before her, so she knew I am ok. So then, all the people would see me coming and their laughter would suddenly change to sadness. That was the effect I had on them, I wonder why? Anyways, knowing this, I said to my Mum, "Mum you go on first, I am right behind you," So when the people on the bus (these people were our neighbors and usually friends of the family for many years) never saw me running before my Mum, they were so happy.

They said, "Oh Mary, Sean is not with you today!" with very big smiles on their faces and sighs of relief. Honestly, they were so joyful of the thought I was not on that bus. Then out of nowhere, here comes Mr. Energy, I bounced on that bus and ran up the center like I was in a race. Man, you could hear a pin drop on that bus. It all went silent with fear and shock once they saw me. Oh, I was so excited and you could see the little bad mind in my face. I am sure my face displayed a message to them ("Ha ha, fooled you all, thinking I wasn't coming eh!"). So they all looked at my Mum and asked, "Why didn't you tell us Sean was with you?" My mum replied, "What do you want me to do. Let him stay at home alone, with no one to watch him?" Moments like these suited me, I was in my element here, I was doing what I wanted to do, and at the same time, ready to annoy others.

Another time was when we went to church. My Mum always warned me to be on my best behavior when we are inside the church. As you may be aware, church is a holy place of worship, a service, where people come together in the presence of God. Obviously, I was normally quiet and did what my Mum requested as I know we would get into trouble with the church staffs. It was so difficult to be in my seat, as I always wanted to move around, I couldn't really sit on one spot for a long period of time. Church usually lasted about 1½ hours and to me, that was so long. So inevitably, I couldn't just sit as told. I had to see what was going on at the front view. I would always see people walking down the front every week and then be given something by the priest then go back to their seats. I never really thought or knew much about what they were doing and what is being given. So, after periods of time watching all that was going on, and also seeing my brother and sister doing the same thing, I started getting nosy. So I jumped up on the seat to get a better view of things. On this, my Mum would grab me by the arm and tell me to get down. But I had other ideas.

One thing I noticed was that, when the people were walking back to their seats, their mouths were moving. So I thought the Priest was giving out sweeties, or some type of candy and I was missing it. So I started to get agitated that I wasn't getting my share. I was asking my Mum to let me go to the front to get some sweeties from the Priest. My mum assured me that it wasn't sweeties and that I am too young to go to the front. Well, that was like showing a red flag to a bull. I was up and down on that seat, trying to find a way of getting down there to have one of those sweets. Well, my breakthrough had come, I saw my sister down at the front and she was heading in the direction of the Priest, so I thought my Mum will let me go if Pauline is there as she can watch me and take care of me. So I immediately asked her, "Mum, can I go down? Pauline is there, look, I can see her. She will watch me." My mum replied, "No Sean, just stay here. Pauline will be back in a minute." I persisted and asked again and again, but my Mum point blank, refused and told me to sit down.

Well, this was not going good for me and I wasn't accepting my Mum's decision. So I stood up on the church seat (bench) and I shouted, "Pauline, get me one of those sweeties." My mum jumped at me, grabbed and held me down on that seat. She was so embarrassed and told me to sit down and be quiet. She said, "You wait till you get home, I will tell your father what you did." Although I knew I was in big trouble, all I was thinking about was my desire getting one of those sweeties. So I know that the Priest often visited our elementary school as I have seen him a few times in school. So one day my Mum was at our school picking me up and all of a sudden we came across the Priest. In those days I struggled with my words, I could not pronounce the letter 'F' and I was replacing it with the letter 'D'. Also I sometimes would let slip a few swear words now and again of which would earn me a slap on the backside and a grounding period of at least one week. So when we were stopped in front of the Priest, he greeted my Mum. Then the priest turned to me and said, "So young boy, what is your name?" I never replied back until my Mum told me to. She said, "Sean, answer Father such and such." So I did. I replied, "Me not 'ducking' speaking to you, you never gave me one of those 'ducking' sweeties on Sunday." My Mum would have loved the ground to open up and swallow her at that moment. She was so embarrassed and totally shocked. She had to apologize very quickly to the Priest and innocently explained that I have a problem pronouncing my 'F' and that is why I said 'ducking sweeties'. I tell you, as I look back, I can laugh at the sense of humor of our Priest. He replied, "Well Mrs. Mc Fadyen, it is just as well that Sean cannot pronounce his letter F", isn't it?" He was shocked but laughing and said to me, "Ok Sean, I will see you in church on Sunday." My mum whispered to me, "Don't say a word, just smile." So I did. But in my mind I was saying, "Yeh right, that's what you wish. You think I am just going to sit in that church and watch you give everyone else' sweeties and not me! No chance wee man!"

You see, when we look back at those moments where we did wrong things, didn't do what we were told and did what we wanted to do, there is always a time when it will come bouncing back to us and it usually comes with a bad result or consequence. As for me, I seemed to just go from bad to worse. I believe a lot of my active moments led me do such things because I was bored, wanted to always be doing something and got fed up very easily. I think, Mum soon realized that I couldn't sit on my backside for one minute as I always had to be moving around, or being involved in something. So to me, the experiences in my early age are one of the many lessons in life. You see, I got into mischief when I was not involved in anything or kept busy. So my mind starts allowing negative thoughts and actions, then that's when my problem starts.

As I've experienced it, find time to occupy your mind with good things and you will certainly be addressing situations in a more positive manner. Even at the young tender ages of childhood, your mind is so powerful even if it's still developing. Psychologists say that, tests over decades of experiments show that a child learns everything he needs between the ages of 5-11 years. So can you imagine the power of the brain in a little child of which he knows not what to do, except use it in a bad way? It is because he knows no different, unless, they are taught or educated otherwise. For me, my outlet was playing outside with my friends. The more I played outside the less destructive I was inside the house, which I guess pleased my parents more, although, they paid the price for the mischief I done when I was out.

My soccer took off as I really started to enjoy playing and I was becoming very focused on trying to become a better player. The main reason I wanted to become better was that, I could always be on the first team; in the first eleven to walk onto the pitch at the beginning of a game. This was a very important point, as if you are playing in the world cup finals. It was just a sense of pride walking out there knowing you are in the starting eleven players. Normally, the first eleven players are the best, so that they can make an impact on the rest of the team to help each other's overall performance and to give the team a great chance to start off the game well. So still at the age of nine years old up to 12 years, these were experimental years. We were still in elementary school and we were all still kids having a great time, learning to mix with other kids and try to understand what teamwork means. It was fun as you know; we all had best friends as such, and when you have best friends, you always tend to be near them, helping them before others. This was good because you learn to build trust in them and therefore start growing or maturing in that friendship/relationship. The more time you spend with those best friends, the more trust you build up in each other, and your relationship grows. This is a great way of learning as an individual, as you are always learning from each other's attitude and actions. I also adapted a more patient and solitude side of me of which is complete contradictory of my years as I grew up, as I started approaching a more intellectual approach of play. I have no idea how this other quiet, silent part of my being evolved. All I know and remember is that, I love to play games, play with toys, and play with anything where I had a chance to be competitive against others. So at the end of my elementary education we had a certain class where we were allowed to play games, such as checkers, darts, chess, puzzles and a few more.

At that time, we were all happy that we didn't have to study, listen or do work of any kind. Our teacher was a big man, must have been about 6 feet tall and 200 lbs or more. But even if he was a giant compared to us dwarfs, we were not afraid, because he was a gentle giant; always nice and kind to us. Anyway, so we all started playing games and really having lots of fun. We hated when the bell rang and we had to leave that class. So I really liked playing checkers, because you get to beat others. You had to think a few moves ahead in order to have a strategy to win over your opponent. Although you have few stored moves in your strategy plan, it is activated very quickly as both players start to conquer each other's pieces on the board. However, even how exciting and very challenging it was, I was not satisfied with it. I needed more challenging opponents. I continued to play as often as possible with school friends, my Dad and my brother. I just seemed to pick it up quickly and became very good at it. I was the best player in the class and the first pupil in our class to beat our teacher. Again I was a very determined kid who always wanted to win. After conquering the checkers board game, our teacher introduced me to the game of 'chess'. When I looked at the board and saw all these pieces of different shapes and sizes, while the teacher explains how they move and the purpose of them, I walked away. It was too complicated for me. I gave up before even trying. I just went back to the game I seemed to have mastered. I soon got bored with winning all the time at checkers and then noticed one of my best friends, Joe playing the teacher at chess. Joe seemed to pick the game up well, he was good. So then I noticed another friend Allan playing too, and Allan was also good. So, this got my eyebrows raised up, as I wanted to now be a part of this action. So I watched and watched until I knew the basics. I would play other classmates as we were just learning and we never really understood how to play. After a while we became better and worked up to start playing Joe and Allan. Still couldn't beat them. But again I practiced and practiced and even bought an 'electronic chess' game. This is a game where you play against the computer that is programmed into the game. I would play for hours every night until I became good. I set myself a goal and that was to be as good as Joe and Allan. It took dedication, persistence and lots of focus. I finally played them and beat them. Well I was so happy, but they also beat me, to be fair with my story. We were all at the same level.

Then the big challenge came, I played our teacher. I was so nervous but so excited because I wanted to beat him so badly. I couldn't do it, he was so good. After all, he was the one who taught us and was the head teacher and at the same time in-charge of the school chess team and championship events. Joe, Allan and I were eventually drafted in to play for St. Andrew's primary school chess team. We were so thrilled. We got to travel to other schools in the area, to play against them. And we always got drinks and food that was provided by the hosting school. One of the best parts of the chess team is that you got away from your normal class duties that afternoon, and for us, that was the best. It wasn't all a bed of roses when we played other schools, our teacher would really encourage us to focus on winning. He always told us to never underestimate your opponent. We were so nervous when we went to these competitions. It was kind of intimidating because we were the visitors. But when we were the hosts, they also came to know what intimidation meant. We would welcome them by shaking their hands but would say, "You're going to get beaten, why you came here?" I know it was bad and not proper, but we need all help for our self-esteem, to win. But we were not consistent in winning, we lose too.

On the last year of my elementary, the school district organized an event where all school had to qualify to reach the finals for a chess competition. So I've practiced and prepared to get to the finals. So after months of scheduled qualifying games, we got to the finals. Allan, Joe, Karen and I were all picked to represent our school with a few others. We were not favorites to win. It was a school called St. Lawrence, who had probably the best player name, Brian Collins. A total of 36 schools participated and we started the competition at 10am to 5pm. It was so exciting! And at the end, it was between Brian Collins of St. Lawrence and me to take the title. However, on my fifth game, I played Brian and he beat me, so I had 4 wins out of 5. He had 5 out of 5. My last game was against another school lad which I finished quickly, so I now had 5 out of 6 equaling Brian. But then Brian was playing his final game against my school mate

Allan Johnson. So if Brian beat Allan, then he would be the overall champion. While this was going on, my other school mates, Joseph Murdock and Karen won their last games. Joseph also got 5 out of 6 wins so it was me and Joe leading the race and another three lads got 5 also. So, going back on the game between Allan and Brian, Allan had already won 4 out of 5 games, so he was desperate to win obviously to be on the winners list but ultimately to stop Brian from taking the title. Man, it was nail- biting stuff, I had no fingers left. It is amazing when you are watching two players and you know exactly what moves their going to make. It's like having one mind, one spirit with them. And here's the result, Allan beat Brian, and we were jumping all over the place with joy. It was absolutely great; six first place winners with a total of 5 out of 6 points. But our school, St Andrews Primary, had won the team prize and received a huge trophy and our school name was engraved in it. For me, it was a great year and ultimately a great way to end my elementary school years. I still have the memories of that day captured on a picture frame in my home. At least when I look back on those 'handful' days, I can still say that I have paid attention at some point and became willing and available to be taught by my teachers.

Chapter 3

SETBACKS

Now, here comes the next stage, getting ready to go to the big school. The high school I attended is called St. Columba's H.S. It was the school my brother Drew and Sister Pauline also attended and I used to listen to the stories they used to tell. One big giant step forward, here I am heading off to the 'big school', as we call it in Scotland. We were terrified; most of my classmates were beginning the same school. It was located about 2 miles away from our home. If you look at us who were going to attend, you would think that we shouldn't be allowed because of our sizes. We were so small, so timid to enter a huge, High School. There were so many bigger boys there, that it was pretty scary to think about it and what was stored for us, wee freshmen. The first couple of weeks were pretty cool as we never really done much, just registering for all the classes and trying to find our way around. It was also a time to get to know your classmates and build wee friendships. We soon realized that what we had in our last elementary years was completely different from what we were going to experience in our new school. No more chess and checkers, the wee boyish games we used to play and me at the playground area. Nope, things are going to be different. We were very shy as you can imagine, small boys in a huge school for the first time, and majority of the other boys that were already in the school, and even our new classmates, all seemed like giants compared to us. Well, that was just how it was going to be, we would just have to get used to it. I was 12 years old when I entered high school after completing 8 years at St Andrews primary school. So in grade terminology, this would by my 9th grade.

I was excited about my new move to the big school and I knew it was a new adventure for me, something else for me to work on and find what I would like about it most. The next few months was very challenging as we started getting into our class' work. Man, I never thought or could have imagined the type of subjects or work I could be involved in, or have to do. There be so many different subjects to learn about and experiments that were taking place, specifically in the Science room. The great thing about the starting of a new class in a new school is that, everybody is very nice to each other, your making new friends each day. This was cool for me as I really liked to meet people and have as many friends as possible. Once we all started getting to know each other, it was great; we would all hang out together and play games, like chasing each other round the school, hiding from each other, and then when we got the courage we would start annoying the girls. This was amazing! You know how girls are very snobby and don't really want to talk to boys, or be associated with certain types of boys who were just looking to cause trouble, or be a pain to them! Well that was us. We fitted right into that category. I seemed to take my wee cheeky attitude that I had from my elementary years with me to my high school years.

I remember always looking out and observing which girls were the quiet ones and I would start annoying them. The reason being is that, normally they wouldn't retaliate or even say anything to the teacher because they were just so nice and didn't want to cause any trouble. But that was the fun part; the serious part was during class. It was very difficult compared to elementary days; it was a lot more serious here. Not as much flexibility and the teachers never let you away with so much too. As soon as you open your mouth just to talk to your friend, the teacher would catch and stop you right on your tracks. It was like a moment of freeze. You would just look at them with fear, just wondering what was coming next. We thought our wee cute smiles would work with the teachers the way it worked in elementary, but it didn't. This was when we realized we had a battle ahead of us. The more we need to kick into action and work away around the teachers. So as the months go by and we were getting settled into St. Columba's, it was cool. We started to like it, many new friends, and a few enemies. Yep, I already encountered a run in with a group who were like the leaders of the whole year, as in all kids our age joined school at the same time. These guys were scary; they were much taller than me and looked like real thugs. They would roam around the school during break times and would harass and bully kids like myself, who seem pretty helpless against them. They were always in a group of around four, five and maybe six or more. They were all smoking cigarettes so they were classed as being the hard men. Indeed they were because not too many people stood up against them, so they seemed to get their own way at all times.

For me, whenever I saw them, I would walk the other direction or hide or just disappear, I didn't want to be in their path. So we have the good part and now the bad part. I guess that just seems to be the way it goes. Even when I look at schools nowadays and hear many stories, it has got a lot worse now that in my school days. Still you have to carry on and get through the day the best way you can. I really loved school due to the fact we were always playing around and it seemed there was no really urgency in what we were doing in class, no real pressure or understanding on what we had to learn or pay attention to. I must say our teachers were really good, very friendly and always showed an interest in us and done their best for us to learn and succeed. But as always, it's down to us and the choices we make. As young kids growing up in a pretty violent and mixed up environment, our decisions could somewhat be the wrong ones. But again, we were always learning about life, correct? We were only observing what we see others doing right, we were just following the rest of the crowd. A lot of the decisions that we are making, especially at a younger age is merely influenced by others, by friends, family, or somewhat elders who seem to always know what is best for us. But that doesn't stop us making the choices that we want. After all, at this teenage life, it is all about what we want, when we wanted it, and what we are going to do to get it.

During my first year in high school, I would try everything I could to annoy the teacher and disrupt the classes that I would attend. I would start whistling in the class and my classmates would start laughing and the teacher would get so annoyed because they don't know who was causing the disruption. I would rip out paper from my notebook and crumple it up and throw it to another class mate across the room, and then it would come back and then others would join in, and this would drive the teacher crazy. Before you know it, there was a paper war going on inside the classroom. When I got bored with those ideas I would start to be more creative. I would take my bubble gum and throw it to the girls and hope it would stick in their hair. This was so nasty due to the fact; it was so difficult to remove it and that they had to cut off that part of their hair. Wow, they were not pleased at all with me. I believe, for the girls, this is when I started to have some enemies. And ultimately, that hit a blow to my chances of ever getting a date with them. After a while, the teachers were so annoyed at this behavior that they would ask the person responsible for this disruption to come forward and no one would ever own up and no one would dare to tell on someone because you would get names such as, a 'grass' or 'tell tale' or even being called 'teacher's pet'. And you definitely don't want to have any of these labels on your head, because you would be picked on by others in the class and then the whole year, other kids in our entry level would know about it. Its punishment would be like, getting cast away to a desert island or something like that; you would basically have no friends. I have witnessed it and it is not pleasant to go through.

Anyway, once the teachers were not successful in asking the culprit to come forward, they took dramatic measures; since they had no person to punish they decided to punish the whole class. Man, this was a shocker to everyone. So the result was, we were asked to write a 'sentence' on our notebook which is lined individually for writing words So the sentence we had to write was, 'I will not disturb my class', in a shocking scribble...five hundred times! My star rating started to diminish slowly, because most classes I was in, we would all get writing the sentence as a punishment. So you can imagine the response I was getting from some class mates now. Anyway I got worse, because writing the 'sentence' was not completely stopping the carrying on inside the class, the punishment got more. The teacher would start punishing us by giving us 'detention'. Detention was, being kept behind after school in a certain classroom for a specific period of time. This started off at fifteen minutes of which were a piece of cake, it was nothing. Then it got longer and could be up to one hour. Well, that was a different story. One hour behind was an hour off your playtime at night. That was the most painful time, as I never had much time to play after school. I was only allowed out until six pm, meaning I only had an hour to play. So evidently, I was becoming very unpopular in school, no one wanted to play along with my little games or schemes as they also wanted to enjoy their play time after school. Well, all the funs and games ultimately had an effect on my education. I was obviously not paying much attention in class so when it came to handing in my homework, I would fail miserably. And if I could not do the homework, which helps me build up my overall knowledge, then my chances of passing my class' exams were very limited, hence, the reason my subject grades was far, far behind. As the 'sentence' or 'detention' wasn't working very well, the ultimate punishment was given. The teacher started giving me the 'belt' as it was famously known. This was a hard leather strap with one end having two or three loose straps. The teacher would normally hold the end with the loose straps and bring down the other end onto the palm of your hands. Man this was like sticking your hands into a hot furnace and then having someone stand on top of it. It was so painful! In the early days of me receiving the 'strap' or 'belt' I would cry. Again this was so embarrassing, because if you cried in front of the class, they would laugh at you and give verbal abuse forever. Well, at times I could not help but cry as it was so painful, and me not being the 'largest' or 'well built' boy in the school, it just seemed to hurt even more. It was just like someone whipping the bones of my hands with a cane. Also, it wasn't as if it hurt for a second or two. It's like it was stinging for fifteen to twenty minutes, or even longer. Sometimes, it wasn't that straight forward either, the strap was supposed to just hit the palms, but the teacher had to be good with their judgment. Remember, they are standing a few feet away from you, and you have your hands stretched out in front of you and in front of them. They have to swing this leather strap from behind their shoulder and aim it onto your hands, so there is some form of coordination and precision when they strike you. There'll be few occasions where one of teachers misjudged the strike and the strap ended up on my wrist. Man, you should have seen the mess of my wrist. It started to swell, and when the teacher noticed it, he was a little shocked and showed extreme concern. I was sent to the school nurse to have it treated. She just put an ice pack on it to reduce the swelling and it came back to normal after an hour or so. But that was the most painful experience I ever had and yet it never stopped me from acting up. This was all part of me enjoying my pre-teen years, taking the risks, getting caught and having to receive the punishment that followed. Ultimately, the more I focused on creating diversions in the class, the less attention or focus I paid to my Academics. Even when I was coming through my elementary years, I don't believe I gave it my best, not even my second best. For whatever reason, my attitude was just to have fun and let others worry about school subjects. I just wanted to carry on and have so much fun and not to worry about anything. I really started to make some good friends and was always an observer. I watched people; how they act, what they say, how they interact with others. This way, if I like a person's attitude or character, then I will try to get their attention or get them to notice me. I didn't watch people in a way they would know, or would make them feel uncomfortable, or like a stalker kind of way. No, it was merely a friendly or curious way to try to make contact, but from a distance of course.

Well, I believe at a young age I have that acuteness of judgment. For some reason I was able to really work it out, or look into the motives or intentions of people's attitudes, or their behaviors in certain issues or situations. I think this may have been my reward since I was not having much success in my school classes. This gift really was a major contribution in the choices I made when it came down to making or hanging out with friends, although, I didn't get it right all of the time (you will know as the story unfolds). Being in early teens, life was just all about having fun and getting as much enjoyment as you can at no cost, so exciting, it was like I had no worries at all. Even on money. When I borrow from my Mum, sister, brother or even friends and they will tell me not to pay it back! Or even when they want to buy me something, of course I won't stop them. It was great being the baby of the family as I would always be spoiled. I would get pocket money from my parents along with what my brother Drew and sister Pauline give, as they were working, which was so cool. My spending money felt like it lasted forever. I guess there wasn't a lot we could buy with a few pounds. I got seven pounds altogether, which I thought was great, although I wouldn't have said no, if they offered me more. I would normally just buy candy with my pocket money at the beginning and hoping my family would give me more next time so I can buy more things, but can't complain. I still enjoyed my sweeties.

When you go into a bigger school with bigger boys and girls, then things start to get a little more challenging, a little more open to the ways of the world, a little more difficult, due to the situations you put yourself into or become involved with. I was still very much into soccer and loved the game. Although we were getting older, I wasn't growing much in height or physique, so eventually it was a little more difficult to make an impact. Being pretty skinny, I thought I should become a runner, as all runners are skinny and they can run forever. So I thought I can just put on my shorts and t-shirt and run round that track and beat everybody. Ha ha ha, what a slap in the face that was. There were even boys in the year below me, running faster and lasting longer than me. Well, being the little determined, cute kid I was, I couldn't take this insult of being beaten by younger ones. What could I do? Well the only thing to do is train and be a part of the Athletics team. So in order for me to be part of the team I have to attend regular training sessions, meet certain criteria and show a consistent level of performance. At first I was thinking, "Hmmm, rules, rules, rules. I don't like rules and discipline. I don't like being disciplined". Remember, I am the kid who just wants to have fun; no worries, no concerns. So I thought to myself, "There goes the idea". After attending few sessions during lunch breaks I got more excited as I was watching the other kids take part and the competition part was brilliant. I watched how they were so determined to beat each other, to win their races and still laugh together. I tell you, each one of those kids wanted to win their races so bad, I saw the determination in their faces and it showed in their efforts. Obviously not everyone can win at one time, but we can all be winners, by that, we can set ourselves small goals, small objectives to reach, to go for, and when we reach them, then you can classify yourself as 'a winner'. From that point on, you can then push yourself to work harder, focus harder to develop your talents, skills and abilities. Seeing this really encouraged me to want to take part in athletics. Of course I used to watch all this on television; I watched all the 'track and field' events for hours. It was always exciting to watch professional athletes; it gave you that inspiration and motivation that you need, to push you to take that first step, or to push you to the next step.

Anyways, I took those steps. I started bringing my running clothes and shoes and was ready to do my part. It was difficult giving up my lunch breaks to do running as I always look forward to eating my lunch and taking time to enjoy my breaks. It was a huge sacrifice for me, as I was used to chilling out with friends and eating burgers, fries, and all the bad stuffs. And now I was reduced down to 10 minutes to eat usually a couple of bags of chips or 'crisps' as we know it in Britain, and a 'quenchy cup drink'. Pretty poor nutrition, I know, but I had to eat something quick and I couldn't go out of school anymore due to time restraints. Now I can see how I remained skinny, not eating enough food or not eating enough nutritious foods that my body needs. So things were going well, as soon I realized that maybe I had to sacrifice things I really liked in order to do, or take part in something that wasn't normal for me to do and see what may progress out of it. At the time of taking part in the lunch time athletics team, I never thought of the bigger picture that was potentially in the horizon. I was just joining a 'running' group to try and become a good runner (at the back of my mind I was thinking, that if I became so fast in running, the police cannot chase if I do bad things). I was not really having any ideas of what I may or could become, or what real benefit I would get from it. I was now at the very young age of 13 years old and I'm really going through the enjoyment of teen life.

Being a part of the school athletics club and also being a team player with our local soccer club, St. Andrews, I kind of fell away from the chess playing scene. But sports with more exciting interaction and challenge physically not mentally, is where I loved putting efforts as it showed in my school grades. The more time I was spending running, the better it was making my performance on the soccer field. It was building up my strength and stamina in my wee skinny chicken legs. Overall, I loved every minute of my sporting activities. It wasn't long that I started running in the morning before I go to school. I would wake up at 6am and go for a jog and would start with 20 minutes. I would build up to 30 minutes, then eventually up to 60 minutes. It's funny, this used to crack my brother Drew up. I would return from my jogging and he would just be waking up to get ready for work. He used to tell me, "There is something wrong with you; you're not right in the head." I used to laugh, probably thinking to myself, "He may be right." So now my schedule was, 1 hour run in the morning, 50 minutes training at lunch time, soccer training once per week and a soccer game on a Saturday morning. Little Mr. Fitness was doing well with outside activities or sports but how were his academic activities doing? Well, sad to say I was pretty much failing in my subjects. My grades for my main subject's Math, English, Science, Arts and Crafts, and Social Studies went downhill. I failed all my major class' exams and homework assignments. I never ever completed any homework, therefore when it came to applying the class work I would always be kind of lost.

Assignments are a part of the progression of class studies. So inevitably, I was not making the mark. My teachers would try to get my attention, they would ask me questions but I would just flunk it and say, "I don't know." This would always allow them to then ask, "Did you complete your homework?" again I would flunk and say, "No." It was somewhat embarrassing when I would get asked questions, as I knew; I would not be able to answer due to my lack of paying attention, and not keeping up with the class. I know that the other kids in my classes would laugh and make fun of me when I couldn't answer, but I couldn't do anything. It was clearly my fault not paying attention and letting myself be distracted from studies. Well at that time, I wasn't really caring about class, or subjects as

I had it in my head, I want to be a soccer player or professional runner, or athlete of some sort. After school, I would start playing video games; I would go to friend's houses and play. This was cool, you would get so much fun doing that and it was so challenging, fun, exciting, I loved it. I loved going to my friends house, as they had the Nintendo, or spectrum game consoles (equivalent to XBOX or PS3 of today) and always their Mum would get us snacks, (he he he), always had to have the snacks. I never invited friends to my house because I had nothing for us to play with. It was so boring at mine and embarrassing. We never really had much, we were not a 'well off' family. Some of my friends in school were also my friends outside and some also played soccer with me at St. Andrews club. We were becoming very good friends, and we were the kind of good guys, in a way. Although we were not doing well in class on our other subjects, we never really done anything wrong in a bad way. Not yet, anyway! Well, the next year started to determine where I was going academically. I was 14 years old and in 2nd year high school. This was when you had to start choosing your subjects (if you passed the grades) or the teachers choose for you (if you didn't pass the grades). Well, have a guess which one I fall under? Yes you got it! The teacher's choice! Earlier I said, I failed all my major subjects being English, Math etc. Well there were other classes that I failed the grades. These were called 'Foundation' classes. Foundation classes means, it is a class where you go over the basics of what you never passed during your previous year, but also allowing you to potentially catch up or grow your knowledge or understanding in that topic. Unfortunately, I belong to these foundation classes; such rewards for not paying attention or focusing in my previous years. Everything you do has a purpose, irrelevant of when you do it, or how small you may think it is, everything has an importance to it, or it wouldn't be there for you to do it. So here I go, into a new class, a new environment, meeting students I have never met before, or had any conversation with. Quite honestly, they were dif-ferent kind of students. One or two of my friends I played soccer with and games outside of school were in these classes also. So, I guess I wasn't all alone. You see, sometimes you can play a major part in where your career leads you, by your previous actions. This you will see in the next pages and chapters.

So now here I am, this wee skinny, athlete who has dreams of becoming a soccer star, or running sensation is in this low level academic classes. It wasn't long before I realized the intention or motives of some of my other classmates in the class. I was not perfect at all, my manners and attitude towards teachers was poor, my lack of attention in class was pretty disgraceful, but I think I met my match. The students I was now sharing a class with were outrageous. These guys were so disobedient, it made me look like a star (and that's saying something). But as time went on, I was getting used to their actions, their tempers, their distractions, their bad attitudes. I would always watch carefully how they address or treat the teachers; there is no respect for them at all. I would also watch how the teachers would deal with this type of behavior. There's not much the teachers could do. No matter what punishment they would give, these lads would somehow seem to get worse. It was like their mission was to cause as much annoyance and disturbance as they possibly could. Well, being in this type of environment soon catches up with you, if you are in it long enough then you eventually start being influenced by their ways and you start inheriting the behavioral patterns. I would start seeing myself acting the same way. It wasn't too long before I started having an attitude towards the teachers. My tone of voice would start changing; I would start raising my voice, in a cheeky or unpleasant manner towards the teacher. This act was part of my trying to be accepted in my class, a form of showing off in front of them, so that they would like me, so that they would allow me to be their friend. At the same time, it was making me become a handful or more of a difficult person to deal with, for the teachers. I believed it was building up my reputation. Come on, a 14 year old boy wanting to have a reputation! Where on earth did this come from? Anyways, off I go on my new journey, new friends, new class, new subjects, and new direction. After a while, I started taking my breaks with some of my new class friends. I would start picking up on their conversations. I would repeat the words I heard them saying, thinking this was the way to acceptance. A lot of these words were crude, vulgar, nasty, and inappropriate and if my parents, brother or sister ever heard me, I would be grounded forever. But it never stopped me, there I was, such innocence in the eyes of my family, such a cute boy who never does anything wrong. Oh yeah! I was such a great little actor. I would play on the fact that my family thought I was innocent. That way, when I did eventually get caught, the punishment would not be as severe as I would blame others and they would tend to go on my side and have some sympathy for me, just another way for me to get away with it. I mean, I would still get questioned, and asked to explain what I did and why I did it. Then my Dad would ground me for few days. This was our punishment; my Dad would always ground us, as he knew we hated that because we were stuck in the house while other friends were out playing. My dad used to tell us that he would take his belt across our backside if we mis-behaved, just as a deterrent, but of course, that didn't stop me. I would always push the limits, I would always test him. Sometimes he would put me over his legs, take my pants down, take off his belt and be ready to strike me, but by the time his belt came off, I was screaming, asking him not to punish me and telling him I am sorry and won't do it again. Well, it always worked, he stopped and never carried it through, but that was when grounding part came in. He had to follow through with some form of punishment.

Sometimes, I wish he would have just hit me with the belt so I can go out to play. Well it wasn't long that I started wanting to do other things outside of school that I hear these class' friends are doing. Once a month we would have a school disco that allows all the kids to attend this night of music where you can chit chat with others, dance, play around with all seems innocent right. But it also allows you to be away from your parents and be in the company of others that you may not normally associate with. This is when things started to change for me. The first couple of times I went, I was kind of shy, just keeping a low profile, staying in the background so I could do my 'observing others' part. I would look to see whom I knew, whom they are hanging out with, watch what they do. This is when my eyes were open up to what school kids could really get up to when not in school and away from their parents. It was scary to see what was going on, I was so nervous at first. I wouldn't interact at all. I would see kids sitting in corners, drinking alcohol (of which they sneaked in) smoking in certain corners, couples kissing each other, it was really wild. After the first couple of months and getting to know other kids, I started relaxing. I was getting comfortable with the surroundings. So, when you are in such environment and mixing or socializing with one's who drinks, smokes, kissing girls and other naughty things, then it can be just a matter of time before you start doing it also.

Well, at 14 years old I started going down that road. I was now taking part in what I know was wrong. I started having a couple of cups of beer at the school disco night to loosen up. It wasn't before long that I was up on the dance floor (yes, me!), a little innocent boy, the apple of his mother's eyes. I'll tell you, once I had those cups of beer in my blood, and got on that dance floor, I thought I was 'John Travolta' or 'Patrick Swayze'. It was only me that thought this, no one else did, so yes, I probably was making a fool of myself, but I was not caring, as the beer was numbing all my sense of self-righteous. Once you start going down that road of having a few cups of beer, and getting to like the feeling that it gives you, that sense of, 'I can do what I like and don't care about others', then it drives you into wanting to have more on a regular basis. It soon becomes a habit, even at such a young age that you start working how you can get this little fulfillment into your life. I used to start thinking about how I can get beer and where I could go while I was in my class. I used to ask my friends, what their plan is for the weekend. I always hoped that someone's parents would be going out for a night, so we can all go to their house and drink. Well, most times it worked because there were many of us; there was always a house to go to. That was great, the first part of the puzzle was over, now came the hard part, getting permission from my parents to go to my friends house.

If you think that is an easy task, let me tell you, getting permission from my Dad to be out the house was like prisoners trying to escape from Alcatraz. My Dad was so strict, so protective over us, that he smothers us, and no, not with kisses. So, knowing that I had an almost impossible task of getting out the house at weekends, I would have to devise a plan or scheme. My ticket out of the house had to be something really good, something strong, something genuine, well, there's nothing better, nothing stronger, nothing more genuine than...you got it! My mother...knowing how much my mother loved us, same as my father of course, I saw an opportunity if I could warm up to my mother then she could be the one to break the question or idea to my Dad. If I asked my Dad outright, then there is no question at all, the answer would be 'a big 'No!' So here's the answer, the 'Mother dear'. This is my gateway weekend to boozing and fun. At first my Mum was not keen on the idea either, she knew what I would be getting up to. Kids, just in case you think your Mums are a little stupid, or not there with the times, or don't really have a clue what you get up to. They do, they know everything, and they know every trick, every little cunning scheme that you're devising. They just let you get away with it because they love you so much and want you to be so happy. Let me tell you this, they know that it is just a matter of time before you come running to them, to get you out of the trouble, or situation that you have caused yourself. So it really took a lot of persuasion for my Mum to build up the courage to ask my Dad to let me out the house. At the first couple of times, he point blank refused. This was a shocker to me. I thought it was a sure thing to use my Mum in my little deceitful plan. I know that if she couldn't persuade him, then I was done. I would never get to go out. My Dad is not stupid either, after like 10 times I would use my Mum to ask, he would get angry and tell me not to get her to ask again. So this I thought was the end. Still at the age of 14, second year high school, I couldn't even go out at weekends. Well, drastic measures had to be taken, I thought of every cunning little scheme I could imagine and it never worked. So I thought, why not play the emotion game? This is where I would sit in front of both my Mum and Dad, I just sigh out loud. I would huff and puff and blow trying to win their affection and sympathy. That didn't work really well either, not at the beginning. Believe me; I didn't just try this once or couple times a week, or month. I tried this half a dozen times a night, every night.

My Dad would get so fed up and annoyed with me that he would say, "If you don't stop that acting, I will put you to bed and give you something to really moan about." But me being me, so determined to get my own way, I would never give in trying. I tell you, my Dad would have never broken, never given in if it wasn't for my Mum. My Mum is a champion, she was the one who broke my dad, she eventually would go against my Dad, and said, "Oh c'mon Andy, for goodness sake, let him go to his friends, do you want him to be here every night, like this, he is even starting to make me feel depress!" So when they started arguing eventually my Dad gave in, Hooray!!! It worked; I got my wee wicked way at last. Man, you would have thought I won a contest; I was going crazy, jumping all over the place. At that moment I knew, I had the breakthrough that my brother Drew and sister Pauline never got. Ha, ha, ha, the wee man had done it! I was on my way to "FREEDOM" as William Wallace would put it. Yes my weekend nights out would have restrictions and rules. I had to be home by 10pm, and my Dad was not joking, can you imagine, fourteen years old and you have to be home by 10pm, but I was not about to complain, no way. I was taking the good while I could! So that was it, I was at my friend's; we had our drink, our wee couple of cups of beer that eventually became bottles. We would be so happy telling jokes, and stories, and doing stupid things. At first I would get home at 10pm as instructed, because my Dad would always call my Mum and check up on me. But here is a thing, my Dad was out also, and I knew he always got home around 11:30pm, so I would start telling my Mum, "Mum, if Dad calls, just tell him I am home already." Well at first she wasn't into it, but it didn't take long, again she has to give in. I thought this was cool, me out drinking and sneaking in late, before Dad gets home.

Our few beers became more and more and eventually I got drinking stronger alcohol. We started mixing our beer with drinking wine. Bottles of wine were cheap and very effective. I got really drunk on a small bottle of wine. Our local wine was called 'Eldorado'. It was horrible, I mean disgusting to drink. I had to hold my nose while I poured it down my throat, it was really that bad, but the quickness it hit you was all that matters. Now that we're getting older, more mature, and developing as young men, we started drifting into our sexual playfulness. One of my friends would always have sexual magazines, like 'Playboy' or some other men's book, and we would all look at it and have fun over the pictures. This would obviously get us excited and then lots of dirty talks would come out our mouths. Then it got worse, we would tease girls in school about the sizes of their top parts and bottoms. We would even use our power over the weaker girls and start groping them, foundling their top assets and touching their private parts. This was really bad behavior and dangerous and could have got us into very big trouble, with our parents, the girls' parents, or even the police. But it didn't stop us as we were always drunk and lost control of our actions. So because of this, I was fondling girls but in fun. But still it was not the right way to behave. It wasn't too long before I had my first sexual experience. Yes at the age of 14, I had sex with a girl the same age. We both were so nervous and didn't know what we were doing to an extent. It was not a nice thing to do at such age. The consequence of our actions would have made such a drastic change to our life. You hear of a girl becoming pregnant at this age and then have to become mother to a young baby. It affects their whole life, their education, their emotions, their attitude; everything suddenly changes. I will not lecture on what you may miss out in life if you have a child at a young age, but I will comment on the potential lack of maturing as an adult on your own without the stressful, strenuous and emotionally draining tasks of raising a child. We are meant to develop in our way of learning, understanding and experiencing the trials and temptation of life.

Going through such aspects in life is what develops our character, our personality. Raising a child at a young age will certainly bring out a greater responsibility, but I believe there are also certain times or stages in our maturity for this to happen. So getting back to my encounter, after we had sex, it was shameful; it was like we couldn't even look at each other. We were very good friends and yet when that sexual encounter happened it broke our friendship apart. I went in a different direction after that, I was now proudly displaying the fact that I lost my virginity as quickly as possible. And it was a huge thing in Scotland, probably all over the UK also. Well, now that I thought I was becoming a man I was geared up for bigger things. I wanted to be noticed as a 'macho man', a good fighter, so I can be looked up at. So I started getting into music, music that displayed a certain type of character. I would listen to groups like, 'The Jam', 'Small Faces', the 'Kinks', all groups who fall under the umbrella of 'Mod' groups. 'Mod' was a fashion, along with 'skin-heads', 'bikers', 'Nutty boys', of which all came with a certain type of clothing and persona, or character type. Being a mod you would dress in a long parker coat with hood, usually green in color, with trendy pants and shoes, with sometimes wearing a cravat or scarf on your neck. You were mostly classed as quite cool or trendy and the girls liked mods. They were clean individuals and we had cool dance moves, well at least I think it was cool. Along with the slick clothes, girls come with the jealousy and competition. Well, com-petition means gangs or other groups, and inevitably these bring violence.

So here you have it, 14 years old, getting drunk, having sex and in a gang. What's next? The fighting! On most occasions we would still go to our school disco but this time with a mission, or an intention, and that was to start fights with other groups being 'skinheads' mostly. Skinheads and mods hated each other as I think it was rightly displayed in the 60's film "Quadraphenia". This was a huge thing in the UK, especially in England where hundreds of these two groups would meet and try to kill each other; well we would do it in a smaller scale. I wasn't much of a fighter on my own, but when you are in a group of people and they are urging you or 'egging' you on as we say it, then you don't really fear as much, because you have all the other friends around you that will help you out. Well, we use to go to various clubs and look for trouble, especially at weekends. I was kind of breaking away from my innocence, 'wean 'or baby of the family upbringing, as I was having at that time, a very changed image. We started really getting involved in fights and alcohol to the stage that we would not even know what we were doing. I had a great friend, called Joe, he was a quiet guy, much taller than me, and was a good fighter, I never knew anyone who beat him in school, a few tried but never succeeded. We used to play at his house many times, he had a billiard table and computer games also. We used to go to the school disco and dance to the mod music, I think he was a better dancer than me, but I never told him that. Most of the times there would be a prize to play for. I had a few things, like toys, games and he also had some items he would put up. If you think about it, you can call it, small scale gambling. Although to us, it was fun and competition. We would play pool forever; sometimes we would play twenty, thirty, forty games for us to have a longer chance of winning against each other. On most occasions we would be equal in winning, I would win something from him, then he would win from me, and this would go on and on, until we played our master game. This was the ultimate of all games. We would offer our best items as this was the 'grand game' the 'crème de la crème' of pool for us; it was like a 'winner takes all' game. We're so addicted trying to beat each other, the adrenaline that we got from playing to win prizes was amazing; we just wanted to play every day so we can have more prizes from each other.

Well, this is it, this was the finale. I had to offer something that was of worth to me and of value or benefit to Joe. He also had to do the same. So Joe asked me what I was willing to gamble, what was my ultimate prize. I offered my complete set of 'football programs'. Football programs are a kind of brochure or 'booklet' from each or certain football games that are played every week, or on certain special occasions. Like if the LA Lakers are playing against Boston Celtics, then there will be a flyer or leaflet or some type of brochure of that game, explaining highlights or focusing on the specials attributes of a player or part of the game. It would also give all the team player info and other info. It was a kind of hobby to collect these and I collected many. If I can recall, I had around two thousand plus of all types, local games, special European games, limited edition and many more that were so precious to me. But I was willing to put all these on the table and gamble them because of two things. One I wanted to get whatever Joe was going to put on the table. Well, initially, Joe being Joe, he was trying to be wise, trying to offer items that were worth not even half as much as mine. Then we got to a point where I said, "Let's not bother". Because he was not giving me anything that was worth the value of my programs. So, me being me, I had a play, I know exactly what I wanted from Joe. So then I said, "Ok, I will play you for your pool table. Well, he almost jumped out of his pants, he couldn't believe it. He would point blank refuse knowing that his table was worth more. But I would play the fact that, he could buy a table anytime, and he couldn't buy all the programs that I have. Anyways, after a while I called him a chicken and pressured him by telling him that I am a better player than him, hence, if he thought he was better than me, then he wouldn't have to worry about losing. This was my technique not that I was 100% sure that I would win, but I wanted his pool table so badly. I was always jealous of him because he had the table. You see, when you want something so badly, when you want something someone has through jealousy then you will go to extreme measures to obtain it.

Well, the game was on! Here we go, offering our best items in order to win from each other and basically rub it in each other's faces when you win. We couldn't just play one game or five games as we both so nervous. So we thought of playing fifty games to test the consistency of each other, hoping one or the other will get tired. This meant we keep playing until one player wins 50 games, not that we thought this was much or going to be long to achieve. We were so wrong; it took us three weeks to complete. We were so hyper, so excited and so aggressive towards each other. Neither of us wanted to lose. We win games alternately. We would get so frustrated when we missed shots that we would curse and whack the cue of the table. You know our characters and personalities really showed during that competition. When I missed a shot, Joe would laugh and tease me and I would do the same to him. This was us playing mind games with each other, trying to break each other's temper in order for our focus to be broken. Man, we were so mean to each other. At times we would nearly physically fight, or punch each other, blaming each other of cheating. I think our friendship was diminishing as it was getting closer to the finale. Out of all the times we played each other, this was the most vicious, most aggressive, most focused ever. There would be a gap of sometimes three or five games, then it would be equal, well it couldn't have been any closer. We eventually got down to the closing stage. The score was 49 to 49; yes we were both equal on the last game. Man you could cut the air with a knife. It was so quiet and the tension was frightening. Every shot we took, we measured it, thought about it, analyze it, over and over and over again, I think we were both shaking badly with nerves. After a grueling game of strategy, we got down to the last ball, the black ball. We really couldn't believe that it all depended on who potted this little black ball. Well, all things must come to an end. We would play so slowly trying to be careful but trying to win. Well, the ball was eventually potted. It was all over, the prize had been won. There prevailed a champion of champions, a winner takes all, the crown of champions was given to... the winner is...and the gold medal goes to... JOE. It was JOE!!! Wow, I thought my world had fallen apart. It was like my heart and soul was ripped out. It was as if the world just closed in on top of me. You never saw such an angry, depressed little boy in your whole life, while Joe was jumping up and down with joy. I wanted to wrap the pool cue right round his neck and choke him. Man, I was so angry, I hated every inch of that boy. I wanted to pull every inch of hair out of his head. But, he deserved to win; he was the best player at the end. But I so hated handing him over all my football programs.

Well, that was it for me; there was something at that moment that broke my temper. I was starting to become so aggressive in nature, so focused on having to win at everything in order to get my way. I would start being really selfish towards others. I was building a little devilish attitude that would eventually be a stumbling block in my friendships with others. This would certainly be noticed during school. I could be so nasty towards others, although they done nothing wrong to me, I would pick on them, and I would be little them, make fun of them, and try to disgrace them in front of other school kids. This attitude was allowing me to build up my ego that I am indeed a strong man so I will fit into the gangs that were operating in the school. I wanted to be noticed so badly. I was entering my last year in high school and was gearing myself up to enter the big bad world.

My last years in high school were great. I was a great runner, playing regularly in our soccer club, went cycling, swimming all the time, playing tennis and badminton, when possible and had very little academic classes as possible. By this time, I couldn't care less about 'grades' in school. I was having a ball, and I had some great friends and knew many more, and I couldn't wait to leave school. I just wanted to play soccer and get a girlfriend and drink and have fun. Well, it all had its price. The more I wanted to play around the worse my grades got. My studies were so bad that it was a waste of time even attending the classes or taking the exams. I completely failed every test, having no grades whatsoever. The kids that were bigger than me and much more violent than me would pick on me and others. If you have never heard of this saying, then pay attention to it right now. The saying goes like this, 'What goes around comes around,' meaning what you do to others gets done to you. So be very careful on how you treat others, think twice before picking on someone smaller or younger than you, as it can come right back to you. As I was picking on others, innocent ones who do not 'say' or 'do' a bad thing to you, I was getting my payback. There was one boy in our school who was the same age as me but was part of the toughest gang in our school. If you have ever watched the movie 'Nightmare in Elm Street' well, this boy was my nightmare in St Columba's High School. This boy would pick on me through the previous years in high school, but this was the worse year so far. Before, he would say abusive things to me call me names and push me around. Believe me when I say I hated him, I mean, I really did. I just wanted to hit him over the head to stop him bullying me. It is so ironic isn't it? Here I am, feeling useless when this boy keeps bullying me, feeling threatened every single time I crossed his path, and yet I am doing the same to others, 'what goes around, comes around'.

This last year was horrible for me with this school thug. The bullying got more violent. He would stop me in the playground or school grounds either when I was going to class or during break times. He would push me, and then verbally abuse me then here comes the crunch, bang! His fist would come across my face; man I was so terrified. This guy would punch me in the face so hard that it stung for hour's man. Sometimes I would get a black eye and that was so embarrassing. I would have to face the other kids and they would laugh and stare at me. The worst part was going home and facing my parents. They were so mad and wanted to go to the school and see the principal, but I completely refused as this would be more embarrassing. There was no way on this earth I was willing to tell his name, he would have killed me, big time. So I just suffered the pain, the torture, the beatings, I mean, c'mon, how much worse can it get? Hmmm, I was about to find out. That year in class was my scariest ever. Why, because this thug was there in some of my classes. Well I just wanted the ground to swallow me up. I could not imagine myself in the same room as this boy. It started from the 'get go', he would constantly call me names and throw things at me. Oh it was so horrible; this caused me not to attend classes. I would make excuses like I was sick, I had a headache, I went to the dentist, and lots of other lies just not to attend. So obviously, I flunked class again. I received no grades as my attendance was pathetic and I didn't even sit the exam. The worse was still to come. In the next chapter, find out how much more the bullying continued, the beatings intensified, the bruises and marks were more severe, the breaking of my temper and turning point of a new lifestyle and attitude of a 16 year old about to leave high school.

Chapter 4

THE BEATINGS

My second year in high school continued to be the biggest challenge to me in many ways. There was the disgraceful grade results, the intensifying bullying, the changing of a nice boy into a young monster and a rebellious child. Indeed, it was the time for me to grow up and begin to realize that after this school term, these would be the subjects that I would have to use for me to be sent out in to the big world of 'don't know what to do'. But first, I had to get through the last 2 years. It wasn't the most pleasant year of school for me. I was continuously getting ridiculed for my lack of effort in class and gaining no grades at all. I mean, we were graded from 'A' to 'F'. Believe me when I tell you, I was in the 'F' category for all subjects bar two. I was in Foundation English, Foundation Math, and Social Studies; there were no Science class as I was completely hopeless at those and no Art. These were all my 'F' classes, can you imagine! But I have something to boast about and that was my hands on practical skills. I had taken a special class that involved two subjects rolled into one class. These were Woodwork, Sheet Metalwork, this I was not too bad at as I received a 'B' grade for my course assessment work and a 'B' grade for my end of year project. So too me, this was a great result, I achieved something from school, so I thought. My other class was called, EFL (Education for Leisure). I need to laugh here because once you know what it is and how many classes I had, you will drop off your chair. EFL was basically a name for PE (Physical Education). Normally you would only have two or three classes of PE in a week. I was a special child, I had twelve, yes, and you got it, twelve classes in a week over and above my three normal classes giving a total of fifteen. You may be asking how on earth I got to have all those extra classes. Well here is the answer. It was not because I was the teacher's pet and so he gave me more classes than anyone else. It was because; well you know how I told you I flunked all my normal classes like English, Mathematics and others? This is where they put you if you decide to drop out of these classes; the reason being is that there is nowhere else to put you. In short, you failed the normal classes so you have to fill in your day, so what the teachers would say to me is, "Just head over to EFL and do what you want to do over there". This was for two reasons: one was to get me out of their hair, so I don't disrupt the rest of the class, pretty clever of them eh? And the other was to fill up my time. I had no objection whatsoever, in fact I loved this plan, and it suits me right down to a tee. C'mon, you must see my point here, I was doing the things I loved doing. I was playing soccer at least 7 or 8 times a week, I was swimming once or twice and then I was doing my cross country jogging. I was great, I couldn't have been happier when I was in the EFL building, it was my favorite.

This was how I built up my skills in soccer and running, although I wasn't what you would say a classy skillful player at all. But my strength was in running and tackling. I was really a fast runner, so where that would benefit me on the soccer field is when the opposing team would be advancing up to our goal area, and then I would stop them. They would try to kick the ball past me then run to get it before me, but there was no way this little chap was going to let that happen. I would know what they were planning so I was ready to chase that ball and get it before they would, and I normally succeed 100% of the time. Yep, I was super fast man and there's one time that someone caught me off guard and got past me, then I reverted to plan B. Plan B was my stopping plan, in other words, if they managed to get by me, then I would do a slide tackle as we would call it. Meaning I would chase the man holding the ball slide into him and hopefully hit the ball first but hope to bring him down to the ground at the same time. Sometimes I missed the timing and got the player first instead of the ball, he, he, he, that was the best part, seeing them fall to the ground. I know I was Mr. Nasty but that was just the way it was. Playing soccer was the best thing ever for me; I never looked forward to anything in my whole life apart from that. I would join any soccer event when possible; I would play anytime I got a chance. This was my favorite hobby and past-time. I devoted myself to this in every way. I was also getting stronger in my physical ability; I was starting to join a local sports centre down the street from our house. I worked out there and started attending class called 'Circuit Training". This was an aerobic high intensity class where you carried out many different exercises on the floor, like press ups, pushups, jumping jacks, sprints etc. etc. There was in all, about 20 exercises that you do within an hour period and mostly you do the circuit twice, although you can stop at any time or go at your own pace or level of fitness. This was awesome after the first month or so. The first couple of weeks almost killed me though, because you are using muscles you have never used before and you were completely out of breathe due to the extreme intensity of the exercise and lack of time for breaks. But it was amazing and fun. We all used to laugh at each other due to our lack of fitness and almost dying together lying on that floor. But it was so much fun and I am glad I started it at the age I did. Even to this day, I join any aerobic classes I can, as I know it keeps you in good shape, it's good for your heart and lungs and it allows you to meet other people. Anyway, that was the great, fun and exciting part of my last year in school of which I started making more friends who were what we would class as the, 'good guys'. Not that this had made my attitude really change much, it just gave me more variety of friends and people to do sports with. But let's not forget where we left off on the last chapter. I cannot forget or ignore this part of my last year in school. It's the bullying part. As I said, this had gotten a lot worse than those times before. It used to be the verbal abuse, the laughing at me moment, make fun of me being small and stupid, laughing at my grades, make fun of my uniform as it may not have been the most trendiest, or up to date, or stylish as per brand name clothes and all that.

When I mentioned there was one school kid who really used me as his pet body bag, his punching bag, well, he was still around and I think he made it his purpose in life to really focus on me. I mean, everywhere I seemed to turn he was there, so I would try to avoid him and go a different direction or use other means to avoid him as I knew what would happen if I crossed his path. But being in such a small school with only a few options to hide from someone, I seemed to get caught. Man, I was so sorry if I crossed his path. Normally, he would use the verbal abuse to get my attention and then go physical with the pushing and shoving stuff, then the slapping on the head or face. Then it would move up to the kicking in the legs or butt. I thought that was bad enough, but wait a minute, now he was more aggressive. I guess he must have thought these other measures weren't really hurting me, so he started to punch my face and then he would see the pain and most times I would cry in front of him. This is what he wanted to see. This was the ultimate sign of my weakness and that really pleased him as others would see my crying and that would inevitably build up his hard man reputation. He would kick and punch me in the stomach which would make me fall to the ground and he would walk away laughing. During these times and it means, this was on a regular basis, this wasn't just every six months or so, this was weekly or every other week. This was really making my life a misery that is why I was so happy being in my EFL classes where I was safe. I was away from the brute, the bully, the thug of my life. Not that this took away the problem, no, it just temporary put it on hold, as when he would catch up with me again he would make a point of hurting me even more. There was one moment of which I will never forget even to this day, I remember it as if it just happened yesterday. Do you ever have those moments in your life where there are incidences that never seem to leave you, situations that always seemed to be in your memory? Well this is one has never left me to this day. It was a break time and I was running out of the doors heading towards the EFL building to take my class. I was so joyful knowing I was going to play over an hour of soccer while others were going into Mathematics, Physics, and Biology or Geography class.

While I was enjoying myself running around after a ball and trying to be the next David Beckham,(Oh, if you don't know who David Beckham is then look up the LA Galaxy and you might still find him playing there unless, he has moved back to Spain or Italy to play for the big giants of soccer), well here I was, pushing open those doors wide, jumping of the steps and progressing forward until, to my fear, this leg was put out in front of me making me fall to the ground. I got up and was ready to shout at the person who tripped me up, remember I have a little attitude of my own, remember I am also a wee bully of my own. So here I was, full of rage now and ready to pounce on this fool who tripped me, so I got up and looked dead in the face this guy, and who do you think it was? Yes, it was him, it was my nightmare, it was my St Columba's devil in disguise. Well, you can imagine what was going on in my mind and in my heart. I thought my heart just stopped or I wanted it to stop because I knew what was about to happen. I was about to get another slap around the head or punch in the face or some sort of cruel act put on me. I was right, here he is laughing at me falling to the ground and getting up facing him like I wanted to challenge him to a fight. Yeh right! As if I would, that would be the last thing on my mind, let me tell you that. If, I was to challenge him, my parents would be putting me in a box and putting me in the ground at a very early age. I wanted to run as far away as possible from him but couldn't, I was stuck. I was in his way and he was going to do whatever he wanted to get past me, around me or through me. I guess he took the option of going through me, (ha ha ha), I'm laughing not because he got through me but I was facing him and staring at him with so much fear that he must have smelt it, or saw it in my eyes because he never budged an eye lid, he never even blinked, he was so focus on my wee cheeky face that he just stared right through me. After a few seconds of pushing me and saying to me, "Well, do you want to do something? You want to hit me or kick me? C'mon then, let me see what you can do" (with a little extra verbal words in among the sentences of which I won't mention). I mean me? I couldn't even get the words out my mouth fast enough, I just said, "Of course not, why would I want to fight you?" (Knowing I would be killed if I even tried to move an inch towards him). After I said this, he took things into his own hands and made his move, yes here it comes, the worse beating he gave me up to that point. He head butted me in the face and I just hit the ground immediately, I honestly thought I was hit in the face with a baseball bat. Man I went down like there was no tomorrow, I just hit the floor in a second and wondered, "what on earth just happened?" But then the pain in my face soon made me realize that I was just been given a blow to the face and the blood was my evidence of that. I thought there was no more blood left in my body as it was gushing everywhere. I was covered in it and I mean it was like it all happened in a split second and it was over. He never hit me again at that time as there was no point.

There was nothing else to do to me, I was on the ground, blood pouring from my nose and mouth and lying there helpless. He accomplished his goal I guess, once again. Some people around me were saying "Are you ok, do you need help?", I thought, "hmm let's see, you all stood there while this guy just stuck the head on me and put me to the ground and never even stepped in to stop him or even say anything to him, but now, I am lying on the ground full of blood, and now you're asking if I need help?". That's what I felt like saying but I never did, just in case I upset someone else and they took advantage of the situation and maybe they would hit me also. So I just said "No, I will be fine". I headed to the restrooms, to clean myself up, man there was nothing I could do about my clothes as they were covered in blood and my face was a mess already. I obviously never went to my classes after that; I just walked home, wondering, 'How am I going to explain this to my folks'. They will go crazy and my Dad will want to definitely get a hold of whoever had done this to his wee innocent son. When I got home, my Mum was there and she just went through the roof. She was shouting "what happened to you, who done this? Right that's it, enough is enough. We are going to that school in the morning when your Dad is here". Man that was the last thing I wanted to hear. Anyway, I managed to persuade them to let it go and I will sort it out myself. How? I had no idea, but I just said it, so they wouldn't get involved. My Dad flipped his lid, he went nuts, and he wanted me to tell him at once who it was, so he can kill him. So again, I couldn't say as it would get me into bigger trouble. So he calmed down once I said it was fine it wouldn't happen again. I remained off school for the rest of the week so my face would have time to heal. After the second day I had two black eyes, I hid in my room and never came out. I was so ashamed of how I looked, that was the first time I ever had a black eye. Not that it was painful, it just looked bad. I didn't want everyone asking, "Oh what happened to you? How did that happen?" So I kept a low profile until it was away. Well, after a few weeks I never saw this guy and it was great, I felt good, but I was so scared to bump into him again. Anyway time went on, and on few occasions I notice him, but managed to avoid him, hiding behind doors, jumping in classrooms, or completely doing a three hundred sixty degrees turn around and running away. I mean, I would do anything for him not to notice me. You be probably thinking, "You're hypocrite, you are here, complaining and sharing about your beatings and yet you are just the same. As you also picked on other innocent kids in a less violent manner, but still with the same principle, to show them you can bully them, to show them you want to be recognized as a little hard man". And you would be hundred percent correct in saying that, but still, it never stopped me, it actually rose up my anger and temper against others whom I can easily pick on. Although I never reached that point of violence in hitting someone in the face or head butting them, but I would now kick them up the butt, or really push them hard, sometimes even pull their hair. I didn't have that sort of courage or evilness in me yet! So things were good for a while, staying out of trouble, out of danger. I was getting more into my EFL classes and building up my running and soccer abilities. Maybe I was thinking that one day I would need my running skills to run away from this head case. I was still very skinny even though I was training, exercising and working out.

I never had big muscles or be heavy made, just a wee skinny guy. I never really ate much food during school because of my running at lunch times, never really had much time, only about ten minutes then back to class. Normally I would just buy a few bags of chips or crisps as they say in the UK and a quenchy cup drink. A quenchy cup drink was a small plastic cup with soda sealed inside and you used a straw to drink from the cup. I know, not very much for lunch but I didn't bother, I was ok with that. I would normally just stand or sit somewhere for a few minutes or even eat this while walking to the next class. Sometimes I would just chit chat with friends while eating and drinking it. Sometimes I would head down to the school cloakrooms. This is where kids can hang up their jackets leaving there until they are leaving school that day. This was a simple place where there was benches to sit on like a locker room type of bench. Well these places were normally pretty quiet; there would be a few people around just chatting until classes started again. Well, my horror continued, there I was just minding my own business and who pops round the corner? I mean it was like a scary movie, where the victim was trying to escape from the pursuers and no matter where they would run, the person would find them. That's the way I felt, I thought no matter where I go this guy is there, it's like he knows my every move. Man my heartbeats tripled, I mean I was scared stiff now, I knew I wasn't going to get out of this one, there was nowhere to run, nowhere to escape. Well I just embarrassed myself for what was about to happen. C'mon what else could he do to me that would be any more hurtful than the headbutting, which was the extreme right there? To my surprise he just mouthed off to me and never lifted a hand. I was like, "Yes, he has stopped, he has had enough, he is now bored with picking on me". I was so happy and relieved, although he was still beside me and pushing me off and all that, but at this time, he could say all the words that he wanted, it was a pleasure not being beat up, so I was hoping he would continue to keep giving me the verbal abuse, I could handle that part. Then I realized why he didn't touch me, he was with some of his gang member friends? So maybe his friends don't approve on hitting others who cannot defend themselves. Ha ha ha, I was wrong again.

I was approached by the leader of the gang, and by the way, this boy was supposed to be the best fighter in the whole school, like the don of the school I mean, the head haunch, the big fish. No one would mess with this guy, he was built like a rock, and I mean his biceps were probably as big as my waist, he was solid all over. But the funny thing is I was never as scared of him, as I was the other nut. I was concerned because of his reputation but he never ever bothered me in school. He picked on other people but normally those who posed a threat to his name or title as best fighter, that was way out of my league. Anyway, here we are in a situation, were I am in a school cloakroom surrounded by about five or six of these gang members and believe me when they came to me, that place suddenly emptied, I never saw people scatter so quickly in my whole life. They were out there like a flash of lighting. So I was still eating my little bag of crisps and my drink, and then the leader of the gang asked me, "Hey give me some of your crisps". I was like, what? So I said, "This is my lunch". Again he said, "Give me some of your crisps". I looked at him and said "No, this is all I have to eat and I am so hungry". He looked at me and said, "Are you not giving me any?" I said, "No". I mean here I am saying 'no' to the best fighter in the whole school who was also standing alongside this maniac who wanted to take my head off my shoulders with his head butting skills. I really don't know what was going on in my head at that moment. I just can't believe what I was saying to him. I heard on many occasions that they would always take kids lunch from them, or sweets or even money. They were notorious for robbing kids' possessions in school. Most of the school kids were afraid of these guys, but this was my first time to experience them as a gang. Usually I only meet up with the Looney tunes of the gang, if you know what I mean. Anyway, we're here in this confrontational situation where I am putting my head on the block just to save me giving him my lunch, I mean c'mon, it's not as if it was a 'Subway Foot Long' Teriyaki Chicken sandwich or something, it was a bag of crisps, not worth the hassle over. Well to me, it was about food, I loved food, whenever I ate food I ate it myself and I would share it with no one, it was mine and it always stayed that way. I was not about to share my food, my lunch with anyone. This is now going on for a minute or two where he would ask me to give him my lunch and I would point blank refuse. (I am sure his friends are probably saying to themselves, dude are you stupid, are you off your head refusing this guy's request for a simple bag of crisps?) He continued to ask one more time and then I gave in; I was getting tired of him annoying me, so I gave it to him. Here, I gave him one crisp, (Ha Ha

Ha), I am laughing because it was so insulting to offer him just one crisp. Man, he wanted the whole packed and I offered him one. I can now see the steam coming out of his ears with rage, the anger all building up due to me embarrassing him in front of his friends by only offering him one piece. Well, I was not ready for what was to follow. I gave him the crisp and he looked at it and then looked at me. He said, "Are you joking, is this all you're going to give me?", as he held this one piece of crisp in his hand. I had the tenacity, the boldness, the stupidity to say 'Aye, that's all I'm going to gave ye, its ma lunch and am hungry". (This means in proper English, "yes, that is all I am going to give you. It is my lunch and I am hungry") well, it's as if the earth stood still for a moment, there was silence.

Then wait for it, here it comes, bang! Wow, I hit the floor like there was an explosion. I mean, I hit that floor in a split second, he whacked me right in the side of the head, man, I thought someone had hit me on the side of the head with a hammer. The power of his punch would have put a hole in the walls man. But the funny thing was it never really hurt as much as the other lunatics punch or even the head butting incident. But, it still floored me; I don't think it took much to floor me right enough as I said I was a skinny wee boy. So, I got up and looked at him, and that was probably the worst thing I could have done, maybe he thought I was challenging him, of which I certainly wasn't. But he took it different I guess, so when I turned away my head he whacked me again. For some reason I never went down this time, it's as if I was used to it or something. It was such a strange moment what went into my head. I thought, if I don't go down, this guy is going to waste me, he is going to trample all over my head here, but then I paused, even if I do go down he may still do it and this may be the start of his bullying towards me also. So here I am in a dilemma, "Do I continue to go down and take a beating or do I stay up and wait for him to hit me another blow?" Well, I don't know what happened or how it happened but I immediately turned round and whacked him in the face! I mean my punch probably felt like an insect hitting his face, he didn't even budge, and yet I used all my strength in swinging a punch in his face. Well that was it for me, he just whacked me and whacked me until I hit the deck then he started to kick my body and face. There was no fighting back this time, I was on the ground and just wondering, "What did you do Sean?" Why did you do that?" So he just kept kicking me, so I covered my face with my arms so there would be no blows to my face or head. My stomach and ribs took a pounding man. It really hurt! I tried to curl up my legs to my stomach but for some reason he managed to get through my legs, he would then jump on top of me with his feet landing on the side of my body and legs, after a minute he stopped and I just lay there, there was no way I was getting back up. They went away and never uttered a word, it's as if nothing happed. So I waited for a few seconds, just to make sure they were gone, because I watched movies were the victim is hiding or running and then slowly makes a move forward or to step out from where they are and then, bam! They get caught again. So I was playing it safe. I got up slowly and looked around and never saw them, so I sat up on the benches holding my stomach, man it was painful, I started to cry with pain and fear I guess. And yet, all that time he was there beating me I never cried. Very strange, but what a mistake I made over just a wee packet of crisps.

Sometimes I look at myself and thought, that could be my selfish side kicking in, or that could be my stubborn side that got me into trouble. Once I am determined to do something I try to stick to it, like this perfect situation where I was not going to part with my crisps. This was a true turning point for me in a few ways; this situation in that cloakroom opened a door for me to refrain from receiving the beatings from these guys. For some reason it worked on my favor. It wasn't too long before I crossed their path again in the school corridor going to class. I was walking towards them and thinking, 'Crap, why me? Why did I have to bump into them?' And yet as I was walking closer to them I kept my eyes on them for a second, I was trying to make myself aware of how many they were, how they are looking at me, if they talking to each other, like planning something for myself. Then I looked away. I looked at the leader straight in the eye, and I was thinking, 'Well, if you're going to do something then I will be ready this time'. I had no idea, not as if I was going to do anything back to him. Nothing happened they just walked on past. I was so relieved, I was so joyful man, and

I was amazed I got past this time without any conflict. I thought maybe they like me now, maybe he will consider me as a friend since I stood up to him. In life, sometimes there will be circumstances where you may have to stand your ground, take that step of courage and hold so preciously. You may be completely terrified, completely outclassed or know you are no match for what you are facing, but there must be a time where your fear and lack of faith in your abilities must be put to the test. In this case, this was one of my tests. This was a test for me that if I never stood my ground, if I never hold my own bravery, even if I was a skinny, feeble little guy with no real strength, then I would be facing these thugs for the whole duration of my school days that I had left. I had to make a stand!

That opportunity came sooner than I expected or wanted. Let me tell you, this confrontation with these thugs was on a continuous basis, every time these guys would pick on one weaker than them, less powerful, less mature in a way and they would always take things from other kids. I and some of my friends would hate them. My big friend Joe, remember the one who beat me at pool and took all my soccer souvenir programs? Yes, that Joe. He really hated them. Joe & I would still be friends and for some reason we were getting closer again, maybe he was my protector. Joe could handle himself as I was saying previously. He was bigger and stronger, although he was a quiet big guy, he was fun. But when time came, he made himself known to anyone who wanted to mess with him. Joe obviously knew of my beatings and suddenly would hang around with me more than usual again. We would have fun as he was in a few of my classes, and he was never interested in classes either. We were both dummies as we would say. Joe really wanted to have an opportunity to have his way with these guys, he was afraid of no one. He would face goliath, and that he did later on. I will tell you a few more stories about Joe. But for now let's get back to how this escalated in to something bigger. It wasn't long before my favorite thug, my head butting friend caught up with me. We met again on the playground, again I was walking out the door and he pulled me up. I thought, "Oh no, not you again". Here we go. Head butt to the face, down I go and the rest is history. He would sometimes just push me and say many crude words towards me, of which, again, I didn't mind, better than getting a blow to the face. But most of the times a smack right in the face. But there was a time I didn't go down or cry. I looked at him as if to say, "Is that all you've got fool?" But it wasn't, he had more, he really let loose with his fists punching me repeatedly and then pulling me down by the hair, and then kicking into my face. He would continue to punch and kick my face, there wasn't a lot I could do back, I mean he had me by the hair, so I couldn't look up or escape so he had control of the situation, but then all of a sudden I heard a smack. Immediately his hands let go of my hair and as I looked up, who was there? Yes, my big guardian angel, Joe. Joe had came to my rescue and jumped in to help me out. Well, Joe started to wade into this guy, punching him in the face a few times, this guy would be shouting at Joe, "What you doing, this has nothing to do with you, this is our fight". Joe would reply, "Why don't you pick up someone your own size? Why don't you pick on me?" I was jumping with joy, my big buddy had my back, and he was looking after his wee weak friend. So, these two were now at it with each other. Joe again started to beat on him. The thug would try to fight back but he was no match for Joe. He was getting beat up by Joe. So I thought, "This is my chance to get this guy back for all those times he beat me up, the punches, kicks and the famous head butt". I went to work. I ran to him and kick him in the stomach, and he looked at me as if to say, "When I get you, you are dead". I really felt that he was saying those words to me. But it didn't stop me, Joe pulled him down by the hair and started punching into his face, so I jumped in and kick him in the face. I am telling you I was still terrified, I never kicked anyone in the face but I took pleasure in doing it to this guy, I really enjoyed it so much that I kept doing it. I would start punching him in the face and saying, "Yep, can you feel it, how do you like it getting done to you?" And I would start to verbally abuse him. If my parents would have heard the words that came out of my mouth, I would have been grounded forever. I hope if they ever read this book, they will never ask me what those words were (probably, they will have an idea, because remember the story about what I said to the priest in the earlier days?

Well, this was down the same road, similar words except much more vulgar and aggressive). Yippee, payback time! We finished on top of this thug, he was on the floor just lying there, and pretty much helpless, the same way I was when he was beating me up. Man, what a feeling, paying someone back for the things they done to you. Although I knew, that if I meet this guy on my own, I am dead meat, I mean, my days will be over. Anyway, we left this guy lying on the deck and I felt like I could take on the world, when I was beside big Joe. I was feeling so proud and was looking around to see if anyone had witnessed what I had done to this guy, so they would know not to mess with me (He He He), I was thinking I was some sort of big guns now. Joe paved the way that I was on a mission to prove I will not be bullied again or people will suffer. Well, news did travel fast in school; you know what it is like. Man news spreads as fast as the wind blows. People were coming up to me and saying, "I heard you gave so & so a beating. Is it true?" Well, I would say with a smile, "Of course, he pushed me too far". Man they were so amazed, as people knew, I couldn't really fight and was too small to hit or bully anyone, especially of his caliber and standing. Anyway, I was enjoying every minute of the attention while it lasted. Well, life went on, and this started a trend of fights now for me. Strange things happened in our area, even in school or out of school. When you have been in a fight with another guy who has a reputation, like this guy did, and you were lucky enough to beat him, well it opened a can of worms with others. The reason being is that people around the same caliber or better than the one you beat would all of a sudden want to take you on. It was like contests were all you were doing was making it to the next round and the next opponent would be a little more difficult. It wasn't too long before I got my next challenge put in front of me. One of the gang members that this thug used to be a member of also challenged me to a fight. I never really had much dealing with this new bloke who wanted to smash my head in, probably because we beat up his friend. So he obviously wanted to get me back while I was on my own. Well, I had no intention of taking this guy on, he was bigger than me, which most people were anyway, but I never dreamed of coming up against him. I always thought he was an alright guy, I never heard any bad rumors against him, or bad dealing he had done, except he took drugs in school. Anyway, he started pushing me around and mouthing off to me, provoking me to fight or hit him. I would just keep saying, "I don't want to fight you, I have no reason to fight with you". He kept saying, "Are you just going to let me push you around and not do anything?" I still refused, and then he dragged me by the hair and was dragging me around on the ground, I was getting angry, but I knew, I couldn't beat him, so I still done nothing, then he started punching me in the face and that was sore, I felt it, his hands were like steel hitting me. It was so painful man, then I was thinking, this guy is going to waste me here whether I fight or not. So I said to myself, "Stuff it, if I don't hit back I am going to suffer, and if I do hit back then probably I will suffer more, so may as well get something in return for my suffering". So here I go, I wrestled to get up on my feet, then I got loose from his grip on my hair, then I started to swing punches, I don't know if they were making an impact or even hitting him, but I was swinging anyway.

This was crazy, here I was like a little madman, swinging punches into the air, but all of a sudden, I caught him with a punch, and man I saw the look on his face as if to say, "I didn't know you could punch that hard" Well that was all I needed, I knew I hurt him a little so I punched him, and pulled his hair, he was big and it was awkward to pull him down, but somehow I managed to get his head down and I started to punch him in the face. I was on a roll, it was like the adrenalin just kicked in and I was in control now, he is sort of giving up in a way, probably he was shocked to have me taking over and being in control of the fight. I wouldn't stop; I was like a crazy man. I was shouting all sorts of words at him, but I think that was just the shock, fear, and the rush of having control. I was making sure people around me were noticing me. I made sure he paid the price, I was continuing to punch him and then I got him on the ground and I started kicking him on the face too. I was so much enjoying winning; after all, I was always on the losing side until Joe helped me out with my bully friend. Well the fight lasted about five minutes with me eventually shouting at him, "Do you give up, do you give up?", I was hoping he would say yes so I could stop and go home, just in case he managed to overpower me and start winning, there was still some fear there although I was winning. He eventually said, "Yes, I give up, you win". Man when I heard those words I could have jumped up and touched the stars, I was so ecstatic, my first ever winning a fight on my own against a good fighter and a guy with a solid reputation. So I let him go, and everybody who was watching were all cheering for me and shouting my name. It's as if I was a superstar. I was enjoying the moment, even though I had blood on my face and shirt again, I wasn't caring because I also had his blood on me as well (He He He). As I was walking home that day from school, I kept thinking of that fight, on how I managed to beat this guy, I really couldn't believe I done it. I was also thinking, what will happen once word gets around among his friends, I mean the reason he came up to me was because of what Joe & I did to the thug. So I am thinking that the same is going to happen again, some other gang member is going to take me on, someone who is even a better fighter.

So again, I had days of panic wondering when that moment is going to be, and who it is going to be. I was having all the people in their gang in my mind and saying, "Well if it is this one then I am dead, if it is that one then I am dead". There was one or two who were just 'hanger-on', meaning just hanging with these guys for protection, they could not hurt a fly, they couldn't handle themselves, If you said, "Boo" to them, they would jump. I would love to have one of them come up against me, but that wasn't going to happen. That is not how it worked on those days, if you beat one member then you would always be facing one who is a better fighter or who has a tougher reputation. That is the joy of fighting, you need to move up the ranks, you don't' go back the way, you only go forward. Don't get me wrong, I was not looking to fight the world or even looking to be in fights every day, I would rather not be in any of it, as long as I could just pick on ones I knew would fight back or be able to defend themselves. But unfortunately, it was like once you go down this road, then you seem to have trouble come to you whether you like it or not. Even out of school, when we would play soccer. It is supposed to be a friendly sport, a sport of skill, speed, strategy and above all, of entertainment. It is, most of the time, but there are occasions were you get head cases that would spoil the game. We were still young and still very much learning the game and having fun at the same time. I was still playing for St Andrew Football Club and at the age of fifteen, I was still relatively young. I was supposedly maturing as I was in my last couple of years of school. Once you get to the last years, people look up to you, you are the elders of the school and should be leading by example.

Out in the soccer field it never really showed at all. I mean we were getting violent as a club, with young boys just out to hit a ball around. We were not the best soccer team in our district, we never really win anything, any championships, or leagues, or even cups, but we tried. We were a team of young boys who loved to play and loved the excitement of playing other teams that were favorites against us. Meaning, we were not expecting a great result each week, but we put all of our heart and soul into the game. We would run up and down that park for the full ninety minutes, we would be tired, but we wanted to win so badly that we were just running on pure adrenalin. We were not the worse team in the district but were not in the top half either. We had some great teams to play against; it is like the champs Manchester United playing a number of low level teams and is expected to win. Most teams we came up against were much favored to win also. On occasions, we would cause an upset and win a game against a top team. Man when that happened, we would celebrate all week and we would be ready to face goliath the following week. But that is just the excitement of winning. It helps boost up your confidence, like in any sport or activity, if you win at it then it makes you feel great and it encourages you to do even greater the next time. Especially in the case of schooling, you do your projects or homework every night, (except for me), and then you hear the result from the teacher when you submit your work. Whatever the result is that comes from the teacher and they way it is expressed back to you can make all the difference in how you will approach the next project or homework. I mean, if you get a great mark on your project and the teacher really praises you for the work and effort, then you will feel great and it will boost up your confidence and make you feel positive towards that class or topic, correct? But if your teacher gives you a poor mark and make comments that your effort was poor, or lack of thought went into your work, then you will be disappointed and will feel hurt. After all, we are all human and have emotions. So, the next time you come up against that teacher, or even that subject, you will not be too enthusiastic about it, or maybe you won't even want to be there or take part. But these are the challenges we all face in our lives, some things go well and we're encouraged to go on and do even better, but sometimes we don't do so well but just need to focus a little more and set a goal and aim for a better result next time. The same was with all of us on that park, we would be all hyped up going on to the field and would say to each other, "Ok lads, let make this our game, we can do this, keep it tight and let's make it happen". We would always be encouraging each other throughout the 90 minutes. It was very important that we do not get discouraged if we are losing or having a bad game, because all it takes is for one person to lose that positive attitude and the rest of the team can go down as well and before you know it, we have thrown in the towel and it is really sad when that happens.

There were some occasions where this happened, we were playing so bad and everything was going wrong and one player would just say, "What Is the point? We are crap, they are much better than us". Well, I was always a kind of mouthy person on the field; in other words, I would always be shouting words of encouragement, positive words to lift up the team. I would hate to be depressed while we are all playing a game that we love; it just needed a little more passion and effort. I would directly go to our player who was feeling that way and really try to boost him up. I really knew the consequences if we give up, because once you give up, then there is no chance that you will win. Believe me when I say this, your opponents know when you have given up and they will not be your friends, they will go all the way to humiliate you the best way they can. There are no friends on the field, both teams are there to win, it's as simple as that, no prize for second place. I know with my loud shouts and rants, that I would be annoying others on the field, especially our opponents. But I wasn't caring about that, my goal was to encourage our team and I would go on for the full ninety minutes of a game. I thought I was being positive when I was trying to build up our team's confidence and get them focused on winning.

When I look back and remember those times, now I can see how much I annoyed others on the field. I can see why these guys were so angry with me, many times I was told to shut my mouth, or give my mouth a rest. Man that was like showing a red rag to a bull, it got my temper up and I shouted even more, just to annoy them. That was me, you tell me to do something then I will do the opposite, especially if it will annoy you, or be a hindrance to you. So now, my passion for the team was growing more and more, and with a few enemies against me I was raring to go. I was the one who was like the raging bull on the field, you didn't have to show me a red flag, I was always ready for action, always ready to attack when given the chance or opportunity. Now, go back a few pages to what we have just learned about the series of bullying in school, me standing up for myself and how my attitude went from a timid wee school boy to this hero who had beaten up one of the renowned fighters of the school, so I was up for it, I was ready to take on the world. So here we are, on the field running our wee legs off, trying to impress our manager and supporters. Of course, we were the underdogs, as always, but we were still there and we had a job to do. Most of the players on our team all grew up playing soccer together and even played for St Andrew's since we were 8 years old, so we all knew each other very well, we knew each other's strengths and weaknesses, we knew where each of us should play on the field and how we worked together. But I guess the issue was, we were not just as skillful as other teams, individually. You may have heard the saying, 'more hands make light work', well it is simple on the field, if we all put in the same effort then it makes it much easier to put up a fight against our opponents and at the same time you are not making things easy for them. The harder a team works together against the opposing team then the harder they must work to get the results that they want, so then you have a battle. As individuals, we must strive to give our best at all times, we must have the desire to succeed and want to win, we must have the passion in our heart that will drive us forward in achieving what we set out to achieve. This is all a combination of many things, when we talk about soccer we talk about few very important factors that will evidently have an effect on your performance.

Let's talk about strategy first, we must have set a design or play on how you think we could win the game, there must be a specific way that you feel you can overcome your opponents. Normally, you will have some background on the team you are playing; your manager or coach will have done his homework on the team you will be up against. This is when he will discuss these measures of his strategy with the team, normally we don't listen, we just want to get out there and do the stuff. However, he must inform us of their continuous performances up to this point. If a team has won all their games leading up to your games, then they are going to be full of confidence, they will be on fire, and they will be looking to add another victory to their belt. In this instance, they are going to come up gunning for you; they are not going to let you get in their way of victory, just like any other sport or competitive game. On the other hand, if they have been playing poorly and have lost a few games or they are on a losing streak, then the coach will use this to build you up, to give you confidence to say that this team are not really that good, hoping you will pick up on it and go out there with a positive attitude to win. The second important factor is how you have prepared for the game. There are loads of issues that can relate to this, but the most important factor is your attitude. Have you come to the game fully focused and ready to give it your all? No matter what else is happening in your daily life, you need to find a way to put it on the back burner, you need to find a way to deal with things after the match, the reason being is, if your mind is elsewhere, then you are definitely not going to give the rest of your team mates the best you have, and you're certainly not going to give your manager your best, or show him you true talents or capabilities on the field. There are many distractions that can cause you not to focus on your game. A few is, being personal, family, school, friends, or you just may lack interest that day, you may want to be somewhere else except on that field. I can tell you in reality this is real, there have been occasions where my mind, my heart and my soul are completely elsewhere, and mine was mostly on girls.

I would suddenly wonder into a dream and start thinking about a certain girl in school or situation with a girl and then not pay attention to the game, and then all of a sudden, the ball would go flying past me, it is quite funny, as all I would here my manager shouting is "Sean, pay attention, get the ball". Then suddenly, I would snap out of the wee dream and run like a maniac after that ball, man it was embarrassing, because sometimes I would be too late and the other team would score a goal, I felt bad. I would be thinking to myself, all my team mates will be hating me right now, I can imagine what they are all saying under their breath about me. So, that is why it is so important to focus at all times no matter what area of your life you are in. Even at our young age and playing sports, if you want to develop and become great at that event or certain activity, then you need to do your part. Put in the effort, put in the time, put in the dedication and commitment, and surely only positive results will come out of it. Another great factor that you should build into your individual game and performance is respect. You should have respect for yourself, for your team mates and your opponents. In the first instance, you should respect yourself, meaning you should have a certain attitude or demeanor that you display on the field, in front of your fellow team members and in front of your manager. This is where I mostly failed in. Although I was so determined, so enthusiastic, so passionate about winning and playing the game, I would let myself get carried away and lose my composure on the field. Maybe when I think about this part it may have been because of my loud shouting and my ranting and raving for the players, maybe I came across as an aggressive person. I would always watch the attitude of the other player, especially our opponents; I would monitor them very carefully and see if anyone was like a trouble maker or instigator (like me,) then I would keep an eye on that person. I would watch how they would react to my screaming from the top of my voice, and as I said, if it annoyed them, I continue to do it even more. This was a kind of way for me to distract them, to try and put them off their game, after all, we needed all the help we can get, as I said before. On several occasions as I would be screaming, it would also be because we were losing and I am not a good loser at all. So this losing and my screaming may have led to a little anger management problem and coupled with my aggressive-ness in fighting in school ultimately led to me carrying the violence onto the field. Yep, you guessed it. I started to lose my cool on the field. This was not a normal thing to see or watch; not very often would you see or hear of such acts on the field. If there was any circumstances were a fight broke out, or a player assaulted another player then they would immediately be ordered off the field, they would be red carded. No one wanted that because you get pun-ished by the official league committee usually suspending you for a few games, man that was a killer; it was so annoying not being allowed to play. Also, our manager would normally punish you also, because you brought a bad reputation to the soccer club name, and that wasn't good. Well, it wasn't before long that I got started on my reign of terror on the field. I mean, you cannot visualize me in this scenario, I was one of the smallest on the field out of the 22 players, and yet you would know I was on their team because you would hear me before you could see me.

Yes, I was the loudest on the field and I made sure I was heard and people knew I was playing. It was my trademark. When I was shouting, it was mostly for encouragement to my team players, as I mentioned, but this excitement and anger started mixing, about ninety five percent of my shouting was good for my team, but the other five percent was towards the opposing team. Ha Ha Ha, I can laugh now because when I look back at my antics I should have been banned from the sport forever. That five percent of shouting towards the other team was really nasty and was not showing respect at all. All I needed was a little reason to go off and I did, I would go on a total tantrum and start shouting abuse at the other team. I would curse at them saying, "C'mon lads, this team are a bunch of 'something', we can beat them". That was the beginning, and this would really get them annoyed, but at the same time they would be shocked at the words coming out of my mouth. I got that bad that their manager would complain to the referee to get me off the field. Although that didn't work, the referee would some-times have a word in my ear and tell me to relax and calm down. This would normally work for a short while, depending on how we were playing and if I really didn't like the team we were playing.

Our main competitor at that time would be Gourock Youth Athletic Club; they were very close to us in the same area but different town. Their playing fields were only like three to five miles away from ours but their park was smaller and very unusual. Most teams didn't like playing them, they were very good and not many teams would beat them on their home ground. Gourock were probably the best team in our whole district, but for some reason we were never afraid when we played them, we loved it, we were all geared up for those games against them. Although most times they would beat us, it would be a very close game. They would win by one goal only. There was never any fighting with us and them, we were like friends as we all went to the same school together and know each other very well. But a strange thing happened, all of a sudden when we went to play at their home ground they could not beat us, it would always end in a draw. A draw for us is a great result, because we never expected anything but to lose against them, so we were so happy when we got a point out of the game. These games were our best games, our team came out against them and played with all of our hearts, these were the most entertaining games for us, and we all loved it! But I can't say the same comments about some of our other competitors, as I was saying about my emotions getting the best of me, my excitement and anger taking over on the field. Here's the drama of it.

There was this one team, they were from Glasgow, and man, when we played them, I don't know what happened, it was like that incident when a red rag was thrown in the face of the bull, I was that bull. Even before the game started I had this very nasty attitude knowing that I was going on there to cause trouble. I really don't know how it managed to build up, or obtain this attitude against this certain team, as they never did anything wrong towards us except beat us, maybe that was all the excuse I needed. Or maybe, it was more of a religious act, after all they were called Rangers SC and we were called St. Andrews SC. In Scotland there are two main soccer clubs that dominate soccer in the whole of Scotland; they are 'Glasgow Celtic' & 'Glasgow Rangers'. It is so ironic that the two best teams come from the same city and are within close proximity of each other and one is of 'Catholic' religion and the other of 'Protestant' religion. These religious acts between catholic & protestant go away back well before our grand fathers and great grand fathers; it has been brought up through the generations and continues to play a very big factor in the separation between both sects in the church and out of the church. It used to be a very strict regime that only men of a catholic background would be accepted to play for Celtic and that a man of a protestant background would only be accepted to play for Rangers. Anything else is not just going to happen. This ultimately continued to cause the division between the religions and between players on and off the field. It is also a major concern when it comes to where your house would be situated, what area or town. As there are towns which are predominately catholic and towns that are protestant and depending on which one you are, then you do not go into the other area, or you will be in big trouble. It also played a major part in what school we would be attending. Again, there are schools specifically for children who are catholic and who are protestant, and believe me, whatever one you were you were not allowed to go into the other religions school, it just didn't happen for obvious reasons. I was brought up in a catholic family environment and everything was either catholic or nothing. There was a serious problem in relation to this catholic and protestant thing, it was like you were not allowed to be associated with the other religion, it was like totally forbidden. In some occasions if your school colleagues found out that you had a friend who was a protestant they would give you a hard time and also they would wait for your friend and give them a beating and tell them to stay away from you. This was so serious that whenever you came across someone of the other religion, they would hurl insults at you. They would give verbal abuse, and depending if you answered back, then you would get a beaten, and the same was for us. If we came across a few Protestants and they were on their own or even with friends, if there were more of them, they would give us the abuse, and if we retaliated with our words then we would get the beating. So it was actually the same on both sides, no one side was better than the other. You know the old saying 'it takes two to tango', well; we were as bad as each other. Now you have a little picture of how this religious thing affects every aspect of our lives even as being raised in our homes or in our school and now we take it into sports as well. So here we are the catholic team going to play against the protestant team. I really can't remember if I was the only one who was up to take this team on in more than just a soccer way. I wanted more, it wasn't because I knew anything about catholic against protestant, I think it was just because of whom we were and the division was already created for us by the generations before us. I know that we all knew the difference and that we went to a catholic school and all that, but soccer is soccer, it is only a game, right? Wrong! It is all about winning, even to this day on the professional field where Celtic and Rangers continue to compete; it is about winning, beating the other team. I mean, these supporters are called 'die-hards' meaning they would give up everything to follow their club, they would give up their jobs, their houses if they could or had too, I believe.

Don't think for one moment that I am the only guy in Scotland that wanted too, or took part in fights, no, even these adults who follow these professional clubs and who pay large amounts of money to follow them, have their way of causing fights against each other. Every time when these teams meet, there are casualties of the game. The reason is either over religion, upbringing or could be generational curses. This has been imparted to us from the generations and it is a hard thing to break, there is such thing as generational curses, wherein the younger generations are left with the scars to face and the traditions to follow that has been carried on and passed down to them, and they don't even know it. We all just do as we are told to do, or made to follow or understand, what our ancestors or parents want us to. Well, of course as we all grow, get older and get more mature in life, we should have the right to choose what we want to do, what we want to follow or what we want to leave behind or step away from. Sometimes this is easier said than done, especially, if it is imparted to us from a family tradition, carried on through friendships and/or where we have to be raised and schooled. Well, I was among that era where we went to catholic school, had catholic friends, raised in a catholic environment, followed a catholic soccer team. So, here we are on the playing field with a protestant team of which were pretty good because some of their players would be recognized from the main Rangers FC that I described earlier, so they were much better than us, but still we were ready for them, I was up for it big time. Bring it on man! This was the first time we had played this team but we heard that they were a good team and because of the name they carried 'Rangers FC', we were already intimidated by them, but we had to go out and see what we could do. So we're here, at our home park, playing in front of our home supporters, which is really a huge help in these game where you are up against great opposition. When the referee blew the whistle to start the game, our supporters were all cheering like crazy for us and it was really giving us a massive confidence boost. Always in the beginning ten minutes, we are all running around like headless chickens chasing after the ball, not really having any true focus except win that ball. Then our manager would shout as us, "Right, settle down, think about what you are doing, and pay attention to our strategy". We would all seem to get our heads together and start positioning ourselves correctly as to where we should be playing on the field. We would start looking around to see where we are weak, either lacking players in the middle, front or back. I would as usual do the shouting from the back and try to advise my co-players of their positions and if they seem to be wandering off or not. There was always a weakness of our part like we would lose a goal at the very beginning and that would throw us off a little. It made it harder then because we are coming from behind, and now the opponent has an advantage over us. I believe that was always the cause of us not being organized at the start and not playing in our correct positions. We would always look at each other when that other team scored to say, "Who's fault was that?" and normally, the defenders would tend to get the blame. Well, when I see this team rejoicing over scoring a goal then it would really get by back up, it would get me angry and then I am much more determined to get back at them. My shouting starts to get louder and much fiercer, it tends to lean towards the one who scored. I would normally shout out, "Don't let him get past us again", and that was the nice way of saying it. I didn't always say things nice once the game was progressing on. I would make it a point to do what was necessary so that, that boy never got passed us or me again. I was always looking at the opponents to see who were their main players and what position they played or what role they had in their team. Most times, it was the forwards whom I would be marking, me being on the left side of defense, I would be marking the right side forward player. When this player realized that he cannot pass me due to my speed then he would swap over to the left side of the field hoping that our defender at that side will not be so fast. But my job was to mark him, so I followed him, these guys thought they were cute; they would take you for a walk. In other words, they would walk around hoping that you would give up and not follow them around giving them the freedom to play, there was no way it happened, unless I knew that the player coming in at my side was faster than him, I would tell my colleague to mark the one I was marking and I would take this guy who was faster.

Anyway, that is the tactics of the teams and you just run with it. Well, there was one guy on their side, the one who scored the first goal who I had my eyes on. I knew that he was going to play a big part in this team's success and our manager already warned us about him. So I gave myself the task of marking him, I was going to make it my job not to let him pass me or to score, wherever he went, I followed him. I know I was annoying him but that is also part of my tactics and make them lack focus or concentration then hopefully his game would suffer. Well, it wasn't too long into the game and because of my continuous shouting and encouraging my co-player, this guy started to make some comments to me. He would tell me to shut my mouth for a while. I was giving him a headache. Well, imagine that, this guy from the opposing team telling me to shut up. Funny! As I look back to that game, I laugh. Little did he know he was telling a little monster to shut his mouth, and I know he had the courage to say that to me because I was so little and he was a big guy maybe around 5' 10' or more. That was all I needed, he just threw fuel into the fire, and this little fire horse was just heating up. So when I heard this, I automatically replied, "Who do you think you're talking too?" He replied, "I am talking to you motor mouth". Motor mouth is a term we use for someone who constantly talks and never shuts up. I immediately responded, "Is that right? We'll see if you're still saying that once you have that ball at your feet and I bring you down". He said, "You bring me down? I can't wait to see that". At that point he was trying to move away from me, but that was it for me, he was mine. I followed him around that park, I mean, I went everywhere he went. Then after a minute or two, the ball came over to our side of the park, we were both running for it and it was a little distance away from both of us. I was getting their first and he was right at my back, so I thought, if I get to it then I can't take him down. My only intention was to bring this guy down on the deck. So I was making it look like he was catching up with me as I slowed down a little. Well here it comes, he connected with ball and hit it passed me, so he was running for it and so was I, I knew at that point I could catch him no matter how hard he ran, so I waited for the right moment. Both of us running for the ball and exactly once he got his feet to it, I carried out what we call a sliding tackle. Basically, it is when we slide on the ground while trying to hit the ball first and hopefully taking out the player at the same time. Honestly, my timing was perfect, I caught that ball smack in the middle while connecting to his legs and he went down like a sack of potatoes. Man, was I not happy? The smiles on my face said it all.

Another great factor about this tackle was that it was at our side of the park where our supporters where standing, so immediately they began cheering for me and clapping their hands and all that. It was awesome, I felt on top of the world, and when I got up I said to him, "You have not managed to shut my mouth yet, big man, anytime you want to try, just let me know". Well the war was on, I opened up a can of worms, and yet all I done was a fair tackle. But everyone knew the severity of the tackle was no way a friendly one. But still, the referee thought it was good and I never got into trouble, so to me I had a free ticket to do it again. Well, play went on and again whenever the ball came to him I would be right on his tail, carrying out a few more sliding tackles. There came a point where we exchanged words again, and this time, little to my knowledge the referee was watching us and came over to us. He had a few words in our ear and advised us to play soccer and stop the non-sense; it is only a game so enjoy it. So we apologized to the referee. So we went in for the break. We normally got about five to ten minutes rest, to get drinks and for the manager to do his team talk stuff. I was on fire; I was like a crazy horse ready to jump the walls. My manager was encouraging me to keep up the great defending, but keep my head. You're right, there was no way I was going to remain calm, this guy had my back up and he was going to suffer big time. So here we go back out for the second half, we are still losing one goal to zero, but we had plenty of time to catch up. So we were playing pretty good, and through great team work we scored our first goal. It was great, it really lifted us up big time, we were all jumping around like crazy, c'mon, and this wee St Andrew's SC scored a goal against the mighty Rangers FC. We enjoyed the moment. So we kind of took over for a while with great passing and skillful play by a couple of our best players. We had a few really good players, who dominated the midfield, middle of the park area which gave us great advantage. This wasn't being received too well with this team and they started to play dirty, they started doing tackles that were not good, and we were all getting mad. So you can imagine all our tempers were flying high and there was some nasty fools being made by both sides. Here I come again, my friend had the ball and running at me, he kicked it past me and as he was running he elbowed me in the side. Man, it was painful and I shouted out to the referee for a foul. So we got the call. We had a free kick as it is called, in other words the ball is stopped at the area the foul took place and I could kick the ball anywhere I want. So as I wanted to take it quickly, this guy would stand in front of me not allowing me to do what I wanted, so I whack the ball of his face that moved him. He shouted to the referee and then when the ref told me to take it again, I done the same thing, he was so mad. He came running up to me and I was ready to knock him on the ground, but I waited to see what he would do. He pushed me, but I saw the ref coming and thought if I hit him I am of the park and my team needs all players in order to win this game. So I held back and shouted on the ref. The ref came over and gave him a yellow card, meaning a warning, one more warning and he is off. So I was cool that he got into trouble. I laughed in his face and as he was walking away. I was enjoying this moment, the bitter, evil minded wee man, me, was on top of his game, I was winning the personal battle with this guy. So the game went on, and tempers were really heating up on the park, there was a few more nasty tackles.

Then an amazing thing happened, we scored another goal, well, you could hear the cheers for miles, we were so noisy and we're running around that park as if we had won the world cup. We were ecstatic with joy and our opponents were not happy at all. They came to us thinking it would be a walk in the park to beat us, little did they know that they were playing a team with hearts like a lion. So, it was me and my 'friend's' time again, hear he comes with ball, trying to be skillful and trying to pass me, well he hit the ball and ran for it, we were both sprinting for this and again I made a sliding tackle, but this time, I miss judged it and never touched the ball this time, I connected with his legs instead and man, he went flying in the air. Well, the referee blew his whistle and their manager and players were all shouting and screaming at him to send me off, because the tackle was bad. I really had no intention of hitting the ball, I went straight for his legs and I got them, and I brought that guy down so hard on the ground, you can hear the thud of his body hitting the hard gravel surface. He was rolling on the floor moaning and groaning and hoping the referee would take severe action against me. He got it right! I got a yellow card and a warning, that if I done this sort of tackle again then I would be off. I didn't mind getting the yellow card as it still allowed me to play. After a minute, the player got up and he was limping, I looked at him and laughed at him. After that point it became really nasty, I think I started a war. The tackles and aggressions that be flying around between both sides was nasty. They managed to get in a few nasty tackles, taking out a few of our players and were we all ready to battle now. Another few minutes would go by and the ball was up at the other end of the park, but I and my opponent were standing together and we were exchanging nasty words again, then he suddenly stuck his elbow in my face and I immediately hit the ground, hoping the referee would catch it and send him off. Unfortunately, he didn't, so he got away with it, but man, I was so mad at this guy now that I was not caring if I got sent off the field or not. A few of our supporters were shouting. "Wee-man, don't let him get away with that; bring him out of the game", Meaning, take him down so he can't play anymore. Well, I don't think I could do that, as that means like break his leg so he can't play. I mean I am a nasty wee fighting man, but to break someone's leg is a different story. So I would plan on something else instead, I knew I would get my moment again with the ball. My manager at that time was a woman and I was a great friend of the family and I was a friend with her son, as we knew each other through soccer and school. She was called Mrs. Mills, she was a wee energetic woman, always shouting at the side of the park, encouraging us and getting us motivated. She likes me very much because I was dating her daughter Angie for a while, so I was a close friend and she knew my wee temper and knew I was not going to let this guy get away with this. She was trying to tell me to stay calm that it is not worth getting sent off for this guy. But would I listen? No! I had my stubborn head on, on my own mission, to get back at this guy. Well my time came, again when the ball was down that side of the field and I knew the referee couldn't see us, I took the opportunity to whack this guy in the mouth, and I just swung my hand and caught him, bang on the nose. It was so cool, a big guy like him getting whacked on the face by a small guy like me and he went down, groaning like a big baby.

His manager was shouting like crazy to the referee to stop the game and attend to his player and he was shouting that I knocked him down. Immediately, the referee came running over to the player lying on the ground looking at his injury. There was no immediate physical evidence of any violence towards him, no blood coming from his face or marks, so he pulled me over and asked me what happened. I told him, "I don't know why he is acting like this; he just fell to the ground and probably hoping you will think I assaulted him so you could send me off. I never touched him ref, honest. How could a guy my size hit some one of his size?"(Is there anything wrong with a little white lie?) C'mon, this guy deserved it; he whacked me in the face with his elbow, so it was payback time for me. So to me we were even, it was all square now, he got me and I got him, but I was still gunning for this guy. Another few minutes passed and we clashed again, the ball was kicked up to our side and we were both running for it and it was like a fifty/fifty tackle, meaning both of us clashed at the same time which is very normal. But I managed to slide an extra leg in and caught him on his legs running my football studs on the bottom of my boots right down his leg. Man this leaves a bad mark; it scratches the skin off and gives it a very nasty rash and it stings so badly. So he wasn't happy at all at this so he immediately jumped up and challenged me and started to push me, so I retaliated and pushed him back and then that was it, we both lashed out and swinging punches all over the place. It was mental, we were both going at it like wild animals, we would not stop, then one of his co-players would join in and start punching me, then one of my co-players would help me and start punching him and before you know it, there was like ten of us all scrapping away on the field and my manager was going ballistic, she was going absolutely crazy with us. So after the referee managed to break this mad moment of violence on the field, he pulled the two of us over and we got our marching orders, we got sent to the dressing rooms. In other words, we got sent off the field, our game was over. So we were made to sit at the side of the pitch and wait for the game to finish, there was only a few minutes left anyway, so we didn't wait too long. Mrs. Mills knew me, so she kept me beside her so she could keep an eye on me after the game. She warned me, "You better not go near him, you are going straight to the dressing room or your suspended, got it?", Well I just looked at her and said nothing, and I am sure she knew exactly what was on my mind and what I was going to do. I couldn't wait for that whistle to go for the end of the game, I already knew in my mind what was going to happen.

They managed to score a goal in the dying minutes to make it level at 2-2, so we blew our chance of beating the mighty Rangers FC, but who cares, we can always beat them when we play them at their home park in Glasgow. There it goes, the whistle blows and the game is over, so we all assembled at the side as requested by Mrs. Mills, as she knew we could start trouble here. She let the opponents go first to the dressing room so we could not be a problem to them. Well there was a few of us together heading towards the dressing room and Mrs. Mills would be at my side and watching closely. Me and a couple of my co-players would start to edge away from her with a plan to attack the guy I was fighting with the co-players of his that was with him, so we never had much of a window to get to them so we had to make a move quickly, or it was gone. We just went for it, we ran to them and then we just jumped on them, starting to punch and kick them. It was a scramble, they would fight back and before you know it, both teams were throwing punches at each other, it was like something out of a movie. There was punches and kicks flying everywhere, Mrs. Mills was going crazy at us telling us to stop it, it was nuts, we were not caring because we had one intention and that was to kill these guys and make sure they paid for their attitudes on the field. For us it was great, we got the last say in the matter, we showed them not to mess with us down here, no matter who they were, especially if they are from the big city. This fighting lasted for a minute or two until we knew we had beaten them and they gave in and ran into the dressing rooms. We were ordered by our manager not to follow them, she made us stay there until they were inside and she also kept us there until they had left the premises. We were gunning for them we wanted to beat them up more and more. But that was it, they were gone, we really embarrassed our team and the name of the club. We now had a very bad reputation because of probably me and my attitude. You see, not only does your attitude have an effect on your own life but it can have an effect on those around you as well. Because of my anger, my temper and my lack of self control it brought me to include others into my world of violence of which they may not have normally been involved with. Although we all got a thrill from it at the time, now we had to deal with con-sequences of our actions. We paid the price of this during our next few training games; we were really pushed to limits with exercises. Mrs. Mills made us suffer and punished us by giving us 2 hours of pure torture, not allowing us to play. Normally we would do some physical training then play together afterwards, but not now, it is strictly tough exercise routine. Man, that was pure pain for us, we were so disgusted about that but it was completely our fault and we deserved to be punished.

Like all bad works, there is and should be a punishment served, it is justified and is the only way we will learn from our mistakes or bad behavior. It was the same in school when we would do things that distracted the class, when the teacher caught you she would discipline you and rightly so. It is no different in any other aspect of our lives. So here we are being disciplined in a way that was painful to us but also in a way that hopefully would make an impact with us so we won't carry out this same attitude on the field again. This was a two part event, as we played this team at our home park in Greenock; there was also the return game that was to be held at Rangers FC ground in Glasgow. Well, we never thought about that until weeks and weeks later when our manager told us that our next game would be away and up in Glasgow. Normally, we would be so excited in going away to play other teams as it was great playing in others' parks as they normally would have better facilities and football field than us. So were all so excited and were like asking, "Who is it we're playing? Are they good? What are the facilities like and all that?" Well, here comes the blow. She said, "Are you ready for it?" We're like, "Yes, tells us who is it", and she said, "It is Rangers FC". Wow, a massive silence came over the room and we all looked at each other with fear, we looked around and started saying to her, "Can we not change it? Can we not have them come here and play again?" This was not possible due to the fact it is the rules that each team must play each other at home and away to give both teams the same advantage. She said to us very sarcastically, "Oh what's up, don't tell me all the hard men that beat them up when they were here, are now all afraid?" She was pretty aggressive with us and at the same time being straight forward. That's what I really liked about Mrs. Mills; she was always so straight forward with everyone which was her nature. This was really going to be a testing time for us, we are going to a new area and face a team that we tried to ridicule, to embarrass, try to intimidate and even try to beat up. I guess this could be their payback time to us, if they were interested, of which we were thinking that because of their name and reputation they will treat us nice. Whoa, that was the biggest mistake of our lives; man when we got there the atmosphere was so tense. We we're absolutely scared out of our mind, as we didn't know what to expect. Oh, they were all so nice at the start then the fun began, the harsh tackles started coming in and we were hoping the referee would come to our rescue, but it was like he heard about how we treated them while at our place, so he was allowing so many bad incidents not punished. So we knew that we were on our own here, and it was not going to be easy at all. We never really focused on the game because of our fear of what was going to happen. It was no surprise that we were losing a few goals, as we did not care; we were not focused at all. I was being picked on by the same boy that I picked before and I didn't like it at all, I was not comfortable because my surroundings was not in my favor and for some reason my strong aggressive attitude was not there. You now noticed a timid, shy side of the wee monster from Greenock.

During the break, we were all quiet, and Mrs. Mills got laid into us, she was so unhappy that we were not performing to our capabilities because of our fear. It must have been one of our worst performances by far, you can tell we were just not interested in the game at all, we just wanted out of that place. And to make it worse, once we came out for the second half we noticed that their supporters were getting more and more. The whole one side was all their fans and we never had any, it was only our manager and a few of our players. We were totally outnumbered and it even got worse for us. Their fans started singing songs to us and threatening us saying that we were dead at the end of the game. On the park, I was getting pay back from my opponent, the one I picked on, he was doing to me what I was doing to him. I am sure he was enjoying this game a lot more than I was. This was the most terrifying moment of my soccer career and life. This was worse than my school bullying days with my psycho friend, remember the head-butter? This guy was sticking his elbow in my ribs, kicking my legs, punching me in the face, although I did have enough of this crap and I did retaliate, I was giving him a good run for his money by doing the same back, but you know, I had no mean streak in me at this time due to the fear for his friends and supporters. I soon realized that what I did on the park was going to be paid back to me once we were off the park. Every time I looked over at the side of the park I noticed their crowds getting bigger and bigger, man, these guys were ready for a real gang war. I was looking at them and their eyes were fixed on us giving hands gestures to say they were going to beat us up and they even started producing weapons, yes they had baseball bats in the hands and swinging them around. These guys meant business here, I am sure that they were going to kill us that we will never leave that place alive. I shouted to my manager and she was telling the rest of the boys that as soon as the whistle goes we don't go back to the changing rooms that we head straight to the van for a quick exit. So our manager and the boys managed to get all our clothes out of the changing rooms and man once that whistle went, we all ran as fast as we could into that van. We were terrified, and you probably never saw young boys run so fast in their whole life. I mean, we would all have broken the 100 meter Guinness book of records here, all you see was dust of the ground and we were all shoving each other in that van as quick as you could say, "Who's your Daddy?" You should have seen this picture, there was fourteen skimpy, frail wee boys running to get inside a van to save their lives, because believe me, these guys did not bring baseball bats to that game to play baseball, unless they were going to use our heads as the balls. They chased us over to the van and we were shouting to our driver to hurry up and drive, they were getting closer and closer and then they started throwing bricks at the van. Whew! Never experienced this kind of gang before, we heard of gang fights and all that but we thought It would never be at a soccer game or any sports game.

This was the biggest wake up call for us; this was a lesson for us to learn. The lesson here is that you should always think twice about how, or what way you treat others because this is a small and strange world. There is a saying that people often use in this type of situation and it goes like this, 'What goes around, comes around'. It basically means, what other people experience through the wrong doings, behavior or bad attitudes toward them came around to those who give it out. You see, it worked perfect for us, we gave this team such a beating and tried to make them feel use-less and defeated and yet, we were put into the same scenario by them and we did not like one little bit of it. If I can take you back to my school experience, remember I was the one picking on some innocent school kids because I thought I could manipulate the situation or make them feel beneath me or even make them feel weak and frightened? And yet, there I was getting my payback from my psycho thug. Again for me, what goes around, comes around was the scenario in school. I was being a monster to innocent kids who were minding their own business and not troubling anyone and yet when it was my turn to receive the punishment I didn't like it, so it came around me. I believe we really did learn a lesson as a team after that experience because; we were not so violent and aggressive in a physical nature on the field. We still put in the same passion and effort to win and enjoy every game but we were more under control. This attitude on the field also built up our reputation in school as other guys heard about us doing in a team from the big city so we were being more recognized again and I was still on a mission at this age and still at war with my psycho friend and his gang. So I was just biding my time before I came up against them again. I knew that somewhere along the road we will meet up again or, there will be another member of the famous best fighter gang who will be looking for me to beat up on and add as another trophy on their wee list of guys they beat up and to raise their level of ranking. It never took long for this to happen, and it was with the best fighter again and his gang. Well here we are again, gunfight at the OK CORAL, it was like a western cowboy movie where both actors were about to square up to each other and draw their guns, well, we were about to draw our fists, at least he was, I thought. Man to my surprise, he never did anything, he never lifted a hand, no gestures, no verbal comment, he just looked me in the eyes and we walked past each other. Wow, what had just happened here, why didn't he knock me out? Why didn't he give me abuse? So, as I walked past him I caught the eye of the other thug friend, the head-butter whom I feared for so long and I just looked him straight in the eye and was saying to myself, "Yeh, well what you want to do, you want to do this, me and you?" And my legs and body was saying 'RUN FOOL'. He never did anything, no comments, no gestures, no reactions, nothing at all. Man after that moment I felt like break dancing, I felt like I want to jump up and reach the moon. I felt like superman, like I was untouchable. This was a true turning point for me. My mind was going crazy trying to think about what had just happened here. I mean why didn't he knock my head off my shoulders? After I told a few of my friends what had happened, they said to me that maybe they already paid a respect, or they are just waiting for another time to react. I was cool with them saying that maybe they respected me now, I was satisfied with that, but they spoiled the moment when they said they may just be waiting for another moment.

Anyway, I carried on and just hoped for the best that they wouldn't bother me again. Time was going past very quick as were we ending the year and preparing for our final year in high school. There was still no improvement in my grades in class or attitude, I was still the same old kid not even interested in doing better in the main subjects, or even attempting to become more attentive in any class except of course the EFL classes, my sport classes. I was more distracted now knowing that even if I was to do better it is probably too late, no point in trying anymore, just face the fact that I will not be clever and that's it. I entered my last year at high school not knowing what will I become at the end of my school days, but I wasn't really caring anyway. I just went through as normal, attending what classes I had too, turning up when requested too but really not showing any interest at all. I also changed my personal outlook from being a 'Mod' and dancing to the groups I mentioned earlier around the 60's era. I turned to a skinhead, I shaved off all my hair, bought a pair of Dr. Martens black, fourteen **hole** boots of which, I shined every night with polish. The secret of wearing the boots was that you had to 'spit polish' them, meaning you rub black polish on them and then spit on a towel or rag and rub in very short, small motions on the boots until you can see your face in them. This routine could take up to 30-60 minutes or even longer, depending if you have the time and occasion to attend. Then, I would have my long black 'crombie' coat as it was called then and my scarf around my neck with a handkerchief in the top left pocket of the 'crombie' coat. This was pretty cool to wear and it was great during the winter days as it kept you nice and warm. This was very much a style and a fashion statement of who you were, or what you were trying to get across to people. Normally, skinheads were classed as nutters, head-cases who were normally out looking for trouble, and in most cases we were. But a lot of the time, trouble just came to us because of what we were portraying and the way we put ourselves across.

There were a lot of scary moments in those skinhead days and it was all related to violence. We would go into the town centre on nights or weekends and normally with a gang of around ten to twenty. We used to hang out around our neighborhood of Braeside or Larkfield, where we would gather, just drink and have fun. Then once we were fueled up with the booze we would go looking for people whom we could beat up, or challenge to fight. We always like to find the 'mods', the fashion I was into before turning into a skinhead, because these two groups were always against each other from way back in the days, probably it all started in the nineteen sixties. So, here again it shows that through generations and upbringing, then you can be caught up in what was going on decades before you. You can be led into a situation because of your family traditions or friend's upbringing; you will be drawn into a scenario in your life where it is hard to get out of it because most times you are maintaining the family name or tradition. I remember those days of roaming around the street looking for a fight, we had some really good fighters in our group so that was cool for me, as I wasn't really a good one, I would not go as far as some people would. I mean, these guys would hit others over the head with bottles, or stick a glass in their face or really brutally beat others up very badly. I remember we would go looking for this group of 'mods' that lived over in the Larkfield area and sometimes we would clash. It was a pretty fair fight as we were roughly the same in numbers. Then one time we arranged to meet them at the community centre down the hill from where I lived, this was a community centre that was open for youth at nights to keep us off the street, so we met then we had our fight, and it ended pretty evenly. No one was hurt really bad, just a few black eyes, bust and broken noses. We heard that there was a disco coming up in the centre, so we planned to be there as we knew these guys were going too. This was going to be another bloody night of violence. Well, we were all preparing for it. So, we thought that we were going to win this one pretty easily. When our music came on we were up on the floor dancing, then their music would come on and they were up dancing, so we were just roaming around waiting for the right time to pounce on them. Then it happened, I can never forget this song, it was called 'Wooley Booley', not sure if that is the correct spelling, but this was the song that made it all happen. This song was a kind of open song that both groups could dance too. So when this song played, they automatically went up to dance, maybe there was around ten of them at this point, then we all joined the dance floor and there was also about eight to ten, so were we pretty even. After a minute of the song our leader gave us the signal that he would make his move on their leader and we were to just follow after that and hit anyone that was in their company.

So here he goes, he attacked their leader and man, chairs were going flying at each other, there was punching, kicking, head butting, and it was so crazy. I was a bit shocked and surprised that it was as violent as this, I thought it would just be a few punches that we would be throwing at each other, at this point, I suddenly realized that these groups really hated each other and were determined to cause as much pain to each other that they could. But then to my real shock and amazement I start to see the other group pull weapons from their long coats. Some of them had sticks, baseball bats, a few had knives and started waving them around and one guy had a pair of Bruce Lee Sticks on a chain, (Numshacks as we called them).When we all saw this and then there seemed to be more of them enter the front door into the hall, we started to make a run for it as we were out-numbered and not ready for a weapon fight. So we shouted on each other and headed to the back door exit, we ran out of that place and we all split up and started running in different directions. I only stayed at the top of the hill, so I knew I had to make a quick departure and head home and I would be safe. So I climbed up the hill the back way, up over the field where I was covered with trees and bushes, so no one saw me. I went as fast as I possibly could, my heart was pumping hundred miles an hour, and it was scary. When I got home, I looked out the window very discretely so that no one would recognize me if they happened to be there. I noticed a few of them running around outside and looking for us, I saw a few of my friends still running in other directions, but I believe we all managed to escape and nobody was really hurt. We had a few bruises and that, but nothing compared to what might have happened if we were caught. I knew this was another message or warning for me, that if I am to continue to play with fire then I will eventually get burned. I seem to have escaped the bullying at school, I escaped the beating from the thugs on the football pitch at Rangers FC and now escaped the possible beating or even worse, from the group of 'mods'. So you would think this was enough warnings or messages for one person to realize that they were going down the wrong road. Going through my last year in high school was somewhat exciting but uneventful, from an academic point of view. Although I was enjoying my time doing sports, my class subjects were still very bad. The thing about our school in those days was that there was an automatic graduation no matter what your academic level was. When you're sixteen years old, you were allowed to leave and that was you, finished with school. There be no major celebrations, no big grad parties, and no big presents to be given to you by your parents, nope, it was a case of. Well what do you plan to do with yourself now? I wasn't really bothered about it, as I always thought that I would get a job somewhere, doing something.

What a way to look forward to leaving school, not much hope in being someone or hope for an exciting career. But the one thing that had helped me was determination. I was always determined to succeed in whatever I wanted to put my mind and attention too. Don't get me wrong; when I say 'in whatever I want to put my mind and attention too', meaning if I don't want to do something then I won't do it. Perfect example was my school subjects, as you are now aware of my poor grades and lack of interests in class led to poor results and a poor graduation. Anyway, as I was getting closer to the end of my school days, I was going out much more at nights, going to the arcade centre's where I would continuously play video games for hours and also this is where we used to meet with guys in my class. I was always hanging around with different people; it sort of changed with the seasons I think. I started being friends with other boys in the centre and then started to drink more regularly, and it just went from bad to worse. I was again being drawn into the life of alcohol and violence. You must be thinking, how bad can it be for a sixteen year old boy, how much alcohol and violence you can get involved in? Well, let me tell you, I was playing a big role on these two areas. Once I started meeting new people, I would start wandering around the town centre at nights and we would start picking on innocent guys and start beating them up.

Yep! Here I go again, not learning from my previous lessons, I was continuing where I left off with getting involved with fights. We used to walk around what we called 'The Bus-stops' this is where everyone waited to get their bus home and where the fish and chip shop was, so it was always busy. There were always some innocent people there that we would just start beating up. The most unfortunate ones who we always picked on were the guys that came off the boats from the navy. These guys were prime candidates and they would never fight back. I remember our leader was eyeing up these two Navy boys and it was so shameful when I think about it, these guys were just walking around minding their own business and suddenly our leader would walk up to them, he would ask one of them, "Excuse me, do you have the time?", as the boy looked at his watched and gave the time, our leader said, "Are you sure, my watch says something different", and he lifted up his arm to look at his watch, and as the sailor also looked at his watch, our leader smacked him right in the face with his elbow. Man, that poor fellow hit the ground so fast, and then, our leader started kicking into his body and then the rest of us started to kick and punch into his friend, so both of them started to get really beaten up and we would just walk away, as if nothing ever happened.

This was our routine every night we would just roam around and wait for the perfect opportunity to pick on someone. The weekends were the worst time for these fights. The weekends were so busy and everyone wanted to be out in the town as they all waited to get the buses home, they used to run very late. Our last bus was around 11:00pm. We would go in to the arcade, play games, and go out have a few drinks, go back in play games, hang out with our girlfriends, then back out for more drinks, then when the arcade closes at 10pm, that's when the fun begins. By this time we are drunk and ready to go to battle with anyone who is in our way. This was a very quick way in building up your reputation by beating up people. We would also pick on other local people whom we knew were good fighters to help us move up the rank. I moved up very quickly. There was this one guy who was kind of beating everyone and he was well known and no one would fight him. I certainly wasn't going to be the hero either. We were good friends and went around together, but for some reason this night he started acting stupid towards me, calling me names and making fun of me. So I ignored him as my friends said to me, "He is only looking for a fight because he is drunk and has no one to fight with" So I stayed away from him, and there was no way I was going up against him, he was stronger than me and was never beaten by anyone, and we were friends. I am sure you can read into this story for what was about to happen next, I will cover this intriguing part of my adolescent life outside of school, and my last year in high school. This was me supposedly preparing myself to deal with the outside world and try to fit into the social sector with my new found friends whom I would be spending the next few years with, years of which would be very important to me and would play a major role on how, and where my life would be heading as I go on with my life's story. Read on with me to see what unfolds in this intriguing and somewhat strange turnaround of events.

Chapter 5

BREATHING SPACE

Escaped the bullying of high school thugs, escaped the fren-zied supporters on a football field, escaped the weapons of gang fights and now, to the overpowering of innocent young men minding their own business in the small town of Greenock, just off the west coast of Scotland. Here we are, in our small town where there are plenty of bars and clubs, arcade center to host the young and old, pool halls and gambling halls for the hard working and crazies. Normally on most nights it is pretty quiet until you enter the world of drunken young teenagers trying to make a name for them. There were numerous gangs around in our days. Where you lived determined what gang you would be a part of. It wasn't too long before each gang would meet up and try to beat up and over power the other neighborhood gangs. But that was a little far in the distance for this group of teenagers who were mastering the land around the local bus stops at nights. These boys were just learning how to fight, learning how to build up their confidence and their names. Their victims were somewhat those who never defended themselves, who never was in the frame of mind of causing, or being a part of any trouble. They seemed to be in the wrong place at the wrong time. In the middle of this epic tale of gang fights and brutal beatings of innocent people was a young lad who was learning the hard way in life, was also bullied and pushed around, and was always in the middle of most of the trouble that seemed to take part. This boy of whom you all know is "ME', was quite a little trouble maker, he seemed to know how to annoy people, upset people, rub people the wrong way, and be the instigator of most fights that occurred, yes you got it, I am speaking about myself here little do I know, where it is all leading.

Let me continue with the story of me and my best friend. While we were hanging around the local bus stops waiting for our bus to go home, my friend was more drunk than I was, he was making a nuisance of himself and was making lots of noise. He was shouting out loud at everyone he passed or come into contact with, he would verbally abuse anyone, even older men or woman. Everyone was afraid to look at him in the event they would get verbally abused. He started to punch the window of the shops and bus stops; he would just be going off his head. He did pick on one or two boys and beat them up for no reason, our friends would try to stop him because he was getting out of order and it was embarrassing. Ha! 'Listen to me talk', I was just as bad, but now I saw what it was like to be on the other side witnessing the behavior of such a person. But still, he went on ranting and raving and his temper was getting higher & higher. Then the ultimate happened, I was walking out of the fish and chip shop just eating my chips, he caught my eye and came over, he was friendly at first putting his arms around me and saying, "Hey Seany boy, you're my best friend I love you", this is the things you say when you're drunk. He started singing songs and asked me to sing with him, and I said softly, "No it's cool mate, you carry on, and I am eating ma food". He continued to hang around me, singing, shouting, and saying, "me and wee Seany here can beat anyone in this town, we will take on anyone". I was like, 'Yeh right, you're on your own dude'. I was not willing to give an open invitation to the whole town for me to challenge them. After a few minutes he left me and he was in a bad mood, he was cursing at me for not joining him in his wee singing session, but I was ok with that, as long as he left me alone. So I was just hanging around chit chatting with ma friends and finishing ma food, then I saw him walking back down towards where I was standing and I noticed he had a few people beside him, his usual followers. I noticed that he had a bit of speed in his walk and looked pretty serious, I thought that he was challenged by someone and he was coming to ask help from the rest of us. How wrong was I? He immediately made his way over to me and started pointing his finger at me and cursing at me. He was trying to embarrass me and say things to me that were not true.

But I knew his game; this was a tactic so that it would cause an argument so we can then fight. But I would deny all his comments and try to reason with him; after all, I did not want to take him on. I used the same tactics on people whom I wanted to try to pick a fight with, so I knew where this was going. Anyway after a few minutes of this nonsense, he started to push me around, so I said, "Whit you daen mate? Whit ye picking on me fur?" This is Scottish for (What are you doing mate? What are you picking on me for?) He started again saying, "You think you're great, you think you're the best fighter, well c'mon let's see if you can beat me". So obviously I denied all this and refused to fight him, I was saying to him, "we're friends, why you want us to fight, you know you can beat me?" But it didn't matter, he had an agenda, he was on a mission and I was the stumbling block in his way, and no matter what, he didn't want to go around me, he wanted to go through me. I was thinking to myself, this guy is not going to stop until he beats me up or embarrasses me in front of everyone, so I walked away from him telling him, I didn't want to fight him. So again, he was calling me names and all that stuffs and he was following me as I was walking away, then all of a sudden bang, he whacked me in the face, well that was it for me, that was the turning point, I was thinking, if I am his best friend and he can do this to me to prove who he is, then our friendship means nothing, and I am going to have to defend myself here. So we got at it, after he punched me in the face, I quickly retaliated and smacked him in the face, I guess he was surprised that I hit him back because he was not ready for it, and then I just kept on going, punching him in the face, he tried to punch back but I was getting the better of him. Man everyone was shouting out our names so that more people can come and watch. It was like the fight of the year, it was like Pacquiao versus Cotto, although they never fought yet but the build up to this was just as exciting. Man, it was like the whole town came and surrounded us within seconds all cheering and shouting for both of us. I had quite a few friends shouting my name, but I think he had more shouting his as he was more popular than me, and a lot of people were frightened of him, so they were just his followers and part of his wee entourage, of which, most of them were my friends too. But when it comes down to a fight then they will very quickly take sides. Their decision to take side mostly rests on who they want to win and who they think will be the better friend to them, and also be able to protect them more. I couldn't even tell you who were there or how many, my focus was on beating him, now that he started it and I couldn't walk away from it. This was truly exciting to all of these guys watching, as this was classed as two of the best fighters in the gang and who-ever would come out winning would be the leader. I wasn't even interested in that part; I just wanted to come away from this in one piece, because I knew that this guy can throw a good strong punch and he's very strong indeed. I have witnessed many of his fights over the year and he is no wimp. Anyway, as we are battling at it, I was getting the better of him; I was over-powering him to my surprise. I started to pull his hair and eventually got him under me then I started to throw punches as fast and as hard as I could into his face to try and cause as much damage as I can. The reason to do this is so he cannot gain control or I would end up being the one getting the punches in the face. I like my face the way it is, thanks!

So here I am, the wee fighter from Braeside of which I never really had a reputation of being a hard man, or even someone who had a track record outside of school, but I was here giving it my best against a boy whom I classed as my best friend at that time. So as I was gaining momentum in holding him down and punching into his face I put a little more effort into pulling him down more so I can start kicking him in the face. This was a bit difficult due to his strength, it was a real struggle, but as he was more drunk than me, I have an advantage over him, so I used it. I got more control and starting letting swing my feet into his face. It was hard to con-nect due to the height, I had him at and he was now covering his face. I knew at this point I was winning, as once your opponent starts to cover his face or body, then he is in a way submitting or giving in. I liked this part of being in control seeing that he was losing by covering himself up. By now, the crowd around us was too many, that they had to keep moving back and splitting up because I was dragging this guy around and swinging him as I was punching and kicking into him. I was really getting carried away by now and smelling the victory, and that was pumping up my adrenalin. I was on fire man, I was up for this now, I was all over this friend and I only had one thing in mind, and that was to humiliate him in front of everyone as he tried to humiliate me. As I was dragging him around and he was covering his face, he left himself more vulnerable to me to do other things, so I automatically swept his legs away from him so I can make him fall to the ground. It worked after a few swipes of my feet, he landed on the deck and there it all changed for me. I was now in complete control of this fight and made every attempt to make the most of this moment. I knew he was not getting back up from this, there was no way he was going to recover, at the same time I was thinking, if he does get up from this and is able to fight back, then I am in big trouble. So, I ultimately battered away at his face with my feet, all this time I still had a grip of his hair while I was kicking away at him as this was my security that I can keep control of this situation. I tell you, it seemed to last for ages. I was battering at his face and body while he was on the ground and it was as if I was getting nowhere. But at least I wasn't the one on the ground or on the receiving end. I was thinking to myself, 'when is this going to end?' To my surprise, it ended shortly after these thoughts, I was really kicking into him and he was just lying there, I was saying to him, "Have you had enough? Have you had enough? Give it up mate?" There was no comment from him, he just cuddled up in a ball holding his body close together so now I let go and really thrust my feet into his body kicking any part of him I could see an opening for. I was focusing on his face, his stomach, his back and legs. I was jumping all over him like a crazed madman. Then it all ended, some of my friends and his friends said, "That is enough Sean, he is beat, stop it". But I wouldn't stop right away I was making sure of this victory as I might not get another chance. I was thinking, what on earth is going to happen after this? Is he going to hound me for the rest of my life? Am I going to be hiding from this guy forever?

Anyway, a few people grabbed me and pulled me away, they knew he was done and that he was defeated, and didn't want any more damage done to him. So I let them take me away and they said, "Go home, just get out of here now". There was no way I was walking away from this until I knew he was not going to chase after me or retaliate with a weapon, or a group of friends. Sometimes that's what we tend to do, if we get beaten up by someone then we get back at them when we a have number of us all together. So I knew the routine here and was making sure all was good. Once they got him up I went over to him and started asking him, "Hey, are we good here, is this now finished?" To my surprise and amazement he agreed, "Yes it is", and he offered his hand to finish this fight and make a deal that there would be no rematch or repercussions for me. He admitted his defeat and said, "Well done Seany". I was so happy and relieved because I didn't know if I could really do that again when he was sober. Well, I walked around the bus stop as if I was king of the ring, I was so joyful inside and so excited about this great victory that I didn't want to go home. I wanted to parade around and feel the joy as everybody came up to me as said, "Great job Sean, he deserved that beating, it was just about time someone gave it to him", as I was realizing a lot of people never liked this guy because he really went around the town bullying & picking on people & showing off continually. So I guess the little statement again comes into force; 'What goes around, comes around'. It was his time that, what was going around and being done to others through his behavior, finally came back around to him. This opened a whole new door for me as in being more popular around town, I seemed to have more friends now than I ever had, I had a few girls hanging around me now which were a great plus of course. I was not a handsome looking guy at all, never had nice clothes, great hair style or even good jokes to tell. I was still pretty normal boring wee guy but now with a heart like a lion, thinking I can take on the world.

So now I was not afraid to walk around the town on my own, knowing that I was a little more respected and had a few more friends to back me up in the event I was ever cornered or picked on, by another gang. But with this great success of being a fighter in town, always brought another challenge. It was quite remarkable as back in school, I was not really in many fights at all, actually I don't think I was in any more before I finally graduated from high school. It was as if I was untouchable, I mean, it seemed like I was walking around with a halo around me protecting me from any danger or bullies. Maybe it was a change in direction for me, maybe the fighting days were now over and I was going to be doing something good with my last months in school. Yeh right! Can pigs fly? Although school was kind of quiet for me in the remaining months, outside of school was certainly not. I started mixing in with a new group, they were from another part of town, this part of town was well known for its violence, and the ones that live there have a very bad reputation. They were always knows as trouble makers but they could really fight and there was always a lot of them. Nothing had really changed in my lifestyle, I was still doing the same thing, having a few drinks then playing arcade games and having more drinks and then more games, having fun with my girlfriend at that time. My girlfriend was a better fighter than me I think, all the other girls were so afraid of her, she was as hard as nails, but I thought she was lovely looking. We would be seeing each other for many months and every night. Sometimes you would think you would get bored seeing each other every night, but I never got bored seeing her. I always had a motive in my mind, Do you have any idea what that motive might have been? Let me tell you, it was 'SEX'. I wanted to have sex with her so badly that I tried every single night; I tried touching her thinking that eventually she will give in and I would get my way. I thought that surely if you keep persisting in doing a thing eventually that person will surely give way to your advances. Man she was so stubborn and persistent in pushing my hand away and she would warn me, 'If you keep doing this I will slap you in the face". I replied, "So you will? I will slap you back". So I would give it a try, slipping my hand all over her and then here it comes, 'Bang', right on my face as she said she would. I was like, "What was that all about? Do you like me or what? I thought we were boyfriend and girlfriend?" She replied, "We are, but I am not like that, and I told you I would slap you in the face if you keep trying to touch me". Man I was so shocked and stunned that a girl, my girl would do that to me, and after all, she was as hard as nails and portrayed a very wild attitude to others.

Normally, we would take the wild girls as easy to have sex with because they seem to be more liberal and ready for action. Man was I wrong with this one. Anyway, I never stopped trying it on with this girl, every single night we were together I would try and still get nowhere. Anyway, we had a pretty strong relationship in such a way that no girl would come near me as they knew I was going out with this girl and that if they tried anything with me she would absolutely kill them. Anyway after a while of this going around the bus stops picking on people, beating up innocent guys we were getting bored, we were looking for something bigger, something more challenging to do. So we started arranging fights with other gangs from other parts of the town, we would all meet in a place where there was no real threat of police being there or catching us all. Remember I was still in my last year in high school and only 16 years of age and never really grew any in size. But I would now face goliath, I had a lot of courage and would face any challenge or situation that came my way. I was getting very active in the gang fights now and we were always into looking to conquer new areas of town. We would still hang around the town bus stops and do our usual thing when we had no action elsewhere. I remember there was another gang in town that we had not fought before, so once we heard where they were, we got prepared.

A couple of guys went home and came back in with some weapons, man I was like no way, what kind of fight are we going to have here, I was never into the weapons things, I was afraid to hurt someone that badly. But anyway these guys came with small baseball bats, kung fu sticks, knives and metal bars. I was not taking anything with me, I was going to have a punch up and that's it. Once we were ready, we searched the town for these guys; we were all acting big and hard because we had a good number with us, there were around fifteen to twenty of us including our best fighters so we were in the best shape possible. We looked everywhere for them and then we finally heard they were over at the other side of town, so we ran towards that area and then we noticed them, we all shouted at them to get their attention thinking they would turn-around and come to fight us, but they never. Instead they looked at us and headed off, they ran away from us. Well we chased them and were shouting at them and hoping they would not get away. They started to split up and run in different directions so we did the same, we split up and followed them in the hope of catching them all. Most of them managed to get away, but a few were caught, unfortunately I never got to catch the ones we were chasing, they knew where to run and escape.

So that was it, we had to walk all the way back to our wee meeting place. This was gang fights at its best, this was all about power and who were the meanest and craziest gang in town. I think we were known as the second hardest gang around; there was one gang who was at the top of the list. These guys were from a place called 'The Strone', this was the nuttiest & most mental place in our area it was classed as the slum of the town. Hope my Mum and Dad missed this part of the story as this is where they were born and raised, "Sorry folks"! Normally, you would not mess with anyone that came from that area as they were all madmen and were mostly in prison. Majority of them were in jail for stabbing people, slashing people in the face with a knife, bottle or a glass, to their permanent disfigurement. They would be in jail for grand theft auto, house breaking, arson and other vicious crimes. These guys would do time and then come out and pick on people who got in their way, people who were just in the wrong place at the wrong time. After all, they are now in a lifestyle of crime and have an emotionally unbalanced life. They are in a situation that they don't know any better and their lives are now being directed by their acts of need, desperation, or lack of self control. These guys were in a league of their own, way above our wee gang of fighters, but still they were in the arena of being noticed and so were we, so we would take on anyone. I am glad I was never around when our guys would come up against the boys from 'The Strone'.

Well after a while, me and my girlfriend would like have a break away from each other, meaning we would just go our separate ways for a bit until we missed each other and got back together, this happened a few times and then we would just go out and find another partner to be with. I would then let the word out that I was not with my girlfriend so that girls would know if they wanted to approach me, then it was ok, it was safe, there would be no reprisals against them. So I managed to hang out with a few girls and we would have sex, it was fun at the time but scary as I was still very young, but as always, I thought I knew everything and never thought that there may be consequences of each act that we do. Anyway, I was with this girl and we were hanging out with friends, and her friends then asked me if I really liked her, as she liked me. I knew the girl well as she was part of the group that I knew, but they came from a different area. We were together for only two to three weeks as I was only getting to know more about her, but what I didn't know or ask was, who her previous boyfriend was, not that I would have cared really. So when asked if I like her of course I said yes, thinking I was going to get something at the end of that night. We sat together on top of a hill and chatted while a couple of our friends where next to us, then I made my advances to have sex with her, one thing about me was I wasn't shy when it came to sex. Here we were, lying on the ground and trying to have sex, but then she was embarrassed because our friends were beside us and watching and listening, and it was pretty awkward for us to do it, so we decided to move. We walked for a little bit looking around to find a better place, we found a door way down the bottom of that hill and we thought this was a good and safe place, nobody around us and no one can see us. So here we go, getting prepared to do it, and within a few minutes, we were having sex on a street in a little doorway just standing where we were. This was so crazy, imagine if a policeman walked past or something, we would be in serious trouble.

But in those instances when your motives are completely selfish then you don't worry about anything else but yourself and what you want. Anyway after we finished we all walked back to the town center area and kept on drinking and the usual looking for trouble. I was a wee bit drunk, but not too bad, I still was in control of my senses and knew what I was doing and all that. After we were standing at the bus stops, some of my friends came up to me and gave me the most frightening news of my life. Remember the girl I just had sex with, well, her boyfriend was just released from jail a week ago but he never got in touch with her. He was in jail for a few years for stabbing another youth. Well I asked the girl I was with, "Are you still his girlfriend?" She said, "No. We split up a while ago", I said, "How long ago?" She said, "A few weeks ago". I said, "What? Are you kidding me?" Well after a few minutes of a heated argument she walked away from me leaving me standing there. My friends told me to watch out for this guy as he is in town. He heard that I was with his girlfriend. Well, that is the last thing I wanted to hear, do I ignore the threat, or just hope he goes home and doesn't find me? I was thinking of how I was going to get out of this one if he caught me. I could act stupid and I could ignore the rumors that he might have heard. This was only the beginning of my nightmare with this situation. As I said he was just released from jail from stabbing another boy with a knife, so my mind was racing at a thousand miles per hour thinking, will he do the same to me? Sure he wouldn't, he is just out of jail, and he won't want to go back in. Anyway, I asked one of my friends who were really close to his friends and the people who knew him, I asked for her to find out if he really knows about me and his girlfriend, and if he does, what are his plans. News came back very fast that yes, he did know about us and that he is looking for me right now, and is on his way to where I was standing. Well just great, I am in for a beating over a girl I just went with for a short time. But that wasn't all, was it? Nope there was more news for me. He wasn't just looking for me to possibly give me a beating, but also had a knife in his possession. Wow, time out here! What on earth was he carrying a knife for? After just being released from prison from stabbing someone, you would think the last thing he would have in his possession would be a knife, if he gets caught with that then he is in big trouble. Again, my friends done their work to find out what he was going to do to me, after all, I can't just walk up to him, and say, "Hey dude, you know I had sex with your girlfriend, and you are carrying a knife with you, so what do you plan to do then?".... Don't think so.

I was then told that he is coming looking for me to stab me for being with his girl and he is just round the corner and knows that I am standing here. Gosh, I could have dropped down dead right there. I tell you, I have never panicked and had so much fear run through my body in my whole life. I thought my life was going to end on that night. My friend came over to me and this girl was also a close friend of this guy and the rest of his group and stood beside me and warned me, "Here he comes Sean; you better not look at him". Man I was terrified, I said to her, "What will I do, I don't know what to do?" She said, "Just act drunk really drunk, I have an idea". Man I was asking her, "Are you off your head?" She said, "Shut up and act drunk, here he comes". Well the fear just kicked in and I went totally numb. I started talking rubbish and scrambling my words and pretended to fall down on the ground and my friend would pick me up and shout, "Stand up, you are making a fool of yourself, stand up". Knowing that this guy was about twenty feet away from me, I would fall down again and roll my head round and act really drunk, again my friend would catch me and pull me up, then here he comes he is standing about two feet away from me and he is asking my friend to walk away from me. She said, "Why do you want me to walk away, I am with him, he is my boyfriend". I am like, "What? What is your game girl; I am not your boyfriend". At that time, I wasn't about to call her a liar or anything, I wanted to see where she was going with this crazy stuff. Again he said to her, "Get away from him; I am going to do him in". That means he is going to stab me. Now, when I heard those words come from his mouth I just wanted to do two things, throw the girl out the way and run as fast as I could and hope he wouldn't be able to catch me or, just start crying and begging for mercy, although I thought the second one would be a pathetic choice and wouldn't work. But I never, I just left my fate in the hands of this girl, and hoped for the best. But during this moment of frenzy, I am now facing an absolute lunatic and head case that stabs people. I was wondering how is he going to do it, will it be slow and quick then he will go away and I will just collapse of the floor in a pool of blood and never see my family and friends ever again? Or will he be a mad man and stab me about 100 times fast and aggressively to make sure I die for what I did with his girlfriend and I will be alive to feel every single thrust he puts in to my belly? Will he stab me so I feel the pain and then end me with a cut to my throat? Believe me this is what I was thinking.

During these seconds of fear, he and this girl were still debating about her going away from me to give him direct access to me. She would not give in to him and would stand directly in front of me covering my body up, if he really wanted to get me he would have thrown her out the way of which I thought was going to be the end result, I imagined her really annoying him so much that he would grab her and toss her away then it would be game over for me. I really had watched too many movies and was ready to act one out, a movie like Halloween where the murderer finally gets his victim and brutally kills him. And there was this girl in the crowd who was covering me from him. Anyway he asked her, "Why are you protecting him like this? He is nothing to you!"

And she said, "He is my boyfriend and you know that. He was never with your girlfriend, he was always with me, so leave him alone, look at him, he is drunk, he can't even stand up on his feet and fight you, just let him go". I was completely shocked and amazed that this girl would say these things and put herself on the chopping block for me, because if this guy really knows I had his girl, then he may just stab her as well for sticking up for me, and then she would be dead for nothing. A great thing happened after that, yes he let it go, he walked away from me and she said to me, don't move, and don't do anything until I say so". As if I would, I would remain standing there acting this way all night if I had too. After a minute she asked a few friends to follow this guy see where he was going, so they did and then they came back and they let her know that he went on a bus and went home. Then she told me he is away, "You can stop acting now". What a performance! I have never experienced anything like this in my life and hope I would never have to experience it again. It was the most terrifying feeling ever and most uncomfortable moment of my life that made me feel completely useless. But I was glad, so glad that I made it out of that situation alive and in one piece. Maybe you are now thinking, what stupid girl would stick her head out for a guy that was just about to be possibly murdered! You want to know who it was, I should have mentioned it at the beginning, it was my previous girlfriend, the one I keep on trying to have sex with and would keep refusing me, yes it was her. She looked after me in a way that probably no one else would have. We went round the other side of the bus stops away from every one and then we became boyfriend and girlfriend again. Not that anything had happened but we just kissed and got back to our normal situation. When I finally went home that night I was so happy to see my parents, I was happy that my Mum was asking me how my night was. I knew I wasn't dreaming this and that it was real and that I made it home. By this time high school was finishing and in the last months. I was ready to leave that place; I had enough of school because I wasn't really learning anything and thought it was just a waste of time. I wanted to get out into the world and have fun drinking and partying, and not caring, as my parents, brother and sister will look after me and give me money all the time. That is one of the benefits of being the baby of the family. It seemed to be that, whenever I asked for money then I would get it. Drew and Pauline were very generous to me all the time, they gave me my pocket money every week and over and above that if I asked, then they would give, they would give a little bit of complaining or moaning just as an act so I don't think I will get every time, but I knew their tactics and knew how to get around them. They were my wee bank withdrawal system where you just put your request in and out comes the money, no hassle at all. Anyway, the last days in high school were so much fun as we were all so excited to leave. I don't think we did anything in the last days, we just had fun, carried on, planned to cause trouble before we leave, because our attitude was, 'What can they do, we are leaving?' Not as if they can suspend you is it? It was hilarious, the teachers were just useless in this situation as they knew we didn't care at all, and were just waiting for our term to finish because they would never see us again after that, so who cares. Goodbye St. Columba's High School, welcome the outside world.

At this point I had no idea what I would do, probably just register for welfare and live off what the government would pay, of which was not a lot. But at least I could just roam around and do what I want, when I want. That is what I thought! My parents told me, "Right young man, don't think you are just going to laze around this house doing nothing, get yourself out there and find a job". You can apply in the local supermarket where you can continue to pack shelves or work in a factory or something". Hmmm, where was this coming from, this was not part of my plan. I thought my Mum would just let me do what I pleased. I don't think so! Anyway, it was December 1986 when I officially left high school and it was

Christmas, what better Christmas present could a kid ask for, leaving school and Christmas at the same time, wow what a situation, just celebration all the way. At 16 years old I was full of life and was so looking forward to not having any real commitments or responsibilities, c'mon that is normal for us kids, we do not want this at our age, we were created to have fun, be selfish and not care about others or what others wanted isn't that right? One of my friends Brian who was part of our gang that were hanging around the arcade and roaming around the street told me of what he was planning to do, it was like a youth government scheme where you would attend a certain training centre and get educated on various aspects relating to a working office environment. This was a one year course and sounded very interesting as it covered topics like Electronic Office, Computing, Electronics and Micro Electronics and the best part was that they paid you a salary as well and covered your traveling expenses. My first thought of this was education? No way, I am not going back into a school environment, I am done with that. But as usual, I never thought the whole thing through and take a look at the big picture of what could be achieved through learning these skills. But as Brian was talking to me he said, "What do you have to lose Sean? What else will you be doing? It will be cool and we can chill, have fun, and get paid at the same time". He had a few good points here, and it got me thinking, but how am I going to get in, my grades in school were rubbish. The great thing about this program was it never required any entry level or specific grades, so anyone was eligible to take part. The only thing was that there was a certain number only, so either you made a decision to join or you lose out. So the more I thought about it, the more I liked the idea, basically, because I was getting money out of it to do my thing at nights and weekends. So I made the decision to join up. It was for a full year and you were based in this big building which had four different areas, all in the same hall. It was split into the four different topics as I mentioned above, and each topic lasted for three months each. The first topic was Electronic Office and this taught us the entire workload of what would be used within an office environment. I learned how to answer telephones in a proper business manner which was hilarious with my slang and who cares attitude.

I am sure people on the other side of the phone must have been wondering, 'Why on earth is this guy answering this phone, it's as if he is not interested on how he speaks or addresses anyone'.

Also I learned how to do administration work like filing, printing files, organizing documents and folders, and creating a little office structured work area. It also taught you about Microsoft office. This entails working on a computer using office, i.e. word, excel, power-point programs of which we know, is widely used in all business today. It was really exciting learning these skills especially working on the computer and playing around with the power-point applications. It is amazing what you can do using this program, man we thought we were geniuses when we learned how to do certain things; it was only the basics at that time. I learned how to touch type, this was funny, they made you memorize the keys on the key-board then when you thought you were ready, they take you to another keyboard of which all the keys were covered up and you had to try and type sentences. That was so hilarious trying to do that, we were all laughing our heads off with some of the words we would type thinking we were using the correct keys. But like everything in life, you have to learn it, practice it and master it, this wasn't easy at the beginning but then after a month or so, you could be typing around 60-70 words per minute which in those days, was good. I loved using the electronic keyboard, this was a keyboard that was powered up and when you touch the keys it was like your fingers were just running over the keys so fast, it was amazing, and it was similar to what we have on our laptops today. So after the three months, you have to go through exams to enable you to move on to the next topic, this was exams on what you learned over the three months so it was pretty easy to pass, and they would make sure you passed anyway. Then you would move on to the next part of the program which was computing.

Computing was the best ever, as I had a computer of my own at home of which I was, never away from. I would play on that thing all the time, mostly games of course. But that is not what we had to learn in this course. This course was very serious indeed; it entailed learning how to read software programs, practice typing in programs, now you can see how the E-Office part comes into play with the typing as most computer geeks can type very fast. Anyway, after a while we started problem shooting programs that wouldn't work, this was to give us an understanding of the computer language and how it all works. This was a very difficult course but very exciting. I loved this course, I never wanted to leave or finish this part, it was just so cool. After the months of training you had your exam to do, it was a two part exam. The first part was to design your own program, using what you learned and know of the computer language. The language we used at that time was 'BASIC'. I believe this was the easiest language to use at the time and most common. Then the second part was, the teacher would give you a program that would not work, that had faults in it and you had to solve the problem and get it working. Well this was not so easy, this was actually very hard to conquer, you really had to know how it worked and go through it step by step. However, I managed to get through both parts and pass, so at one point I am thinking, I cannot be that dumb even if I never got good grades, or any grades from school. It really boosted my confidence up a great deal, it was an amazing experience after six months, I can type, organize an office, produce power-point presentations, problem-solve computer programs and program in the Basic computer language. Wow! What an achievement for a kid who wasted his school years just fooling around and not paying attention. Just imagine this is how Bill Gates started off, in a garage fooling around with computers and games and now take a look at where he is now in his life, not saying I am the next Bill gates or anything, but it let me realize, how you can start off with the basics in life, how it can grow into something out with your imagination or expectation.

I am now going into the third part of the training scheme 'Electronics' as it was called, this part was really different and I never had a clue what it was all about. We were taught how to make microchip boards for computers and other electronic devises. I tell you it all made sense when you thought about it, as inside computers are all little microchip boards that when linked together makes the computers work. This is where we learned all about the components inside the motherboard of a computer. I can only remember a few of these like resistors, capacitors, diodes, electrodes and I am sure there are more, but I can't remember what they are called. So here we are getting all these little components together and have a board of which we are putting them all on, and the metal part of these are sticking out the other side of this little board, then we learned how to solder. This is using a hot iron rod and touching these metal ends of the components and also, using solder to help the joint be strong and be sealed to the board. This was a cool thing to do, but you can easily make a mess if you don't pay attention and take care of how you use the solder and rod. This takes time and precision, it takes a lot of care and focus on this part. Then there is the next stage of the board that you need to join the components in a certain sequence in order for it to work together the way it is designed to do. This part is called 'etching', it is similar to drawing on paper except, you are using little bits of a certain type of tape and you measure it to connect to the components and then make it all fit perfectly. It is just straight lines linking components together in order for the system to function properly. Then to finish the process you have to take the board in to what is called a 'Clean Room'. You have probably seen this method on many movies today where they use clean rooms for processing of materials or evidence. This is a very serious part of the process, you also have to wear aprons, gloves, mask and head piece, and there cannot be any exposure at all, from dirt or materials that would contaminate the process. After this is carried out, the board must be stored in a place to let them dry off and then they are ready to be put in the mother board to create a working computer system. At that time it was all so exciting even if I did not know what it was all about, I just loved working with my hands and being very hands-on. It was not an easy process to manage or follow, and it was so easy to make a mistake. Mistakes usually were not a popular acceptance as it normally meant you had to do the whole thing all over again and it just wasted the teacher's time. Well, this was the end of the process so we then went on to assembling the motherboards with various PCB (Printed Circuit Boards) as they are known that we created with all of the above process steps that I mentioned. I tell you, when you watched the end product and what it does and that you were the one, who created it, was truly an amazing thing. When you have accomplished this task and if anyone ever asks if you know how the insides of a computer are made or what makes a motherboard work, then you can confidently answer them. Here comes the new IT whiz kid…… C'mon, we all have to start somewhere right? I mean if Bill Gates can start in a garage and then build an empire, then why we can't start in a small office based on youth training scheme environment? I was at the third semester of my training program, only one more session to go and that was 'micro electronics'.

Micro electronics was the next stage of learning up, from electronics of which I just covered except, it meant dealing with more integrated units and technology. To be honest, this was the only part of the program I really never had a clue about. I did not pick this part up at all. The teacher would teach us all about sound waves & frequencies and it went straight over my head. We used equipment such as oscilloscopes, and others that I cannot even remember now. Shows you how much attention I paid to the information and subject. Anyway, I know it's all connected with each other to provide a bigger in-depth knowledge of the complete Office/Operations environment. The program that we enrolled in was through a company called 'Intec Inverclyde', which meant 'information technology'. Now you will probably see where the resemblance of what we were learning came into effect for what they were preparing us for. As we know today, all businesses are about information, and we all use some form of technology to gain, display or share this information. Notably, the most convenient and most popular form of having this information available to us is by the use of our personal computers or through the World Wide Web. So when you think about it, this information has been entered by someone for others to view or use, so it most likely is all entered through the computer system of which is created by what I described above. So it means by having learned this process and know how and what makes this computer system function, means that you are already in the industry of the IT world even if you do not realize it, you're in the manufacturing part of the business. Also, there was a great thing happened to me during my year at 'Intec' it was where I met my next girlfriend Sharon. This program was open to both sexes, and it was kind of a surprise as it was more of a program for males due to the nature of the electronics and computing elements. So when we saw some girls attending as well, then obviously it made it that more interesting to us, if you know what I mean! Although there was a shortage of girls to boys, it was a case of just getting in first if you like someone. I immediately fell for Sharon due to her sense of humor and personality; she was very joyful and bubbly person and was always laughing her head off when we were having our breaks. I was kind of shy as it was not my normal surroundings and was not all comfortable being surrounded with others during break times, so I was pretty embarrassed, and I wasn't very good at telling jokes or stories, so most of the time I was just listening and laughing at the other ones who were always cracking jokes. At the same time I was watching how Sharon was acting and what she responded too, this is how I knew to get close to her. When everyone was laughing and joking I was really desperate to make an impact, especially in front of Sharon, so I was waiting for my moment to jump in and say something. Well my moment came and I took it. I can't remember what I said but I know it never went down too well, do you know how the advert goes with the cell phone network when they show you dropping calls and it all goes quiet? Well that was my glorious moment, I opened my mouth when everyone was just finishing laughing at a previous joke and I jumped in and said my peace, man I could have dug a hole in the ground and buried myself, the whole group went quiet and they all just looked at me as if I was an alien. I could feel my face burning up and going red, I think you would have been able to fry an egg on my face.

I was so embarrassed, and as I looked at Sharon she faced the ground and started to snigger, not because what I said was funny but, that it was not funny and all the others were like sniggering as well. So watching those who sniggered at me made me feel even more stupid. Anyway, people started moving off their seats and I was shocked as it was only me and my friend Brian who was left. And he burst out laughing at me and said, "That was the worst party stopper ever, you cleared the room in no time at all". Well I just laughed with him and from that moment on I kept my mouth shut and just went with the flow and whoever was funny I was just laughing with them. Anyway, at the end of the program I had the courage to ask Sharon out and she said she will think about it, man I was very persistent and kept on annoying her (not like me at all) till she said yes. So, eventually we went out and we lasted for about one year and it was a very pleasant relationship and we both had lots of fun, but we were still very young to have anything serious going on. We parted very good friends and even to this day if we pass each other on the streets we will stop and have a quick chat and see how each other is doing. Well, as I was graduating from my youth training program I was going to miss all this training and also the money part. I didn't know what I would do. Getting a job was still pretty difficult and having no proper high school qualifications would not have helped me one little bit. I got talking to the trainers in the program and asked them what I could do, and it was amazing what had happed, the week before I was about to leave, the local government council association opened up a second year program and for those who have complete the first year may be eligible to take part in the second year program, depending on how well you did and how your attitude was. Well, when I heard about this new second year program, I jumped all over it; I was so excited and pushed to have my name put on the list for it. I had no problem with my attitude during my first year, and I believe I did pretty well in my course work and ultimately passed my end assessments. So I should have been in good standing, it really just depended on how many others applied for the spot. You know, sometimes you may hear people say 'in the right place at the right time', and I believe that this can be the case in certain aspects of our life. For me, it was truly being in the right place, talking to the right people and at the right time. I was the first candidate to be chosen for the second year program, it never really occurred to me about what number I was, I just wanted on the program, but to be chosen first, out of all the other applicants meant so much to me. I realized that whatever it was I had accomplished, it made an impact during my first year, and it was recognized by the teachers and management of the program. This was absolutely fantastic news for me; I was overjoyed and ready to start my next assignment.

The second year program was so different from the first and when I heard what it was, I was pretty nervous. For the whole second year you were send out on placement to a professional company to work for them in whatever business or industry they were involved with. Our duties would relatively be in an administrative role as this is where most of our experiences were focused towards. Although we could also be put into a computer or electronics environment, but I guess there was no placements in these industries. So here I go, I started work as an 'Administration/Payroll Clerk' for a Heating, Ventilation and Engineering Company called, 'Hillhead Filtration & Engineering Co. Ltd. I had never heard of this company until now, as I had no idea of the market place due to only having one year of work experience. The company office was situated on the outskirts of our local town center, about three minutes walk away, so there was no problem with me getting there as the local transport would take me to the town center and then I can walk over there. I was so nervous on my first day, I didn't know what to expect, or who I was going to meet or work with. After all, I was the shy type remember, I had no clue of how I would talk with strangers, and at the same time try to do what they would ask me to do on a daily basis. Well, I was sweating buckets man, I mean you could literally fill a bucket with my sweat, as horrible as it may sound, it was a horrible feeling, so uncomfortable. I guess everyone goes through that right? Well, here I go walking up the steps to the main office, I am sure they had cameras on the stairs watching how nervous I was and my actions, and just laughing their heads off at me being so nervous. I opened the door with so much fear not knowing what to expect or, how I would react when I saw these people for the first time. I couldn't have misjudged the situation any wrongly, to my amazement, I was embraced with sheer joy and excitement from the office manager Betty and the office assistant Margaret. This made me so much at ease and it allowed me to breathe normally again, even though I was still uptight about the whole experience, these two ladies made it so much easier for me to be welcomed to the office. I will start off with Betty; she was a little more, 'mature' than Margaret not to mention any ages here or anything and was in charge of the running of the office. Betty was a very organized woman, who knew exactly what was to be done, how it has to be done, when it is to be done and who should do it, on a daily basis. As I got to know more about the business and how things work, I soon realized that the business was on a good standing administratively and accountability wise, by the sheer work ethic and discipline that Betty had established there. This is not to say nobody else was involved, indeed as you will read later, there was many others who contributed to the business in different areas. Betty was strict, I mean very strict, and I noticed that she was a clock counter, meaning she would watch the time when I came into work in the mornings, when I went for my tea-breaks, what time I would go and come back from lunch, and what time I would leave at the end of the day. Oh, and by the way, if you were a few minutes later than your scheduled time, she would let you know. She would jokingly say something to just let you know that you were late and that she is watching your time. At first, it was funny as I would just laugh with her and still let there be a nice atmosphere in the office, but once it became a regular thing if me or even if Margaret was late, she would soon change the tone of the conversation to that of a boss, letting her workers know they were not doing the right thing. These moments started to create a different atmosphere, it brought a little silence in the office now and then, but I guess it was always the right thing to do, after all, it is our fault that we were not on time for work, when you think about it, would you like to have all those minutes you were late for work added up and deducted from your pay checks at the end of the week? Hmmm let me think. Nope!

Anyway, to get back to my first day or even the first week, I was sitting opposite Margaret but with my back towards her, it was not the best of office positions but there was not much space to do anything else with the furniture that was there. Margaret was fantastic. She was Australian and pretty good looking too, with a fantastic personality. She was very funny and would laugh all the time; this made me feel at ease thinking that it was a fun office to be in. I think Margaret's long term goal was to get back to Australia with her Fiancé David. So I guess the long term goal for Betty was to find a replacement for Margaret, not that I even thought about it as I was just new and they had a history of young trainee's starting there but leaving after a while for whatever reasons. I was still a nervous wreck as I would start to meet the other employees. Betty would then take me around the other offices inside the building. Our Boss was pretty clever. He owned this building and built offices inside to rent out to other companies that he had a share in. He would be partners with other people in running these companies but would charge them rental fees and expenses for using his building, pretty smart guy eh, not that this is rocket science nowadays, but back then almost 24 years ago, it was a good money earner. Anyway, I got to know all the other companies and then I got to meet Jimmy, our Contracts Manager. Jimmy was a great man; he has been with the company a long time like Betty and pretty much knew everything that was going on. Jimmy was in charge of all the projects, and all the men that carried out the work on these projects. He had a lot of responsibilities on his shoulders with organizing all the labor for the projects along with doing all the drawings, meeting clients, and all that good stuff that relates to contract management. I believe at that time he managed around fourteen men, including engineers and laborers, little did I know I would be working with all of these guys too. At this time, Jimmy and Betty worked hand in hand as Jimmy would arrange all the jobs and Betty would be receiving all the daily weekly service reports and time sheets in order to invoice the clients that we've done business for and enter the men's timesheets so that they would get their salary on time. They would always communicate with each other and I would be listening to everything they were saying as Jimmy had an office behind Betty, but the door was always open so we can hear everything that was being spoke about. This was to be an advantage for me later on in this story. So my initiation continued, I was introduced to the boss, Mr. Lovell. He was a very smart and sophisticated business man, very sharp with his crisp suit. He was very welcoming to me and wished me all the best in working in his company. He had no doubt that I was in good hands working under the supervision of Betty. It was a short introduction as he was always a very busy guy, and it was better for me as I did not have a clue what to say to him, no words could come to my brain at all. You know, when you get a brain freeze when you eat something cold too quick and you have to take a minute to let it go away, well that was me, my brain froze and no words seemed to come out of my mouth and it was pretty embarrassing moment of silence, but hey, what to expect right, it was my first day at the place and these people were all strangers to me. We went back to the office and I was shown my desk and there was a typewriter sitting there, the first thing Betty asked me was, "Can you type?" Well you all know the answer to this right? Remember, part of my first year training program, I learned "Electronic Office' of which incorporated what? You got it, typing. So I answered her, "Yes I can type". To hear this she was so happy and said, "Well, I think you will do fine here then". Man to hear those words come out of Betty's mouth really made my heart at ease. So I just sat there and got used to the machine, I typed certain stories to get familiar with it, and you know that feeling when someone is watching you, well I had that feeling and I was right. Betty and Margaret were both watching as I type, and then they burst out laughing. So I turned and looked at them and had a blank look on my face wondering why they were laughing, I really thought they were laughing at me because I probably couldn't type so well compared to them, but then Margaret burst out and said, "We are sorry Sean for laughing, but we were expecting you to only type with your two fingers and be very slow, but you can actually type faster than both Betty & I, that is why were laughing, we feel ashamed of our typing compared to you". Man I have never felt so good and appreciated and I never even done anything except press a few keys on a typewriter. But to them, they already knew what they were going to give me, as in, work load, and knew that I would be able to carry out my duties with no problem at all.

My first day was over and I felt good, no real worries, no major issues at all and the people I met so far, was cool. I went home a wee happy chap, ready for the next day. My parents asked me how my first day was and I said that it was great, and just went through what I did, and told them the people that I met. So they were also happy and relieved for me as they knew how I was feeling before I left the house and that whole weekend. The whole week was pretty cool, I was lightly drafted in to the workload and I enjoyed it very much. I also met some of the engineers and laborers as they would come in to the office and hand in their reports etc. But when Monday morning came and I reported to work eight in the morning, then I met all of them as they all had to hand in their timesheets for the week along with any reports that they worked on. These guys were great; they were very friendly towards me and welcomed me to the company. I loved it, there would be a few of them who would tell me jokes and made me laugh so much, one of them was called Owen, he was one of the jokers of the group. He would constantly tell me jokes and stories and he was so interesting, he knew so much about history, and things that really interested me a lot. You will find out later what an impact he had in my working life. Another one of the jokers was Gordy, he was the ultimate comedian, I think everything that came out of his mouth was a joke, and he made us all laugh. So as time went on, Betty showed me what my duties would be, I would be typing the invoices for our biggest customer 'Inverclyde District Council' whom we had a yearly contract to service and repair people's houses that were fitted with gas fires from the council. I would get the information from the service or repair worksheets that the men would hand in on the Monday morning, and then get to work typing so we can get paid. This kind of work was a piece of cake for me, at first, it took me a while to get to know the system and then all the different types of gas fires and the parts for each type. But after I got used to this info, I was away like a house on fire. It would initially take Betty three days to complete the workload and so it was taking me longer due to lack of knowledge and experience. But after a few months I got it down to a maximum of one and a half days which really impressed Betty and Margaret. So because of my typing speed and efficiency of doing my work, I would be asking Betty if there was something else she would like me to work on and learn. At first she laughed and said, "Just relax Sean and take it easy, we need you to make the work last". I thought I was doing great by becoming faster, but sometimes it may not work in their favor. After a month or so, Betty saw I was getting pretty bored; I always like to be working, doing something, so she asked if I wanted to learn how to do the company payroll. Well, my heart fell to the ground, I said, "Me? Learn to do payroll, I know nothing about accounting". She replied, "You knew nothing about invoicing gas fires but look at you now". So I said, "Ok, why not".

Here, it opened another journey for me, to learn payroll and accounts. Betty taught me how to read the men's timesheets in order to pay them correctly, because if you mess up their pay checks, you will have a lot of angry man in your face on the Monday mornings, asking you why? I wasn't really afraid of getting it wrong because I knew Betty would teach me the right way and would not let me do it alone until she was fully confident in me. One thing I realized about Betty was, she was precise and very efficient in doing her work, so with her teachings, I never really had any doubt of completing my tasks either. So here I am, learning to enter timesheets into the accounts software system and at the end, it printed out checks for all the men. The rest of the company staff, including myself, also received our pay checks, but ours were easy as it was salary based and nothing ever changed. I believe I was now three months in the company and was carrying out all local company invoices, answering telephones, entering payroll data and completing salary breakdown for the whole company, not too bad for a simple uneducated 18 year old, would you not say? To all you young ones reading this, If you have the right attitude, determination, enthusiasm and the passion to do something and love doing it, then you can achieve what you set in your mind and in your heart. My advice to you all is, never stop asking, and never stop wanting to learn.

I was completely shocked and amazed one day when Betty asked me to stay at lunchtime as she had something to tell me, well I thought of the worst case scenario, I thought they didn't need me anymore, But I was wrong, I was told that she, and all other staff employees, were extremely happy with my performance and my attitude at work. They gave me a shining report back to 'Intec' of which they were well pleased with, and the Intec training manager Margaret actually came to visit me and thank me personally. To them, this was a sheer example of what they were teaching us at the training center and it was actually working in line with the market place' needs. So everyone was a winner in this case at this time. I was so happy; I felt like I could jump up and touch the sky. You would think I was earning huge amounts of money for the work I was producing, but remember, I am only starting out on life and learning the ropes and of course, getting paid. Yes, I was getting only GBP 35.00 per week which was not a whole lot, but it was a lot if you are getting nothing at all, and at the same time you are paving the way for a career in learning something you can apply anywhere and anytime. So I was a quarter of the way through my placement and all was going very well indeed. I was settling in very nicely and everyone seemed to like me. Going back to my nightlife, I continued to go to the local town center arcade and play games, fool around and still walk around the bus stops and fight with people, some things never seem to change as they say. I also got back together with the one who saved me from the knife welding lunatic that just came out of jail and whom I believe was willing to go back into jail for the murder of a wee Greenockian who stole his girlfriend while he was in the prison. Yes, she was back on the scene again, and she never changed any, she was still beautiful in my eyes, still aggressive and still not falling under my charms to have sex with her. We would meet almost every night and every day during my lunch breaks, we were kind of serious in a way, but both of us knew it could all end very quickly considering our temper and situation. So we just enjoyed the time we had together and enjoyed beating up people. A lot of the girls that hang around the town center were really afraid of her because of her mouth and actions. And also, she had a sister who was probably as mad as her, or even worse. So if you come against one of them, then you have to come against the other. In most circumstances in life, coming against one tough person is bad enough, but having to face two of them, would be suicide. Anyway, as time went by, I was still working away and meeting my girlfriend at lunch times. Then a crossing the line decision came. As we were with each other every lunch time, my girlfriend would try to persuade me to stay off work the rest of the day so we can hang out together. I would always refuse, because I know how Betty would react if I didn't return after lunch with no proper reason. But as time went on my courage was being tested by my girlfriend always asking me not to go back. Well, on this occasion I made the decision to try it, but I was thinking about what excuse I could give. I used to get migraine headaches a lot. We thought we could use this excuse and surely Betty would fall for it, after all, she knows I used to get these on a regular basis. So we devised a plan. My girlfriend called up Betty at the office and pretended to be my Mum (Ha Ha Ha)! What a fool...... I knew that Betty knows my Mum but didn't think twice if she knew my Mum's voice. We were sure we could pull this one off. So we went through with it, I was standing next to my girlfriend and we dialed the office number, Betty answered, and then my girlfriend spoke to her saying, "Hi Betty, this is Sean's Mum, I am sorry, but Sean will be taking off the rest of the day, as he is suffering from a migraine, he should be back in tomorrow". Well, Betty seemed to be ok and said, "Ok, I will see him tomorrow". Wow, what a performance! We did it, so we enjoyed the rest of the afternoon and night together. Yippee! This was awesome; we managed to pull the wool over my boss' eyes, piece of cake.

So ultimately, we were planning to have many days like this, we were contemplating doing it at least once a week. Isn't it true in life that even how young you are, if you managed to devise a scheme that benefits you, or do a thing that you know is not the right thing to do, and you get caught, you know that there will be a consequence. But you will not just be happy doing it once and getting away with it, you will actually do it again and again and again, until you eventually get caught and pay the price. Some of us, when we do get caught we have the skills to talk, or act our way out of the situation and others pay the price. My girlfriend and I were on top of the world that day, so happy that our wee scheme had worked. Next morning, when I went to the office I was not concerned at all, everything seemed to work out well and Betty gave in to my migraine excuse. And now the table turns, I sat at my desk and carried on with whatever tasks lay in front of me, either from the day before, or new work that I have to complete, but you know, the atmosphere wasn't the same this morning. I can tell when Betty was not in a good mood, she goes quiet and does not mention a thing and sometimes would make a little noise so that you know she is not happy. It was a little awkward as I didn't really know how to handle it, so I just make some chit chat and when it was her turn to respond, she was so dry, she let me know she was not really interested in communicating with me. So I got thinking, what could be wrong with her, maybe one of the engineer's upset her on the phone as that happens quite often because of their misunderstand-ings. Margaret also noted the same thing, and she also tried to make some chit chat but again, Betty would not really respond the way she used to. So, Margaret & I would make faces at each other just to acknowledge that we knew Betty was not in a good mood.

Well, the morning went along very slowly and very uneventful, it was really boring and I did not enjoy one little bit of it. Margaret mentioned that she was going to nip over into the town to do a personal chore and would be back shortly, it was almost tea break time anyway. As I was the new boy and the last in, I always had to make the coffees and I know what Betty takes, and she always has a coffee at this time, so as always, I go and make her a cup of coffee and bring it in. I thought maybe she will enjoy the coffee and it will make her feel better, after all, we still didn't know what the issue was. Well, once I made the drinks and sat down, Betty asked if she could have a word with me. Oh, now this is awkward, my brain started racing ahead of me again, thinking they don't need me anymore or something is happening! However, to my shock and horror, Betty asked the million dollar question. She said "Sean, I want you to be honest with me now, the situation yesterday when your Mum called in, and said that you would not be back because you were suffering from a migraine, was that true?" Did you have a migraine? Man, I could feel the walls closing in on me and all of a sudden, I became so nervous when asked that question. I felt so bad and pretty confused by being put under so much pressure, so I replied saying "No, I never had a migraine". So Betty asked why I didn't want to come back to the office. "Don't you like your job or one of us? Was there a problem that you had to deal with or some-thing?" I replied, "No, I love my work and you guys are great, and I never had any problem" So, she then asked me the next question of which blew me away she said, "Sean, was that really your Mum on the phone or someone else?" Well, the shame just came upon me, I was pretty dumb struck at that moment and I had a quick brain thought of, should I tell her the truth, or I lie? After all, how will she ever find out anyway if I lied? I never had the courage to lie, I was caught in the act and I had to own up to it, after all, she is not going to go this far on an assumption. At this point, she knew all the facts, but just wanted to give me a chance to acknowledge it, to make it a workable situation. So I admitted it. Yep, I owned up to doing something wrong. I can hear you saying, "Wow, Sean owning up to something". I know I can't believe it either. So Betty asked "If it wasn't your Mum, then who was it?" So I told her it was my girl-friend. She then told me that I had hurt her feelings and broke her trust, because she never thought I was like that, she never thought I could ever lie to a person just because of my nature and character, little did she know the real Sean. Anyway, after the sad story of how I hurt her feelings, she explained why she was in a bad mood this morning, so it all adds up now.

So Betty started to ask a little history about me and my girl-friend, the usual stuff everyone asks. Where did we meet, how long have we've been together and all that stuff, so I was telling her our story. So maybe after about twenty minutes of chatting she requested me not to ever lie to her again and try to pull a stunt like the one I did. She said "If you want to take an afternoon off, or take a day off, just ask me, I will have no problem allowing you to do it". She elaborated that she would rather have the truth and works out the situation or issue than have her hear a lie. She gave me a great bit of advice that I always think about in situations like this. She said to me, "Sean, whatever a person says, or does, reflects their character; it shows others a piece of who they are, to this day, I have never ever forgotten that because I believe it is so true. It can't tell you all about that person, but it can certainly tell you a bit about them, and it displays a very strong part of their nature and trustworthiness, as a person". So we cleared the air and after that we had a great day, when Margaret came in, me and Betty were laughing together so she was so happy that the atmosphere was different and we were laughing so she asked, "What did I miss?" Well I looked at Betty and she looked at me and I said, "If you want Betty, you can mention it to Margaret as I had no secrets with her at all, she was brilliant and very caring lady". So Betty told her, and we all burst out laughing, she was amazed that I had the courage to try and pull that off over Betty, She said that Betty is like the CIA, she knows everything, she knows all the wee tricks in the book, and she always finds out in the end. But she did say, "You are very lucky that

Betty thinks so much of you, because if she didn't, then that would have been your last day in the company". Wow, what a statement! I asked Betty "Is that true? Would you have fired me if you didn't like me?" She point blank replied, "Yes". Well, I was utterly shocked and amazed, but also so glad that she liked me, because I could have messed up my wee job, my friendship with them, and I would have put a very bad light on my dealing with Margaret from Intec who got me the chance to be there in the first place, and would have surely disgraced my family. We all have heard of getting a second chance right? Well, here was mine. Margaret gave me a very good piece of advice at that point when she said to me that if someone really cares about you and wants to be with you as much as my girl-friend wanted to be with me that afternoon, then why would she not think about the consequence of carrying out such an act? She should be considering what effect that instance would have on you if the worst case scenario had happened, and why would she want you to make up a lie? She said, "Sean, ask yourself few questions and maybe when the answers are revealed, you may suddenly feel that she may not be the right girl for you further down the line, or when you start becoming a little more serious and all that". When I look back now, that would be such an important piece of advice and one that I am sure you would take very seriously, but c'mon, I was 17 years old and I had a mission remember? I wanted some-thing from my girlfriend so I wasn't about to go all serious and mess up my chances with her. So as you can imagine, that piece of advice went in one ear and out the other. Although, now I know she was so true with her advice.

It actually wasn't long before we had split up, pretty ironic isn't it, or was it fate? Who knows? All I know was, I was out of that relationship. I started my usual nightly rounds around the bus stops with the gang, checking on whom we can beat up or annoy, and there were always some innocent victims to jump on. However, there was a strange turn of events for me. After a few years of bul-lying others and beating up innocent young men at the bus stops, one night I found myself drunk and standing waiting for the last bus home alone. Well after a few minutes of just hanging on to the side of the bus stop I heard these three boys saying to each other, 'Is that not that guy that got us the beating a few weeks ago?" Well, I was not going to turn around and look at them, to be sure that it was me, c'mon, how many other guys went around their beating up people? So of course they were correct in their statement, but I was not going to be the one to tell them. Anyway, the inevitable happened, they started walking over to me and then the three of them asked me, "Hey, you were the guy that got us a beating a few weeks ago weren't you?" I immediately answered, "Who me? No. I hardly come around here; I was just out tonight for a drink". They insisted, "Yes it is, it is you, do you think we will forget that beating? There was a crowd of you that beat the three of us". Again, I said, "No I think you have got the wrong guy. I haven't been in here for months". One of them said, "It is you. So where are all your friends tonight then? Are they not with you? So you're all alone, what a shame for you". And then it started, one of them just punched me on the face and then the other two started to punch and kick me all over. I was not going to fight three of them, so I thought the best thing I can do here is fall to the ground and take what I deserve. Well, not too sure if that was the brightest idea, but probably the only choice at that time. So I just crawled up into a ball, and lay on the ground letting them take turns in beating me up. What a turnaround, it was my turn to be on the receiving end, and let me tell you, it was not pleasant at all. I lay there for about 5 minutes getting my body punched, kicked, stamped upon until they satisfied themselves.

It was very bizarre at that moment as I was the popular wee fighter in town with loads of followers and all of a sudden, I was on the ground, blood pouring from my face, and there is no one to be found to help me out. Not one person offered a hand to pick me up from the ground, or to come over and ask, "How are you son, are you ok?" No one, not even a whisper from anyone was heard. Hence, I got up and stood there waiting for the bus, and here it comes. Man, if it only had come a few minutes earlier then I would have missed this beating. But, as I believe, there is always a reason for everything that happens to us in life. We may always feel that we are under control of our situations, or the decisions that we continually make, but not so true in all circumstances. On my way home in the bus I was thinking, what on earth is going on? I was confused and drunk at the same time, so not a very good mixture. I always thought I would be on the giving end and not receiving the beatings, but how wrong I was. When I got to the front door of our house, I was just hoping that it was not my Dad who will open the door but Mum, because if it's my Dad then I would be in serious trouble, first because I was drunk and second for fighting. Hooray! It was my Mum, but she was so shocked at the mess of me and she knew with the smell of my breath and the fact that I could hardly stand up that indeed I was drunk. Well, she just got me in that door and into the kitchen, I remember very well this moment as it was my turnaround. She would just take my shirt of my back and start cleaning the blood from my face and at the same time would be asking me a series of questions on how this happened, and where did it happen and why did it happen to her wee innocent boy, and also who did it to me. All these questions were being fired at me and she said, "I am asking you these now so we can have answers for your Dad, for when he comes in, he will surely be asking you the same things. So you better get your story right." My Mum is looking out for me and she knows my Dad will go crazy. During the few minutes that my Mum was cleaning up my face and giving me a lecture I suddenly broke down in tears, weeping like a little baby. Honestly, I could not control my emotions. I knew I had messed up big time and that what I received was probably well deserved because of my previous actions towards others. My mum, being the angel that she is, she just listened to me and let me get it all out, I think she was pretty shocked once I started telling her what I had been up to. She could not believe her wee baby, her youngest of the three, the cutest of them all, could actually be a little monster and young boy who would beat up others kids.

After another few minutes and after listening to me whaling about what I had done, she told me that enough was enough. I was then told not to go back to that town center or she would tell my father, well that was enough for me, when my Mum told me, "Enough", then I needed to listen to her. Plus, I was not looking forward to facing my Dad and telling him the same story that I told my Mum, he would flip it. So, from that day on, I stayed away from the gangs and the arcade, where all of us used to meet. It was time for a change; after all, I didn't fancy getting another beating like that one, not too keen on lying on the ground getting my face and body kicked. I'm sure there must be something better I could be doing in this young wonderful life. After that night, I changed my ways; I needed to do something else in order to get me out of that arcade and away from the town center. It wasn't easy as this was a habit for me, and all my friends were all from the arcade and town centre at that time. When we all get into a routine and are sometimes set in our ways, it is not so easy to change and step away from our normal settings or things we like doing. For me, this moment was an actual life changing event. I started to make some great friends through playing soccer of which, I still loved and was my favorite hobby. As we were getting older, soccer became more challenging in a way that your fitness had to be pretty high in order to keep up with the game. There were some really fit players out there that if you are not up to their level, then they would leave you standing and ultimately, you would be dropped the next game, unless, you would show some improvements on your performances.

One of my friends George was one of the cool guys that were in our school. He was always a hit with the girls, he could pull any girl he wanted, man, I was so jealous of him, not sure why? (He wasn't all that good looking; only kidding mate). George & I would start to go to the bars and the discos at the weekends. Our routine was, we would buy a couple of cans of beer and drink it in the house before we would go out, to give us a wee hit. Meaning, it would get us in the mood to party, oh and by the way, it would have to be in George's house as my Dad would kill me if he knew it. This was my new life changing event, from hanging around an arcade or pool hall drinking, and going around the local town center beating up innocent people, to sneaking into bars while I am under age and getting drunk. Wow, when I think about it, I think this was one step forward and two steps back. Anyway, it seemed to get me out of the messed up life that I was currently in, so why not give it a try and enjoy it, it seemed to be the more mature thing to do. To me, this was all about maturing and growing up in to a young adult and taking some responsibilities of my actions. No matter what it was,

George, myself and some other boys that we were friends with, either from soccer or from school, met on a regular basis, usually on a Friday or Saturday night and we used to get drunk and have so much fun. We all thought we were John Travolta on the dance floor, man you should have seen us all trying to impress the girls. When I think about it now, that is probably one of the major reasons that we couldn't really get any girlfriends, the other was probably, we're the ugliest guys in the room. Yep! The truth hurts sometimes, doesn't it? I am speaking for George of course (ha ha ha), we really did seem to struggle at that time trying to get a girlfriend. I thought George started to blame me after a while, because he was used to just going up to any girl and that was it, he would score. So with me around he was getting nothing, so we don't have to be rocket scientists to work that equation out now, do we? (Oh please, I still have that cute look at least). Things were great for a while and then the inevitable happened, we were all out parting and we were heading over to another bar, when we came across this group of guys who were at one time, our enemies, but we never thought much of them. But suddenly, they started bullying one of our friends Martin, and were beating him up, so obviously we are not going to sit around and watch our friend get beat up, so here we go! It was a free for all, we just ran at them and we started kicking and punching anyone who came in our way, it was pretty even matched as there was around six of us and same with them, so we just got stuck in and hoped for the best. After few minutes of just smashing anyone we could get our hands on, George noticed their leader was trying to run away, so he shouted on me to go after him, as I was the kind of head case, remember? From my previous activities, my friends knew this. So when I saw him, it was like the bell in a boxing ring going off, I just chased the boy and because I was so fit at that time and was an extremely fast runner, there was no way he was escaping me, I was like Lyford Christie, I was on top of him before you could blink an eye. This was my moment to prove to my friends what I could do, so I never hesitated, I smacked this guy on the face a few times and then he hit the ground. That wasn't enough for me though, I should have walked away at that point and said we had won, no not me. I was always greedy to have more of everything, including beating up people, so I jumped on top of him on the ground and started punching into his face as many times as I could.

There was nothing in my way now of completely knocking the head of this guy and believe me, I tried. It was like a fight to the death, you know when you watch the Gladiator movies and they have to fight to the death or even, if you have watched 'fight club' with Brad Pitt, well it was similar to that. I mean, I was smacking this boy's face from left to right and back again, as many times as I possibly could. Remember, I was pretty drunk so I wasn't even in my right mind of what harm I was putting upon this boy. But did I care? No chance, all I was interested in was beating this dude. When I recall this moment and I tell you, I can picture the boy's face right now, and I know exactly how I had him pinned to the ground. I had both his arms spread out and I was sitting on top of him with my knees pinning his arms down so he couldn't move while I was using his face as a punch bag. He would manage to get free and sneak the odd punch into my face but when he did, I let another round of the blazing guns, landing consecutive punches on his face, so it was better for him not to move and just give in. I could say that I won that battle with him, but unfortunately, as I was too busy enjoying my outraged punches to his face; I wasn't ready for the blow that was coming towards me. Yes I was almost knocked out by one of his friends', as I was concentrating on my demolition of this guy on the ground, his friend came running towards me and took one running kick to my face with his boot. Man that was a hit for me; I just went rolling off to the ground and saw stars. This was a full force kick in the face from someone who was running towards you, so you can imagine the damage that he done to me. My face was a mess, I just hit the ground like a sack of potatoes, and I could hardly get up, then all of a sudden all I heard was, "Run Sean, it's the Police". At that point, all the pain of my face suddenly wasn't important as much as being caught by the police. Just to put in the picture of how the police might have came to know, it was actually outside of a disco that was barely one hundred yards from the local police station. Yeh I know, how stupid can you be. Well, that was us, when you are young, free and full of alcohol, nothing seems to matter to you, and nothing seems to frighten you or even be a warning to you, as you just do what you want to do. We were all running away and because I was pretty drunk and not in my senses due to having my head almost knocked off, I didn't even know where to run, so I ended up being caught by the Police. There I was, on a Saturday night, locked up inside a prison cell! Yes you heard it right, the wee baby of the family, the wee innocent one who wouldn't hurt a fly, the wee spoiled one, suddenly locked up in the local police headquarters prison cell. When you get locked up in prison, the routine is that you must appear before the sheriff at the court the following morning and they decide what your punishment is to be. But the worst thing about my situation was that it was on a Saturday night and the court was not open until Monday morning, so as there was no way I could appear on the Sunday, I was kept in over the weekend. Yes indeed, I spent the weekend in the local Police cell, now can you imagine for one moment what was going through my head during my time inside the cell. I was only thinking of one thing, DAD! How do I manage to escape this one, what bunch of old lies am I going to try and throw at him in order to explain why I am here. Let me tell you that was the most fearful time of my life that I would come before my Dad and explain what happened. I have never experienced to this day the feeling of complete hopelessness, and self pity for oneself that I felt during that weekend inside the prison cell. I mean you had nobody to care for you, nobody to listen to your story or your problems, nobody to show you sympathy or empathy, nobody to bring you a wee cup of tea (with milk and sugar please!) and some biscuits when you are hungry, or a wee piece of toast and scrambled egg. There was no way to go to the shops and buy a soft drink and a bar of chocolate. Nope! You are completely abandoned and you're on your own. Let me tell you this, when you watch movies and it shows a prison cell with just a bed or mattress and a toilet and no real comforts, then this is exactly what it was like inside that cell. It was just a mattress and you had one cover of which was full of lice and who knows what else is in there. You would certainly not use this or let it near your body in the event you caught some sort of allergy or disease from it. Honestly it was totally disgusting. But hey, what do you expect, ice cream and cake? After you, have committed a crime, you broke the law, you were a nuisance to the community and possibly a danger. You know, when I think about it in that context then, I deserved every bit of that punishment and possibly more.

The dreaded day came, it was Monday morning and I was to appear before the Sherriff at the local court room. This was ultimately, the most embarrassing time of my life for me and my family. I was still in handcuffs as I walked up the stairs into the court room and all I could see is people staring at me, it was the most frightening experience I had went through and most shameful. All I can see now is both my parents sitting on the benches with the other spectators waiting for the Judge to enter. I looked at my Mum and Dad with complete fear; not knowing what's waiting for me when I get home, if I managed to. You see, I had already been in trouble with the police before this event but only got a warning but this was still on file as being a nuisance to the community, so here I was again up before the judge for the same incident except in a more serious manner. You could not imagine what was racing through my mind at this time, as I heard that I could even face up to three months in prison if the judge decides to lean heavy on me as it was my second time and because of the extreme nature of the incident. Well, here he comes, the whole courtroom rises to their feet and at that precise moment I thought my whole world had ended. I saw my job going down the drain, I saw me grounded for eternity, I saw all my soccer days go up in the air, and I saw the anger that was going in my Dad's face when he get me home. So here it starts, the judge starts and then the prosecutor takes over and states my actions before the court, when I heard these allegations that were put forward against me, I was shocked, because I never done a few of them, the police were making this up in order to get me a bigger penalty. So then it was my defense attorney's turn and he pleaded my case that I am young, mixed up with the wrong people, and that I had been persuaded to drink alcohol to limits above and beyond my control which lead to his misbehavior and consequent actions out in the public. But, he denied some of the facts that I will share with you in a moment. This was all well put and sounded pretty cool, but hey, you are coming before a judge who has probably heard the same spiel about a million times. There is no getting around the system when you're caught doing something you shouldn't be doing, is there? After my lawyer giving his bit, the judge asked me to stand, he looked at me and I felt like I was going to faint with the immense pressure of standing before him and he read out all the accusations against me, and he said, "Young man, are these allegations all true, that you consistently beat up another youth, and that you were singing sectarian songs that is offensive to another religion, and that you were heavily under the influence of alcohol, and that you also resisted Police arrest?" Man, I could have dropped to the floor the way he put it, I felt like a thirty year old criminal who just committed murder. I was astonished at these allegations, so I had the chance to speak so I did. At first, the court couldn't hear me because I spoke so lowly due to nerves and fear so the judge asked me to speak louder. So I responded, "Your honor, I was not singing any such songs as I don't even know of any songs to sing, and I certainly did not resist Police arrest as I was. Like you said, I was under the influence of alcohol so I could not even resist if I wanted too. As for the, under the influence of alcohol, yes I am guilty of this and for the beating up of another boy I was simply defending myself, the boy attacked me first, so I had to defend myself the best way I could, Sir". He looked at me and said, "So young man, are you calling an officer of the law a liar? That he is making up the story of you resisting arrest, why would he make up such a story, can you explain this to me?" I said, "Your honor, I am not calling the officer a liar, I am simply saying he may have misjudged the situation a little wrong, because I know I never, and would never, resist the law, as I know the possible consequences of such an action". Man, this questioning went on for a few minutes and the more it went on, the more nervous I got when answering. But it was quite clear that there was something going on with the police officer, but I guess he may have misjudged the incident. After a few minutes of questions and answers the judge looked at me and said, "Sean Anthony Mc Fadyen, you have serious allegations in front of you and I have the right to sentence you to three months in prison, but I am going to be lenient with you on this instance and impose a fine and give you six months probation. If you ever come up before me or this court again, I will have no hesitation in sending you to prison. Let this be a very strict and severe warning. You're free to go".

I have never been so terrified in my whole life, the police officer released the handcuffs from my hands and handed me over to my parents, when we walked outside the courtroom, the first thing my Dad said to me was, "Just wait till we get home". Well that was my prison sentence starting right there. You see, in this life, you may think you are clever that you can hide your actions, or get away with certain things, you may even have parents that do not punish you much if you get caught doing something you shouldn't be doing. But there may be that one time like me, when it won't be your parents that will catch you, it may be a teacher, professor, police man or a neighbor and have a complete different outcome, and the punishment may be more effective or even embarrassing. So youth, think before you make the decision that you know is not the right one, step back and assess the potential outcome of what actions you are about to make. Every decision will have a consequence, it may be a good consequence or it may be a bad one, you still have the freedom in this life to make your own decisions, so here is what I say to you. Make the right choices that you feel in your heart leaves you at peace, in other words, your conscience is clear. So here we go friends, I entered the house after my Dad, and my Mum was behind him. Maybe the reason my Mum was in the middle was, in the event my Dad lost it during the way home. I could not stop thinking to myself; what is the worst thing that could happen? What is the most painful thing he can do? I thought of everything starting from how many times he is going to take his belt across my bum, or how hard is he going to hit me and how many times I am not going to get any food, for a week or month? The punishment that I knew was going to affect me the most was, how long am I going to be grounded for? I mean, this was inevitable, it was the thing that I was assured was going to happen. When we got settled, Dad told me to sit down on the sofa. I did what he said and was terrified, I automatically went to the defense role of saying, "I am sorry, really sorry and I won't do it again" and all that stuffs, thinking if I get it all out then it will cushion the blow. Obviously, when I saw the anger in his face I was panicking, I didn't know how he would react to this sudden outburst from me. He just told me to shut up while he got his anger out stating the amount of embarrassment that I have brought to my family, how embarrassing it was for my Mum and him to go to court and sit there and listen to them describing me as a monster, and a terror to the public, a young boy drunk and beating up another boy almost to death. I just sat there taking it all in and thinking when is his hand coming across to knock me out, anytime now I guess...

Dad kept raging on about how embarrassed he was and how ashamed he was of me and expressed his total disgust in me. Can you imagine, their little shining star, the wee innocent baby of the family, the wee cutie who couldn't do anything wrong in life? Well I think I broke their hearts that day. I know, I let them down big time, I knew I crossed the line and deserved whatever was coming my way. After a while of Dad ranting on and on, my Mum as always would step in, she would tell my Dad, "Ok Andy, that's enough. He gets the point you are making". So after my Mum kind of went on my side, that really got the 'hair on my dad's back up', I mean, this made him more mad at me and I thought, "Oh no! I am the one going to suffer for this". I was like, into myself; "Mum, please be quiet, don't make it any worse". So after a few minutes of them arguing my Dad asks me to tell him how it happened and how I managed to get myself into that kind of situation. Whew! I was a bit relieved because it meant I have a chance to state my case and that he wouldn't be shouting at me until I finished my story. So this was my opportunity to possibly lessen the blow of my punishment, I had to make it good and believable. Here I go, this is where I was at my best, when it is story telling time, when there is a chance to exaggerate, then, I am your man. I can make a mountain out of a mole hole, as they say! Well, I started to tell Mum & Dad about the whole saga of how things started with me, hanging around the arcade, and socializing with the wrong crowds who were just a group of young men looking to make a name from themselves that will stop at no cost, in order to prove who they are. Unfortunately, I got caught up in this scene of violence, drunkenness, bitterness, jealousy, hatred and self centeredness, in order to be accepted by a group who probably, never even knew what the purpose of what they were doing was, or what they were subjecting other young men too. They were so bored with nothing else to do that they created their own lifestyle, a lifestyle that drove them into an arena of self indulgence that highlighted to others, how a person can be influenced by others and can be persuaded into becoming a monster. So, I carried on explaining my story to my parents while trying to look at my Dad straight in the eyes, so that I can convince him and he could maybe see the sincere sorrow in my eyes. After a few minutes into the story I put on the 'waterworks', I mean, I let the old tears start flowing from my eyes hoping that my Dad would start to soften up and lean towards my side and understand. How wrong could I have been, after the tears started rolling down my face he just blurted out, "don't think that because you're crying it's going to help you, because it won't". Well that wasn't part of the plan now, was it? Anyway, I carried on, and I think I cried more because I thought my plan wasn't working well and I was in for it, but I just kept going anyway, this was my chance to get it all out, but I had to be careful because the more I was telling him, especially the things that he was not aware of (like the countless nights of drinking and fighting) it was going bad against my Mum and he kept saying to her, "Did you know about this and you never told me?" So that was making him now mad at my Mum and when I was looking at my Mum she was giving me the old evil eye look to say, "Shut up, you're going to get us both in trouble now". So I was still rambling on about how this situation happened and I explained who these other young boys were, and where they came from. There was obviously a background behind it all that led up to this type of violent rage. The more I was talking the more it seemed to calm my Dad down, not that he had forgiven me or anything, no, it was just that he was listening instead of shouting, which was great for me. After about thirty minutes or so with me rambling on and on and trying to justify my behavior and reasons for doing such a thing, I finally gave in and just apologized to both of them and really was truly ashamed that I caused so much embarrassment to them and the family. At this point, I was genuinely sad, because I suddenly realized what I had done and how it affected them, we were never raised in such a way that led me, my brother and sister, to this type of behavior and that was one of the things that my Dad could not understand.

Both of our parents raised the three of us the best way they could, they always tried to teach us to do the right things, 'tell the truth and never lie'. And my Dad just turned to me and asked me, "What did we do wrong that made you go in to this kind of life-style?" Well, I just cried and I said to him, "There was nothing that you both did wrong. It was just me. I let myself get influenced and persuaded to take part in things that I knew, I shouldn't have. This was a decision that I made and I had many chances to come away from this lifestyle and I choose not too". You see, this is a perfect example for you to learn from, no matter how young you are, you still know what you are doing and still know that you can either make the right or wrong decision. I told them that I decided to go down this road and I was aware that it was wrong and very dangerous that I could have ended up being hurt, or even worse, end up in hospital or even dead. I assured them that I will never go back into that arcade or hang around the town center and would stay away from the friends that I was with. I thought, that would be enough and that I would be free and clear, but how wrong could I have been. Just because I managed to calm my Dad down did not mean he will forgive and forget and I would be free from any punishment. Nope! Dad was just waiting till I finished so he could then cast his punishment out to me. It was killing me waiting to hear what my punishment was going to be, I knew I was grounded but the million dollar question was, "For how long?" I don't think my mind could have worked as hard as it did at that moment trying to figure out my sentence. I would ask Dad, "So Dad, what is going to happen to me. Am I grounded? When can I go back out?" He paused for a wee second and looked at me, and just told me not to say anything because he was thinking. So, I thought that this was a good sign, he obviously didn't want to ground me or he would have just said something like; "You're grounded for a week or a month" but he never. I really thought I was in luck here, I really thought that I was going to walk away from this. For me, this was a moment in my life where I completely messed up and deserved to pay a heavy price for my actions, actions that have so rightly deserved a heavy punishment in order to teach me a lesson. You see, sometimes we need to be punished for our wrong doings in order for us to realize the mistakes we made in order to bring it to our attention. So my punishment was....

Chapter 6

MATURING MIND

• • •.........Indefinite grounding rules! "DAD!" So that was the punishment I was going to pay for my foolishness, my lack of self control and the lack of love and respect for others, for my own family, friends and other youths who were just in the wrong place at the wrong time. This is what I deserved, but not to my enjoyment, so I was grounded indefinitely, meaning there was no time period, there was no one week, two weeks or a month. No, it was until Dad decided when he wanted. Man, can you believe that? I mean, you can't do that to your own son, can you? So you should know me a little by now, right? Then you know that I am not going to let this go without putting up a wee fight, so I started to negotiate with my Dad. That was funny wasn't it? Me, who deserves to be punished and yet, when the punishment comes over I want to dispute it? Yes, that is me all over, never satisfied with anything until I get my own way and to my satisfaction.

This little attempt to negotiate never lasted to long, I started to give it my little speech but my Dad soon cut me off and told me not to bother trying as he will not change his mind. Then I tried my little crocodile tears part and that didn't get me anywhere either, and my Mum said very softly, "Sean, let it go son", and she gave me that look to say, "Listen you are so lucky you are just getting grounded, it could have been a lot worse". The moment she jumped in, then I knew I shouldn't push my luck and that I should let things settle down for a while. So I did, I walked away a very unhappy young lad with my head to the ground and went straight to my room, it seemed to be the saddest day of my life. Probably, I shouldn't have been so selfish and should have been so glad I got out of that prison cell. A lesson to be learned here is that, when you make the decisions that are of complete selfishness and with possible disrespect for others causing others harm, and then don't be surprised if you have to pay a severe penalty for your actions. You have heard of the saying, 'What goes around comes around'. Well this was a perfect instance where I experience this, again. And boy, it came around hard on me.

So picture this in your mind, here I am a seventeen year old boy with a nice wee job that I was really fortunate to have been selected from a large application list of potential candidates, a promising young soccer player with a great reputation as a defender, a great family behind me that sticks by me no matter what, and with a criminal record. Wow, hits you in the face isn't it? A criminal record at the age of seventeen! Man what kind of future can this hold for a young boy? I don't know how many times I heard this getting said to me, "Oh! You have a criminal record, what did you do?" Automatically people think you must have murdered somebody and the way they say it, "It is bad enough knowing what you did, and the penalty you paid, never mind others reminding you of it and rubbing it in your face". You see, that is the way certain individuals will come into your life, they are just born to annoy people, to cause harm, to embarrass or ridicule you. When they have situations like this, they use it to make themselves look good and you to look bad, believe me; people get kicks out of this kind of thing. Always remember, when trials come your way there is a reason and a purpose, maybe we cannot understand or work out why, maybe we will ask a question on why they happened, but in many cases that may come your way during your journey through life, there will always be a Superior force that knows why, or what, the reasons are for these trials, and what the outcomes are going to be. What we have to do is try to have the wisdom not do the things that are going to put you in these situations or the wisdom on how to deal with the consequences of making the wrong decisions. In this case for me, it showed a complete lack of self control, lack of wisdom, lack of maturity and that this was probably a result of the last few years of making the wrong decision in drinking excessive amounts of alcohol, hanging around with other youth that were so determined to cause harm to others, and to make a name for themselves. And I put myself in a situation where I was not in control of my actions and not appreciating the upbringing that I received from my family.

Family is one of the most precious gifts that God has given us and probably the first and easiest, for us to hurt or disrespect. Why is that? I am not too sure but I believe it may be due to the fact that we know our family will stick by us no matter what trouble we cause or bring them. We definitely take our family for granted in more ways than we can imagine, as we go through the chapters in this book and as we mature in our life you will see more instances of where I took for granted my family and friends. I didn't really learn my lessons when I was young, I was still very naïve as a youngster. I would be easily swayed into various acts of violence, disturbance, or play a part in some unruly game or activities that would no doubt get me into trouble. But I thought, that is what life is all about, trying different things, do what you want to do, act the way you want to act, or just don't care about what you do, as long as you're happy, right? Completely wrong! While I was still in my teens working in my wee job and slowly maturing, I was still always involved in one aspect of my youth that would always teach me my discipline and that was my soccer days. I still love soccer, it was even more exciting as you get older because you become far more competitive and try to make a huge impression. The one great thing that seemed to start disappearing from me since my previous years was the violence on and off the field. As you would have read in the previous chapters I was no saint, I would love to get involved in whatever way I could, to prove myself and be accepted, even if it meant causing harm to others. As you will read in the forthcoming chapters, that acceptance does not have to come in such a way that you have to do things that you know is not right, or completely go against your ethics and morals. I started to appreciate my friends more than I did before and I started to appreciate other people's skills and abilities, rather than look at them as a threat and want to break their legs on the field. The more I appreciate others, the more I was enjoying the game and understanding the sport. You see, we have great abilities to do great things as individuals, but it is even more amazing when you see what you can do when you act as part of a team, of great individuals. The outcome is far superior and rewarding, I mean, imagine me at the back of defense, chasing that player and ball and making sure they don't get passed me, I could do that all day and probably I would win the ball or get the player, either of the two at least ninety nine percent of the time, because as I said my skill was running. But I couldn't win the match just running up and down and stopping the other team. I couldn't skillfully dribble the ball past the opponent and take them all on, or get the other team's goal and score. No, it took a team of individuals to work together, to work out a plan, to have a game plan in order to complete the full task of winning. You see, when we are so young we don't see the full picture, all we see is us, all we see is what we can do, all we can see is our success and not the success of others, until you see the vision, on the field it's the vision of winning.

In our lives, it is much more than just winning in everything that we do, it is much more than succeeding in everything that we set out to succeed in, it is much more than conquering all our goals and being the best, it is about sharing your success with others. I mean, if God has given us individual talents that allow us to progress in our lives, to strive for bigger and better things, to achieve most of the things that we set out to achieve, and then why not do it, with the presence and influence of others? When I look back at how I carried out my young adulthood life it was certainly not in the way I am describing to you now. Why? Because I never knew any better that's why. I was such an individual young man, wanting to do things my way, on my terms, and in my time, such a selfish wee boy.

It certainly helps when you are among those people who are in similar thoughts or frame of mind, in other words, if you socialize with people who are just out for themselves then it is very likely, that your expectations will not be that of a high level, or you will not be setting yourself up for achieving great results, as this is hindered by your self-indulgence or pride. But if you are with people who are striving for great things, to be successful and are not afraid to share in their ambitions or goals in life, then your chances will surely succeed. Take for instance any team sport, since we're on the subject of soccer, look at how champion clubs are made. Forget about the money part of them buying the best players and all that stuff, think about why they need eleven players on that field? Do you think it is possible for David Beckham to win a game for Real Madrid on his own playing against eleven other players? There is no way, it's not possible. It doesn't mean that because they have the best players, or even a lot of great players, they can win alone. No, they still have to perform together and work on a game plan or strategy. The one great thing they all have in common is the desire to win. We have to have a similar desire inside of us in order for us to push ourselves to a higher level, may it be on a soccer field, in the classroom, in the work place, in our family lives or in our spiritual lives. You may have heard of the saying, 'Go the extra mile'. Do you have any idea of what that could possibly mean to you, or even how this could play a very important part in your life?

I believe I had to go the extra mile for myself at this point in my life. I had to go above and beyond my current situation that I created on my own. It was a time of my young adulthood where, I can either continue on the road that I was on, that was surely a road to destruction or, I could go that extra mile and change my attitude to one that will direct me on the right pathway. This may sound easy to some of you but I tell you, it definitely wasn't easy for me. You build a lifestyle through your decisions and actions, your emotions and convictions, your passions and ambitions, your dreams and desires, along with your failures and shortcomings. I had built a really nasty lifestyle up to this point with being involved in violence on and off the field, created a terrible attitude toward others, got involved with gangs, lie on behalf of a young girl, be deceitful to my parents, and show lack of respect to my family. When I look at this I wonder, if you can get much worse. The answer is 'Yes'. But, you have the choice to overcome any circumstance or situation in your life, there is always a way out of your current dilemma if you just know how to deal with it in the right manner. So here I am, wondering what on earth I am going to do now, how do I pick myself up from this tragic moment in my life, I now have my picture in the local police department and no doubt in the whole country.

For some reason I never seem to give up that easily, when I seem to be kicked in the teeth and feel like the whole world is falling apart around me. Somehow, I can lift myself up and move on. It does take a lot of effort and will power to be able to carry yourself through such an ordeal and believe me; you cannot just shake it off as if it never happened, it stays with you. What you need to do is remember the experience, remember the cause of this issue, remember the hurt, torture or pain, remember those that were involved and those whom you may have hurt or insulted, and then use this as a stepping stone on building your defense system to help you work a way out, and a way forward. Being in this situation I realized something very quickly and that was, I was hurting the people I loved and who loved me, so I knew that there was definitely something wrong with this and there had to be a change. I thought, one of the best things for me was to concentrate on my job. I had a great opportunity as a young trainee to have a full time job at the end of my second year youth training program and if I wasn't careful with my personal life, then this could possibly all disappear.

So, I went back to work and I tried to put this horrible experience of being convicted of a crime behind me. One of the biggest challenges for me at this moment was, do I tell my boss and co-workers, or do I try to hide it from them? Well, you know from my past experience with Betty in the 'telephone call' that I wasn't that good in lying, so my chances of getting away with this was in the low side, plus I wasn't sure if this incident was going to be publically announced in the local news paper. I asked the wisdom of my Mum, as she is normally right all the time anyway. I trust her advice. You know I couldn't really ask my Dad as he was still very mad at me, so Mum was my best choice. Mum advised me to be honest and tell the truth, as she has always told me in the past, although I never listened, and look where that got me. So I did, I told the truth and I was upfront with my boss and was ready to face whatever decision he would give. I told Betty and Margaret first as they were the closest to me and they were absolutely gob-smacked. I mean, they could not believe it, as they always thought of me as a wee cute, innocent, lovely boy who was always very nice. Once they finished asking all the questions of how and why, I would tell them the whole story. I would share to them what I have just shared with you. I mean the whole Monty. Nothing spared, every little detail and you could not draw their faces, let me tell you this, and it was as if I was a member of the mafia, the 'Don'. They paused for a while before commenting and Margaret just sat there looking bewildered at me, not knowing how to respond. While on the other hand, Betty as I said, is pretty straight forward just burst out laughing and shaking her head, I think it was with unbelief of what she just heard.

Betty was the one who was asking me all the questions throughout my whole story as she was really interested in really knowing who this wee office boy she is teaching to take over her duties, assist her with her work load and who is constantly looking after him in the best possible way. When I was telling the story of what I did during those years and how it eventually led up to this point, I felt the shame coming over me and it was a terrible feeling, it was humiliating actually, as I recall those moments of pain, torture, suffering and embarrassment that I put upon many innocent young men, just to put on a show for others. Just to make a name for myself, to be accepted into the society of hooligans. If you have every carried out such acts like the ones I have been sharing with you, or even situations in a similar fashion that ultimately, had a negative effect in someone else life, find someone to share that experience with, it could be a best friend, a family member, a neighbor, a colleague, a pastor, a priest, a brother or sister in Christ, find someone to release it to. Then write to me and tell me how did it feel, tell me what went through your heart and mind as you were reliving those moments, tell me how it affected that moment between you and the person you shared it with. I would like to know if it pierced your heart the way it pierced mine, if you felt shame the way I felt, and you wish you could turn back the clock and never have done it in the first place, the way I wished. If you never felt anything like me, don't worry, it must have been not that bad. Your time will come when your heart will be open, to how God will make a way for you to understand that certain issue and He will show his loving mercy upon you. After like thirty to forty minutes of me telling my wee stories and with a mirage of questions for Betty, I finally felt relieved after getting it out in the open. I was so terrified that she would just tell me to walk straight out that door and never come back. Well, she never. She accepted that it was a phase I was going through and it was a simple case of hanging around with people whom I shouldn't have. Not that she condoned what I did or agreed that it was alright. Oh no! Betty made it very clear that I was in the wrong side and that the things I done was outrageous and very cruel. But Betty was always clever with her words and she had lots of wisdom and great advices and strangely enough, she was very supportive of me, even if I was a little monster as Margaret called me. Margaret had her hand over her mouth the whole time in absolutely amazement and was truly shocked at what she was hearing from this little cute, shy boy. She was completely astonished and was just staring at me, not knowing how to respond, the first thing out of her mouth was, "You little monster". And I laughed and so did Betty. That broke the ice as the moment was so tense. So the moment came, I asked Betty what I should do about telling the big boss, thinking he will surely fire me on the spot. Betty just said, "Leave it with me for a while; I need to think about it".

I was still very nervous, as I only past the test with Betty and Margaret and that was only the first hurdle. I had to pass the finish line of which was how to tell the boss. I knew that whatever Betty was going to do would be for my best and only way, so it was all in her hands. Betty knew our boss; after all, she has been working with him for so many years and knows exactly how to approach him. It was all down to timing according to Betty. You have to sense the right moment where you can approach the boss with something so sensitive like this, even though it would not affect him directly in anyway, but the fact that he is now employing a criminal in his ranks of which, is not a good thing and wasn't the norm in those days. Well, I would ask Betty everyday and at least a couple of times a day, if she has told him. I needed to know, to make sure I am still in a job and when I pass him on the corridor or meet him face to face, I know how to react or deal with him. If I was walking up to him, and he moved to the side with fear, then I would know Betty told him, as he would be terrified in case I would jump on him and start beating him up (just kidding about that comment). Betty would just tell me, "Just hang around Sean, I will tell you when I told him". I think I was annoying her, not like me is it? Time was passing, and day by day I would be wondering, if this is the day I get kicked out and end up claiming unemployment benefit? Is this day my Dad really cracks me in the head for losing my job? Then it came. Betty told me that she had told him, well, my heart stopped a beat, I was all ears. I asked her what happened. "How did you start the story? How did he react? What did he say? Is he angry? Am I still in a job?" Betty stopped me and said, "Sean, quiet and let me tell you". I just sat there like a wee dog waiting for instruction from his master, waiting for the sign to walk out that door. You know, there are so many situations that you will experience in life that you may not understand the outcome, or the reasons why things happen the way they do. I mean, I have just been convicted for committing a criminal offense and yet, here I was, still in a job and my boss accepting my circumstances. Yes you heard it, I was not fired. Hooray! I was still in a job, but I was so anxious on how Betty knocked this one off. Obviously, the way it was put across by Betty was the reason for the outcome to be as it was. If I went in there and started rattling off my story, I would probably not even get finishing it and would have been removed of the premises, but not Betty. I told you she speaks words of wisdom and has a great way of communicating things.

Anyway, Betty explained to our boss my story like this... I was so young and very naïve of what goes on in the world and that I was influenced into being part of a gang. And in those days, being in gang means, you have to justify yourself to what others requires and obliges you to do. So in this case, Sean was unfortunately drawn into this web of alcohol and violence that resulted in him being eventually caught by the police and he ended up spending a few days in the local police cells. Betty also expressed her joy to the boss that I was caught in order for me to be released from continuing this kind of behavior and that I have learned a very hard lesson of what is right and what is wrong. Wow, can you believe this, this is awesome. Betty should have been a Psychologist or something; she was great with words, people & dealing with situations. Betty also commented on the fact that I am being punished severely from my parents as this is not the way I was raised and they are taking this matter very seriously indeed. So after hearing all these, the boss agreed and took the side of Betty, as he always did, because he knew Betty is always ninety nine percent right and that he trusted her judgment. However, there was one stipulation that the boss made and it was to be directed to me. That was, if I ever got into trouble with the police again, or he hears of any of the same kind of behavior, then I am finished, I am out. To me, that was a very fair deal, I mean I didn't even deserve a second chance and yet here I am still hanging on, but I was on very thin ice and had to tread very carefully, if I wanted to remain there. That was enough for me, I was over the moon, and I was so overjoyed about the fact of still being employed. So I took the advice from Betty and went on my way to change my evil ways. I was coming to the end of my second year placement and I was learning a lot. I managed to take sole control of all the invoices for the contract that we had for the local council, and was in charge of the payroll for the office. I was in a pretty good position in order to hopefully be kept on full time with this company upon the completion of my training program. During all these, I was still playing soccer and we were getting a little better but were still not up to the level of the top teams. We were always arguing on the field with each other due to the mistakes we would make and how we expected others to perform and help out. But we were all just growing up and maturing and none of us were really getting the bigger picture of how to know each other, and work together as a team, and not as individuals. When we would play other teams and they were much more skillful than us, much more aggressive, and they seemed to know where each other would be when it was time to pass that ball, I wished the same for our team. They would constantly be talking and directing each other, guiding each other as to what to do and when to do it. We would just be running around like headless chickens trying to stop them and getting frustrated at the same time. But I guess, at this stage in our young lives it was indeed a learning stage. As they say, 'you have to crawl before you can walk'. We were definitely in the crawling stages but taking giant steps towards reaching the goal. We were definitely improving but had a long way to go before being capable of finishing at the top. We would try our best in every game but it seems, we were just not good enough as the top teams, but we would always try to achieve one thing, and that was to beat our local team called Gourock United FC. I mean these guys were the best, most skillful, quickest, the toughest, and they had a great reputation behind them throughout all the years. They were always the top team in our league. The funny thing was, when we would play teams that would struggle against Gourock, we would get smashed. It was always very close, it would either be a draw or they would win with one point. It was always a mystery to us and to them. I believe it was because in our hearts we wanted to beat them so badly that we would give 110% effort on that field and we would not give in to them.

This is a very important aspect of the learning cycle in our lives. No matter what you will be doing, whether it is at work, on a play field, in a classroom, in a group surrounding, even in a relationship, you will have the choice to give that skill or talent that you have, in order to achieve the result you want or desire. You look at all the soccer players, all the NFL players, ML Baseball players, NBA players, racing drivers, golfers, tennis players, CEO's, engineers, architects, nurses or teachers to say a few, they give all they can in order to achieve that ultimate result of winning, the result of success, the result of accomplishment, and the result of their chosen field. They all have a choice like you do even at this young age, they all have a path that they can follow that would take them down a road of achievement, success, accomplishment, satisfaction, gratitude or gratefulness, or they can follow a path that would take them down a road of resentment, bitterness, hatred, lies, destruction, devastation, hopelessness and/or regret. They have a choice like you and I. At the beginning, I made my choice of going down the second road mentioned and look where it landed me, in prison and not to mention many enemies. That as a result, made me watch over my shoulder at all times. I'm not saying that the same things will happen to you, not at all, it just means that there are consequences for every choice that we make, every decision and every action that we take. You will not work it all out at this young age, because there are so many different challenges that comes along the way with maturity and experience, but you just have to try to work out what are the right things to do, what are the wrong things to do, and then identify the right path to suit those right things. It seems to be difficult in choosing the right path every time as it seems to go against the way of the world, the way of our selfish desires, our greed, our lack of respect or mannerism, our lack of compassion. But there is a reason for that, and I will share it further. But just believe, that above you and I, there is a Force to be reckoned, that will allow you a way out, that will allow you many chances to make the right choices, that will pull you out of that pit when you fall down, that will bring many great things your way that you will not think possible or couldn't achieve on your own.

Now don't get me wrong here, I didn't turn Mr. Nice overnight, no, this was just a wake-up call for me to change the direction that I was allowing my life to take. My youthful day was still in full force. I just changed direction and stayed away from the arcade machines and the town centre bus stops where our gang would operate. I took my party life to the next level. I started going to actual bars and get drunk in there, after all, it seemed to be safer and a more friendly place and environment to be. Not to mention that there were loads of girls of which, made it more enjoyable. I got to be honest with you here, all we ever thought about was booze and birds, or in proper English terms, alcohol and girls. You will be thinking, hold on a minute, how can he get into bars when you are supposed to be eighteen years old of age to enter theses establishments? And if you recall, I was only seventeen years old and I was so small, so how did I get in? Well, there be some other things that we did in those days in order to get into the bars and clubs, and it wasn't correct, but we did what we had to do. We needed access to the alcohol and girls. You must be thinking, you have just told us about your horrifying ordeal inside a prison cell, embarrassment of facing your boss and co-workers, possibility of losing your job, and even being grounded by your parents of which, you embarrassed to no end. And yet, here you are again? Well, that sums me up doesn't it? I was just a boy at a bad age who never wanted to learn from his mistakes and take the right path in life. This is where the selfishness in all of us and the 'conforming to this world' comes in to effect in our lives that can direct the choices and actions that we make. Going back to the time of drinking, in order for us to get alcohol before we go to the pubs, we had to buy from outside and then drink in your house before you go to the bars and clubs. These little shops were called 'liquor store' or an 'off-license'. These were small grocery stores that mostly sell alcohol and seemed to be easy to get served. I still had to use my influence to be able to buy alcohol from these stores because I was so small and never looked my age at all. I was actually only seventeen years old so they would ask me some questions to try and catch me out, but I was prepared. Once I was served a few times they got to know me and they wouldn't ask anymore, pretty bad sign when an alcohol establishment gets to know you by face isn't it? Well this was my next step in the process of enjoying being a young-adult, buying alcohol, taking it to the house, drinking it and then hitting the bars and clubs, not my house, as my Dad will kill me if he knew, no, we would go to my friends house and drink there. So here we are with a new hobby, drinking in the house and hitting bars and clubs. This was the 'in' thing as everyone our age was doing it, so we had to be 'in' too. Again a perfect example of being influenced by the society we live in and conforming to the desires of this world. But what do we know at that age, we're only learning about life, right? Our parents did the same thing; they made the mistakes and got it all wrong, so why should we be any different? Well, that is the whole essence of life, living in a way that you make the right choices that do not put you through the same scenarios or situations that our ancestors went through or experienced, but that just seems impossible in this day and age, as there is just too much distraction and temptation around us. Time went by and we were seemingly enjoying this new found lifestyle that we knew was wrong at the time but still, didn't stop us from carrying it out. We were having a ball, going to parties, getting drunk, getting girlfriends and feeling great, knowing that you're out there getting seen by others and trying to impress the whole world. It wasn't too long before I met a girl who wasn't in our school and I didn't know her at all, but she was a friend of friends and we all ended up together in a disco, I ended up going back to her house at three in the morning. We were both drunk and she was quite a beautiful young girl who was the same age as me. So here we are at 3 in the morning at her house and we were sneaking in so her parents couldn't hear us. Her parents were very strict and put up with no nonsense, so we had to be careful. It was funny, we were sitting on the floor of the kitchen just kissing and talking and then I asked, if we could go up to the bedroom. I know, I shouldn't at that age but we are young adults we are allowed to do these things. Anyway, after like twenty minutes of persuasion she agreed but stipulated that nothing is to happen. So we start sneaking upstairs very slowly and quietly so her parents wouldn't here and man, what happened next? We heard movement upstairs in the parent's room, so we sneaked back down those stairs as quickly and silently as possible, and just sat back on the floor. It was so funny; her dad comes down and starts shouting, "What time is this to come in? And look at you, you're drunk, you should be ashamed of yourself young lady. And who is this that you have brought into my home at this time in the morning? Look at him he, is drunk too". He keeps shouting and pointing his finger at her and telling her to get out the house, then, her Mum comes down and start shouting at the husband. The husband walked away shouting at the wife telling her that she always sticks up for her daughter even if she is in the wrong side. I was like, 'way to go Mum that is the game'. Then she turns on her daughter and start shouting at her and I am like, "What is going on? This family is crazy". Then both parents go upstairs and the father shouts down, "I want your boyfriend out of here in five minutes or I will throw him out". And I am like, wow! I am not getting tossed out a house. But then, I remembered he was a big man and looked pretty mean, so I was all for leaving. Then my girlfriend started to cry very hard and I was like, what do I do? I don't even know her and she is lying here bubbling like a baby in my arms.

Well, being a sensitive guy and pretty shy at most times I just held her in my arms and let her cry out, after all, I have no idea what her family life is like and what goes on among them. All I can see is a very upset girl and a pair of angry parents. Not that they have no right to be angry, we did wake them up at three in the morning so I guess that was deserved, but the throwing me out part, well that is something else isn't it? So after like ten minutes, she stopped crying and we just kind of sat there and we kissed for a couple of minutes which was cool. I liked that bit very much and she was a good kisser as well, which helps. We knew we had to make a move before the big gorilla came bouncing back down the stairs and grab me like a piece of meat to throw me half way across the road. As I only stayed a few minutes away from her house, I just decided to walk home, I was pretty drunk anyway, so I didn't feel the coldness outside and I wasn't really bothered any, I was just happy, I got a girlfriend that night. Let me tell you, they were far and few between. I told you I wasn't the most handsome looking guy in town, so when I got a girlfriend I was over the moon, and yes, it didn't matter if they were nice or not, girls a girl, right? But it just so happened, this one was pretty good looking I thought. Nice figure, nice face, great long curly hair and nice lips. Man what else do you look for and she was funny, we had a great laugh together. She was a pretty sensitive girl as I noticed from the crying part. Well, I took her number so I could give her a call for us to go out another night. We met a few times and then I visited her parent's house again when I was not drunk. Her parents had a very nice house and they lived in a very posh area, an area where only families with good jobs and money could live. I loved going to their house as it was much better than our house, and they had all new furnishings and it was a very comfortable place to be. As I got to know the family, they were very hospitable and friendly but pretty strict. As time went by, we started to see each other every night as this was fine with me, I wanted to see her every night anyway as I was getting very attached to her. We would continue to go to her house on many occasions and also go out at the weekends. We would still go to the bars and clubs, drink and dance the night away, we were at the height of our teenage life enjoying every part of the freedom. At this age, we were not worried about anything, I had a job earning money and at the same time getting pocket money from the family and my girlfriend was working in a hospital, so we were pretty good. I wanted to see her every night and she was up for that too. You must remember that in Greenock where we lived, there was not much to do at nights, and it was always freezing cold and raining most times, so we had to create our own entertainment and that's where the pubs and clubs came in to play. There was no way that as young as we were, and with so much energy, we were going to just stay at home and be nice little boys and girls and do what Mummy and Daddy tells you. Nope, we were out to party.

So were going strong and my job was also going well now that I overcome the 'being a criminal' part and still being accepted by my boss. We were in our first year of our relationship and we couldn't be separated. I mean, there was nothing else we wanted, than to be with each other, I guess they call it 'puppy love'. Whatever it was, it seemed to be working, we were both happy and enjoying every moment we had together. I was coming up for my eighteenth birthday on January, and my last days work at Hillhead in my second year program was on the last week of December. So I was coming to a very crucial situation. This was to be the moment where I would find out what lies ahead in relation to my career at Hillhead. As I mentioned before, this was only a two year program, there was nothing else after this. No third year, no fourth year, no extension, nothing. The only opportunity that may arise from this was, if the company that you were working with for that whole year liked you, subsequently, they have the option to employ you full time. Being employed by them full time was a financial commitment as they then had no more grants to pay for my expenses or towards my salary. It will come out of their funds, meaning I would be a cost to them. Well, as this moment was getting closer, I was not even in the picture as to whether I would be employed at the end. I would try to ask Margaret if she heard anything or knew what the boss's plans were, but she knew nothing, and if she did, she would have probably been told not to tell me anyway. I would also drop a hint to Betty, if she would let slip any information on me, again, she knows nothing. I think both of them were telling the truth, because the boss had to work out exactly what cost I would be to them and what benefit could I really bring to the table, meaning, would I be worth employing, and how much money will it cost the company to keep me? I was getting so nervous. I had like a week to go and was still no further forward in knowing if I had a job or not, so I was preparing myself for the worse. I started to think about going to the job center and checking what other jobs there were to see if I could fit into them. I didn't like the thought of having no money. Having no money means a lot of things, like no alcohol, no clubs, no new clothes, can't take the girlfriend anywhere or buy her anything, I mean, that is major right there, you know girls, they like to have things bought for them, right? I was also thinking, man, this would be a crap birthday present if I never had a job on my birthday. How could I really celebrate and be happy, knowing I am not working anymore? Probably, at that point without even knowing it, I got my first experience of what pressure is like, I am glad we were too young to understand what effect pressure has on your health and physical status.

It was our Christmas party in the office, so there were quite a few of the engineers around and staffs from the other companies that worked in the building that our boss was partners with. Betty suddenly called everyone into the main office to have a toast with all the workers, she thanked everybody for all their hard work over the year and said it was a very successful year and then she started handing out a bonus to everyone. We were all having some drinks as that is the normal thing to do in the workplace at Christmas, everyone has a few drinks to celebrate another year of working with each other and it is the start of everyone's wind down to the year. And, it also puts you in the party mood to start celebrating your holidays that you will soon be on. Betty started calling everyone one by one, and handed them each an envelope with whatever bonus amount you were given. I wasn't too interested at that time with any bonus; I wanted to know if I was still in a job as it was my very last day of work. The bonus was normally one or two week's salary depending on how well the business done, or if the boss was feeling generous that year or, if he was in a good mood. Anyway, for some reason I was not called, all the other office staff was being called then the engineers and then the higher management were called and it was boiling down to me being the last. Well, I wasn't comfortable with this at all. On the first note, I was thinking, man, I am not going to be included in this because they are not going to keep me employed, and that they will tell me when everyone has gone. On the second note, there goes my bonus too. I will end up going home with nothing. And lastly, I was feeling left out and embarrassed, as I hate being last in anything, and thinking that I am not a part of the action. I tell you something, I was really feeling bad about not being called. I felt worthless, ashamed and totally embarrassed by this, as my nature is that, I always had to be in the action, always a part of the moment or the situation, and I felt I was being left out for a reason.

Well, here comes Betty, called my name and announced that I was the last employee to join the company (so that is why she called me last). Now Betty can be very sarcastic at times if she wants to be, but this time she was pretty funny although it probably never showed in my face that way, because I was feeling sick and nervous. She gave a little background of my joining the company at the beginning of the year as a trainee on a special program, that their company had never entered into before so they were pretty new to this trainee program. And honestly, they never held much hope in it working properly or even me, working out to what they were expecting. So, after a few minutes of introduction of my background, she then commented on my work ethics, discipline, and attitude and how much they were extremely satisfied with my work and

How much I have learned over the year and with the responsibility that I was given at such a young age. This was the funny part; she also mentioned that although sometimes I would test her and does things I wasn't supposed to do, also there were times where I was really going through a very difficult time with the local authorities (meaning the police), and in that, everyone laughed. Well that seemed to break the ice for me as everyone knew my story about going to prison for the weekend for fighting, but it was a kind of sensitive issue that was never to be really spoken about in the office. That was because my boss never wanted to remind me of the incident and just hoped that he made the right decision in keeping me in the company.

Now that Betty has mentioned everything about me, she then thanked me for my service to the company over the past year. Well,

I tell you something; at that point I thought it's all over. I am getting kicked out and my face hit the ground with sadness, I really thought I was going to cry. I felt my emotions building up and was saying to myself, "Come on Sean, you can't break down in front of all these guys". But then she gave me my bonus and then another piece of paper. I was wondering what the paper was, until she asked me to read it. I was thinking, 'what on earth is she doing? Why does she want me to read this?' Until I looked at it, the heavens opened. The letter was an 'employment letter' offering me a full time position as an 'Administration / Accounts Clerk'. It was a great moment for me and I was so happy, I just shouted in the air, "Yes, I got a job". You need to remember that in my teenage days there wasn't a lot of options out there in Greenock, and as I wasn't the ripest banana out of the bunch, or in other words, not the cleverest out of the group. So you're odds are much less in landing a good job. So, when I was offered the position, I jumped with joy and I was truly amazed and overwhelmed with the rest of the people at work. They all shouted and cheered for me as it was announced, and that made me feel so great. It was an amazing feeling that made me believe my co-workers really liked me and were happy for me. This was truly fantastic and great moment in my way to becoming successful, so I thought anyway. Could you blame me, I was feeling on top of the world with my great news, so there was nothing to spoil this moment and the way I was feeling. The end of day was nearing so the drinks were starting to flow around quicker and quicker, the guys were ready to wind down for their Christmas holidays. I wasn't allowed much drink from Betty as she still treated me like her wee boy, but the engineers would sneak me some bottles of beer when Betty was busy, or I would go out of the office with the guys and we would down a few bottles. That night, was a celebration night for me. I went out with my friends and we got really drunk and it didn't end there, we spent the whole weekend getting drunk and celebrating my success. I had a great Christmas that year. I felt like I could fly to the moon, I was so excited and couldn't wait to start work after the festive celebrations were over. In Greenock, and I'm sure in all other towns and cities, Christmas is the bomb, it's the best time of the year because everyone is happy and we all get gifts, and usually they are pretty good gifts. Now that we get older, we want like cell phones, branded clothes, computer games, football boots and strips and all those nice things. We would normally not want Christmas and New Year to end because of the parties and getting together with family and friends. Well, not so much with the family as they are always a little old fashioned when it comes to parties and having fun, if you know what I mean, so mostly with our friends because they know how to party. We are still young or you can call us 'young adults' by now.

Anyway, After Christmas was over, I started work at my new position of administration / accounts clerk of which I felt, I was so important in the company now. I really felt like I was worth something and not just a little trainee office boy who nobody bothered about. You know that feeling, when what you do seems irrelevant to others because you are so beneath them in your position, and they always seem to remind you of that, now and again. Well, I was over that part, of feeling like nothing, or feeling like I wasn't even around, or was not contributing to any part of the company success. Have you ever been there? I mean, no matter what you do or how you do it, it never seems to matter, it doesn't seem that important to others. I was there, and now I am not. I was a little bit early on that first day because of my excitement, and Betty was so happy to see me, she had a big smile on her face, I was so joyful to see her too. She congratulated me on my first day as a full time employee and I was smiling from one side of the room to the other. Well, I sat down and got on with my duties that I was carrying out as a former trainee, but now, I felt like I had to really put all my effort and time into making sure what I do, is perfect. I did things as quick as possible so I can then do more work. I was out to impress. And let me tell you, I've done a pretty good job of it. The local council work that I was in charge of processing as a trainee, I would normally take two to three days to complete, and there was a reason for this. I thought I was being smart during that time because although I like my work, I only wanted to do as little as possible, you know what I mean, less work for more money mentality. So, I would allow my work load to drag out for a couple of days so that, Betty would then give more work to Margaret to do, I know it is bad, welcome to my life! Well, this was about to change, as now I seen a different light ahead of me, I saw a vision of what I could possibly run one day. I saw Betty retiring and me taking over as office manager, the reason I saw this was because I know Betty was always wanting to retire or even go part time as she has been working for so many years already and someone, would have to take over. Somehow, someday, someone needs to fill her position and do the things she was doing. At this time you may be wondering, what about Margaret? Well again, me being the wee nosy boy that I was, I knew Margaret's long term plans too. She and her fiancé David were planning to go back to Australia after two or three years, so that wiped her out of the picture, and there was no one else except me.

So now you can see where I was going with my vision and how it came about. I had plans, big plans, and I knew I would love to run the office and be in charge of all the administration, accounts, invoicing, payroll and just the overall running of the business from an office stand point. I would have control over the engineers pay, their time-sheets, their paper works, the whole Monty. Well, we have to dream don't we? Life would be worth nothing if we can't dream of great or big things, right? I was on a one way ticket to stardom here, I had a point to make, and I planned to do my very best to make it work. This was a great opportunity for me to shine, to really show that I could be responsible, reliable and be consistent in my performance of carrying out my tasks ahead of me. But you know one of the great things that I was to expect at this time of starting my new role as a full time employee? Have a guess. The salary increase, yes! I was getting a pay check and it almost doubled my salary. Now, can you see the smile on my wee cheeky face? Yep, big bucks now, like I am in the big league. My salary jumped from thirty five pounds per week, to sixty pounds a week, but still, that was a lot of money for an eighteen year old, after all. I never had any bills or loans to pay, so it was all mine. And you know that wasn't all, Betty was so kind to me; she even gave me another five pounds per week on top of the salary for traveling costs, can you believe it? What a jump in salary benefits and above that, I was still getting pocket money from Drew and Pauline, my brother and sister. But don't ever tell them how much I was getting a salary or they will come after me (if you read this book before them) as I was telling them, I was still getting low salary because I had no experience so they felt pity for me and continued my pocket money. All was going well with my new position and I would buy myself better soccer boots and some soccer strips, so I can look better to my friends when we played soccer. I would buy a better computer, bicycle and other items for myself.

Although I had more money, I never spent it on any of my family, just myself; I guess that was the bad thing about me. I was very selfish and believed, it was all mine, because I was the one working for it, so I deserved to spend it on myself. I did want to spend some on my girlfriend at that time, but she probably was earning more money than me, so she didn't need mine too. And she was very kind, she would always want to buy me something and pay for things, so I let her. Before you say it, I know, not the gentleman thing to do. But hey, I am a young adult, what do I know about the right things to do in life. Remember, I wasn't the best at making choices before, was I? Look where my choices in life got me, a beating, a couple days in prison, not the right way to follow now is it? Anyway, my relationship was getting a bit stronger now since we were seeing each other for over a year and most nights we were together except, the weekend. I would always have a Saturday night as a boy's night out. This was the lads night to go out and have fun, get drunk, talk rubbish and see if we could have a fight with some other youths, just standard stuff really. We were all the same in those days I guess. Once you got a wee bit of the old booze in you then anything goes. I think as we were getting older, or maturing is a good word, we were coming of the wine, and when I say wine, it is not white wine or red wine or any rich bottle of 'Cordonbleu'. No, it was the cheapest and most disgusting wine ever invented. I will tell you the truth here, this stuff was brutal, it was absolutely disgusting and tasted awful, but it got you drunk in no time. That was the benefit of drinking it. We would go out every single Saturday night without fail. There would be six of us, we were all very close friends and stick together like glue when we were out, if anyone come against one of us, then they face the six of us, that was the rule. And even if we were in the wrong side, we still stick together and sorted things out as a team. I liked being in a team play, it felt really good.

Back to my work, things were going great at this time as I was battering away in carrying out my duties and doing it very well. Going back to when I said, I would take two to three days to carry out a certain task for the local council work I was doing. Well it was only taking me between one and one and half days to complete and that knocked the socks of Betty and Margaret. I mean, they were absolutely astounded, shocked, couldn't believe I could do it so quick, so much to their amazement they were expecting loads of mistakes in my work, or I would be invoicing the wrong items or not accounting for everything I was supposed to. But nope, there were no mistakes, nothing missed and everything was accounted for. I was so focused in doing great as I wanted them to acknowledge what I am doing so I can get a pat on the back all the time. You know that can be a danger in our lives today. We are striving for recognition or acknowledgement for what we do or how we do it. Sometimes, we may forget about others and let all the focus be on ourselves, isn't it? Think back and assess the last thing you've done, the last task you carried out, the last duty you performed, or the last time you were asked to do something and think about what you expected in return if you completed it very well and to the satisfaction of those who gave you the task. Did you look for gratitude or a pat on the back, and for someone to say to you, "Well done, you done a great job?" I have done it many times, and sometimes it is even hard not to want that little recognition in today's society. After all it makes us feel good doesn't it? If we have to be honest, it is a feel good factor; it lifts us up and allows us to feel important or accepted. Well, there is great news for each one of us, even this early in my book I will share with you the justice of our being here on this planet and what my book will hopefully reveal to you, and it is certainly not for recognition, it is not for acceptance, it is not for justification, it is not for proving what you can do, or can't do as an individual, it is not how successful you can be at your profession. No, it is for the love of others, in other words, it is how we can show compassion to others when there is no compassion shown to us, it is how we care for others when others don't care for us, it is how we go over and beyond what we can do for others and expect nothing in return, it is about how far you are willing to go to make a difference in others lives, it is about what kind of impact are you making in the lives of those around you no matter what color, what race, what religion, what background, what education, what circumstances they are facing or going through. That's what it's all about, and I will share more on this in the coming chapters.

Back to the office scenario, after a month or two, I was approached by one of the engineers in the company. He was kind of, one of the senior engineers and was with the company for so long with another few of the men of which I will mention later. This engineer must have taken a liking to me. In other words, he liked me in a way that he wanted something better for me in life. Not that, I knew the answers to everything as I was so young, but he was thinking of my future. Anyway, he asked me if I would like to become an engineer, and do the kind of work that they were doing. I just laughed at him and said, "Yeh right Owen" (that was his name). He said to me, "Think about it Sean, it is a good job, you get good money and benefits, you get a van, tools, and all your expenses paid for when you travel, you will have work for the rest of your life, and you will have a qualification that nobody can ever take away from you and you could travel around Scotland". Well, if that doesn't sound fantastic, nothing will. He really got me thinking, but for only a minute, knowing it could not happen. So I just blew it off and said "Thanks, but no thanks. I am happy here doing what I am doing", so he walked away. But I will tell you something, when I thought about all the good things he told me and all the benefits, obviously, I know he wasn't lying about the money part? (Remember who does the salaries?), 'Me'. I knew exactly how much every engineer was taking home and I knew who was earning more than others, and that is because certain men were working away from home and others choose to work close to home. Anyway, after a day or two, it went out of my mind, I was focusing on my wee work at hand that I loved, and was doing well. After another month went by, Owen would approach me again about becoming an engineer and asked me if I thought about it, and I told him there was no point because I can never become an engineer. He asked why not?

I told him that I am only an office boy, I know nothing about engineering and I cannot go to college. Again he asked, "Why not?" So I told him about my high school grades or brutal to say, lacking of high school grades, so I would never get into college and that I also hated school anyway, so I would not be interested in it and would fail terribly. He disagreed, and told me that I don't have to have any grades and that it would not be like the other colleges where you have many subjects. It was an engineering college, and it was more hands on, than theory. When you know that something is not for you, when you know that the obstacle in front of you would be to overwhelming for you to accomplish, or too big to handle, well that was what I was thinking in my head about this particular issue. I thought it was too big to handle. Owen, being the consistent man that he was, continued to ask me to think about it, so I did, and again, I never had any other answer than forget it, it won't happen. My finishing point of this topic to him, just so he could leave me alone was, even If I wanted to go to college and become an engineer, how on earth am I going to pay for it, and what would the boss say? He said to me, "If you tell me that you are interested, really interested, then I will do some homework for you and get all the particulars of what the college fees would be, materials, books, all expenses and then, I would put it in front of the boss and ask him to send you to college". I just laughed at him and said "You're off your head mate? That will never happen; you're wasting your time there". I was almost six months into my new role and all was going well, Betty was getting closer and closer to her retirement I think, as that was all she kept saying and she was confident that I would take over her spot, so I had my eyes on that position more than this fairy tale of becoming an engineer. I was still eighteen years old and going strong with my girlfriend, had a good job with a potential growth, a nice family of whom everyone was working, Mum and Dad was still working, Pauline and Drew were still working. So everything was good. But don't get me wrong. We were not well off, or rich or anything. Pauline had her own life; she was living in her own apartment with her husband as she was married very young. Drew was just out on the town most nights having fun as a young single man does, so I was taking after him I think. He is getting the blame anyway, sorry Bro! Mum and Dad were just the same. Mum would enjoy her nights at the bingo and Dad would be out at the pubs with the men, mostly other men he worked with in those days.

Things were going along nicely, then again here comes Owen with his portfolio of information on how to send me to college. Well, I was really looking forward to hear what he had to say and offer and his way of convincing the boss to send me to college. I let him speak, so he went on about the college and what course I would be taking, the length of the course, would be involved in order for me to finish it to become a fully qualified engineer, and what the costs would be. I was laughing at him because he wanted me to go to college for four years, in an engineering college of which, costs thousands and thousands of pounds and many more related costs like books, materials, travel, and others, that I obviously couldn't pay, that the boss would have to cough up with. So, to me it was just a waste of time. Then he dropped the bombshell on me, he said that, all these costs and even one half of my salary will all be covered if I get accepted, under the government grant scheme. I almost dropped to the ground, I said "Owen, how is that possible? How would a government grant pay for all those costs?" He said, "It is a way for the government to encourage young people to go to college in order for them to have a better education, and a better future ahead of them". Even though this all sounds nice and all costs are taken care of, two obstacles still lie ahead of this great master plan. First, the boss should approve such a request and take on such a responsibility for four years and second, me not having the brains to complete those years of engineering college. Owen really went to town on this, I mean, he covered all angles and went out his way to prove to me it can be done, and that I could be accepted. I asked him, "Why would you go out and waste all your precious and valuable time, obtaining all this information for me?" You know what he said to me? He said, "Sean, I think you are a great young man and you deserve to have a better future ahead of you than stuck in an office, you are a clever young man you're certainly not stupid, or you wouldn't be in charge of a company payroll system. You wouldn't be in charge of our biggest business accounts; you wouldn't be in charge of the administration of almost twenty engineers' payroll and times sheets, on a weekly basis. You wouldn't be in charge of all supplier invoicing and credit control that inevitably allows us all to get paid every week. So don't tell me you don't have the brains to go to college and complete this course, I have been on this course and I know you can pass it, I know because of your determination and discipline that you will succeed". All this time, he was saying these things, Betty and Margaret were in the office listening to him and I turned around and looked at them and said, "Do you not think he is off his head?", they started laughing and we all just had a quick giggle, but then Betty in all her wisdom said, "You know, it is not a bad idea, and I believe what Owen, said that you can do it. Why not give it a try, put it in front of the boss and see what he says. But Sean, do you want to become an engineer? Can you see yourself doing what the guys are doing? You know exactly what they do on paper; can you see yourself doing the same on a practical term?" Margaret also agreed and told me, "Give it a shot, what is the worst thing that could happen? The boss will say no, and that's it, you just carry on doing what you're doing right now". I turned round and said to Owen, "Ok, give it a try, but if he gets angry, then it was all you're doing, not mine".

Owen took all the documents and information he had and went to the office of the boss and presented it to him, he was in there for a couple hours and Betty said, "If he is in there that long, then the boss is certainly listening to him and giving it some thought". I was so nervous, I couldn't believe what was happening, I mean, I only got promoted six months ago and now I am being negotiated to be sent to college to become an engineer. Betty's internal phone was ringing and it was from the boss, he asked her to send me over to his office, well, I was shaking like a leaf, I tell you, the sweat just poured from me. I went in and he was sitting there with Owen and lots of papers spread over the meeting desk in his office and he asked me, "Are you aware of what Owen has proposed in front of me?" I said, "Yes sir, I am". He said, "Do you know the kind of commitment and dedication that is required in order to complete such a course?" I said, "I believe it will be a lot of hard work boss". He asked me, "Do you want to do this?" I said, "Yes sir, I do?" Then he asked me to go back to work. Man, I couldn't get out of his office quick enough. I was in a mess, as I thought he would give me into trouble for wanting to give up my job of a clerk, after just being promoted.

I went back through to the front office and sat on my chair and Betty asked, "What did he say to you?" So I told her everything and she made no comment, so that made me even worse. Normally, Betty would comment on everything and it would always turn out to be good, or even if it wasn't, she would of know the answer to all things. So I let it be and just waited till Owen came back out. After another twenty minutes or so, he came back and was all smiling and said, "The boss is going for it, as long as all the grants get awarded and he has to pay nothing". I shouted out loud just to show my joy of such an opportunity to become an engineer, although I had at the back of my mind, that I have no chance whatsoever in passing these exams, as I knew, how bad I was in school. At least it was a step forward for me attaining an engineering qualification. When I went home and told my parents they were absolutely gob-smacked, they didn't know what to say, but the question came out, "How much does it cost and who is paying for it?" I laughed and said, "If successful, it will be paid for by the government on a 'CITB' grant scheme". CITB means, City of Industry Training Board, this is the organization that allows young people like me to go to college on a government funded grant in order to give them a trade, allow them to become professionals. I could have chosen to become a carpenter, and electrician, a plasterer, a construction worker, a plumber and many more, but I chose the HVAC (Heating, Ventilating and Air Conditioning Course) as that was related to my company and what they do, and probably that was the only reason my boss agreed to send me on this course. This was a fantastic government funded program that really allowed young ones in those days, to try and get a career, they made all roads possible by completely funding every part of the four year course, and can you imagine? They even paid half of my weekly salary, so my boss was really coming out on top with this to the extent that, if I passed my exams and graduated, then he would have a fully qualified HVAC engineer to use at his disposal and charge out the same rate for me on an hourly basis, as he does the other engineers. One thing more that stood in the way of it, becoming a reality was getting awarded the grant from the CITB. I really don't know what Owen had to do, or explain in order for me to get approved, but I was sure that if they asked for my high school GSE results, or pass grades, then I would be totally stumped and that would be the end of that fairy tale. I was honest and I said to Owen that I have no grades at all; I hated school subjects and never passed any except for the Physical Education subject. He just laughed and said he failed all his subjects while he was at school, and look where he is, so he said, "Leave it up to me". One thing about Owen that I must tell you is, he is a gab. I mean he can talk for Scotland, he never stops talking and telling jokes, he is so funny and he is really a good guy. Owen was once an alcoholic but was turning his ways and joined the AA (alcoholics anonymous) to keep him off the booze, and it seemed to work, although he was a little mad at times, but I guess you can't come away from a life of violence and alcohol without having some set-backs right? Anyway, he did nobody any harm so to me he was a great guy. Things were getting pretty tight for this to go ahead as there was only one stipulation that the CITB was very strict on and that was that you must sign on the course and be approved, up to the age of eighteen. If you are over this age then you cannot be granted to attend college. So here we are, I was eighteen, and it was in the month of August and the college course starts on September. I had only one month to get approved and awarded the grant and then start college the next month. I will be totally honest, I never thought I had a chance of getting it anyway, plus to have this time frame put in the loop was another hurdle to get over. So all the odds were going against me, and to tell you the truth, I would not be too disappointed if I wasn't awarded the grant, as I was terrified of the thought of going to college and failing terribly in front of people, like I did my high school years. I was so nervous in those coming weeks just waiting for the news, then one day, Owen walks in the office and slams the paperwork on my desk, "Right young man", he said, "Get ready, in four weeks, you're going to become an engineer". Wow! Could you imagine the joy that came over all of us in that office, Betty and Margaret jumped up screaming the heads off, and I was just smiling and I immediately got up out of my chair and thanked Owen for doing such a great job. Up to this day, I still don't know the true reason on why that man bent over backwards for me, in order for me to get college education. Owen went that extra mile for me to have a better chance in life of achieving something great, allowing a fantastic opportunity to come my way, and not ask for anything in return. You see, this is an example of what I meant by my earlier comment, are you ready to go 'above and beyond' for others? Are you ready to go that extra mile for others? To those you don't know, who don't really care about you, or what you do for them, for ones who, in your eyes, may not deserve your attention, or love, or gifts? Are you ready to raise the bar on your behalf to help out others, because let me tell you, this is one of the many reasons I believe, we have all been created for, to care for others better than ourselves.

So here it is, I have couple of weeks to get my act together and attend college in Springburn, Glasgow. This college is well known on the HVAC industry as a lot of engineers in those days, were working in that profession from the west side of Scotland and mostly attended the same college I was going to. This college was called, Springburn College of Engineering. It was not a very impressive looking college, it was old and not very well maintained but, it had a great reputation for the engineering principle in teaching engineering students like me. I didn't care; I was just terrified at the thought of going to college and being stuck there for four years and failing at the end, or not even getting through each year. You see, this is the wickedness of this world that plays in our minds, that whispers in our ears that we cannot make it, we are going to fail, and we are going to let others down. But we have a Greater Being who gives us hope that allows us to trust Him for the answers, that allows us to focus on His promises, ensure us of a great and prosperous future "Can you see where I am going with this?" Yes I know you do. But at that time in my life I never had any experience of this great hope, this future of prosperity, this way out through the maze of failure and doubt. I just had the wee fickle mind of a little young man who had failed high school but had managed to keep a job down and has now been given a chance to enter a renowned college and take a four year college course on HVAC.

Not that I was into reading the Holy Bible in those days, or even cared anything about it, or any other religion, but there is a scripture verse in the bible that relates to this hope and future and it says, "For I know the plans I have for you", declares the Lord, "plans to prosper you and not harm you, plans to give you hope and a future". You can find this in the book of Jeremiah Chapter 29 verse 11(New International Version), look it up! But if God is really who He says He is, and promises to do what He says, then maybe, just maybe, this was already promised to me and God was bringing it to life for me, at this time. Not that I would recognize it as the work of God but, just the work of man, or an amazing coincidence that all things work out just on time. Get you thinking a bit doesn't it? Anyway, here I am, eighteen years old and now starting college as an apprentice HVAC engineer, can you believe it? I went to college for the first day and I was so nervous and I met all my other class mates, we were all guys no girls at all, so I thought, 'hmmm, what a bummer'. Anyway, I guess it was for the best, as I had to focus on my passing these courses. I think all of us were pretty nervous for the first few weeks as we never knew each other, although there were a couple of students who have worked on the same projects in and around the city. But for me, these guys were all new and they were from bigger towns and cities than where I was, so I was little intimidated by a few of them. Let me tell you, I thought I was from a rough town until I heard of some of the places that these guys were from. One guy was from Cranhill, a place in Glasgow that is known for murders, shootings, stabbings, drugs related. You name it, and it's a part of that town. And there was another one near Ferguslie Park in Paisley, of which, is of similar report, so my wee town of Greenock was like an angel town compared to these places. But these guys were cool, they never showed off, they never tried to bully anyone, they were here for the same reason I was, and that was to come away as a college graduate with a career ahead of them. They actually became my very close friends. The CITB organization gave us a book that was full of individual modules or activities related to each month's topic at college, you have to complete these modules and have them graded by your supervisor on how well you accomplished these tasks. If you never accomplished them, then you were not allowed to progress on to the next month. It was like a monthly exam. We had two types of modules in the book, one is when we attended college and the one is when we were actually on a building site or project, and carried out similar activities or work related issues, as per the books requirements. So meaning, we would attend college for one whole month, learn different parts of the course and then get marked on our performance, then the second part would be to work on a project away from college for a whole month and get marked on how you preformed during this time. Our college was on a month to month basis, so we were only in class for six months a year. So it was pretty cool, not like college nowadays, you stay longer and a full time student. As we were getting along in the course we would become better friends with each other and then we would start to relax, and just mingle and socialize more. After few months, we would start going to the local pub every Friday in Springburn. It was just a minute from the college building. This helped our relationship with each other quite a lot; in fact, it built stronger friendship with everyone. We would not go overboard, just have a couple of pints of beer and a bag of crisps and that was to be our Friday lunch. We panicked one day when we saw the teacher of one of our classes at the pub. He looked at us, and we all thought we were going to be sent home and taken off the course. We really freaked out and he just looked over and laughed and said, "Don't be late for class lads". Well, we thought he was the coolest teacher after that, and after a few times we saw him in there we would go over and buy him a drink, and that made him happy. That was our weekly routine during our month at college. I was driving an old Chrysler Alpine that was bright orange in color. This car was good for driving around my wee town but to go those miles every day, then it would surely start giving me problems. This car was my first car that my Dad had bought me. This was my prize possession. I loved it, it was so cool and in perfect condition inside and outside. My girlfriend and I got talking, and after about six months into my college course and everything seemed to be going well, as I was starting to earn more money, we thought we could buy another car and pay the costs on a monthly basis.

We were getting pretty serious in our relationship and we started to share on most things and I thought, why not go further with a new car, for reliability, as we always went around in my car because she couldn't drive. At the same time, I was starting to pick up some other students from Paisley and then take them to college and they would pay me for the gasoline. So this money actually goes towards paying the monthly cost of the car. So we would not be losing anything on a financial aspect. So, I asked my Dad for his permission to trade in my Chrysler as he was the one who bought it for me, and he said, "Of course, as long as it gets you to your college safely and benefits you". So we did it, we went and bought a brand new car, so this was our first new car at the age of nineteen, and you are probably wondering what kind did I buy. Maybe a Ford, a wee Honda sports coupe, or maybe a BMW!!! Nope it was a Fiat Panda, one of the smallest cars you can ever buy. It was like a super-size microwave, I am not joking. The reason for choosing this small car was that, it was basically for the two of us and it was the most economical car around for my college driving. There was only one issue that I didn't take into consideration before buying such a small car. One of my friends from college whom I picked up from Paisley, was about 6ft 6inches tall and he struggled getting in and out of my little Fiat. The first day I drove up to his house to take him to college he laughed and said, "Where do I stick my head, out of the sun-roof?" And the other three friends in the car burst out laughing. It was so funny him saying that, and he was right. But we all managed somehow to squeeze in to that little microwave, the scary part of this was, when we were heading to college we had to drive over a ramp that went across the freeway and it was a sharp bend, so we were all hanging on to whatever we could because when we were going round on the ramp we actually thought the car was going to overturn and we were all screaming like crazy people. I am not joking; we were literary hanging on to the bars inside, hoping this thing don't flip over. Well it never, we made it safely every day but when the winds came hard, it was pretty scary, let me tell you. We were all saying that one day, it is going to take a tumble over this ramp onto cars below. Thank God, it never happened. When I was nineteen it was a pretty exciting time of my life, I bought a brand new car, I started my first year at college and now, I was going to take a major step in my relationship with my girlfriend. Yes, we decided to get engaged and I know you're probably thinking why so young what are you thinking? Because believe me, everyone was asking us the same thing, but when you're young and in love, you don't listen to people especially, when they don't want to agree, or go along with your plans. Because that is just what we do when we are young, we do what we want, when we want, where we want, how we want and with whom we want and if you are not wanting to be a part of it, then you're out of the circle of friends. The attitude I had in those days could possibly have a comparison of some young people today. It is not that they are bad, or I was any better. It is just our society, our human nature, and desires that drive us to this type of attitude, I guess it does come down to a little lack of respect, lack of maturity and lack of understanding towards others. But do we care at that age? Certainly not, and those are big words to be letting lose among young adults. We're only kids and we are learning from our mistakes, right? Nice excuse to get you out of a stick isn't it?

Anyway, we took the plunge against many wishes of our parents and friends not to, but we went ahead and done it. We got engaged, and shortly after that we took an even bigger plunge, we went and bought our first house. Yes! Can you believe it? It all happened in one year. We bought a house, a brand new house up next to the hospital where my girlfriend was working. So she can walk to work as she never drove at that point. Everything looked to be working out perfectly. I was doing good in my college and passing every module and exam with high marks for a change, we had a great wee economical car that I think, one full tank of gasoline would have taken you to China and back (jokingly of course). We got engaged and we bought a brand new house, what a story to tell the kids when we have them. I look at the young adults today. I don't see too many taking such a plunge as we did on those days of which, is probably a good thing not to jump in too quickly. You see part of my problem was that, when I saw something and I wanted it, then I did whatever I needed, in order to have it. Similar to my younger years and my lifestyle, as I got older, as you will see in the forthcoming words. So we were now living in our wee house happily engaged, and living the American dream in Scotland with our little microwave Fiat Panda car thinking, this is the life. Then all of a sudden a bomb was dropped on me (what happened next was to change our life in a drastic way), my girlfriend announced that she was pregnant. Well, if that didn't move the earth for me, then nothing would have. I was blown away and never had an answer to counter with, I was speechless for a change. We both sat down and just looked at each other with complete fear and hopelessness. We just never knew how to handle that kind of situation and weren't really ready for such responsibility, although we had many responsibilities at that time with house, car, bills and all that, but for a baby? No, not yet. Well, that is a different story and to be honest with you, I still don't recall how I truly felt inside as I was just so numb with shock and didn't understand what I would have to do as a father. My girlfriend was only six weeks pregnant so it was at a very early stage but we still had to prepare and then go about our life to try to better ready ourselves for this addition. We were absolutely terrified of the fact that we had to tell both our parents, as I knew my parents would flip their lids. And knowing my girlfriend's parents, they would have kittens. This was not a pleasant situation to be in at all. So young ones, when you have a few issues of your own that you have to deal with, a few circumstances that you can't handle, or figure out a way how to solve them; trying telling your parents that your girlfriend is pregnant at nineteen years old, and then you will feel what pressure and stress really is, and probably feel the back of your fathers hand across your face. Well, this put a different light on to our relationship and a lot more pressure thinking of all the consequences of her not working, raising a baby, me being away from home, working two weeks at a time and her left alone with the baby. All these thoughts were playing into our minds but we seemed to be ready to work it all out. Then after a few days a dreadful message came out of my girlfriend's mouth asking how I feel about getting rid of the baby. I said to her, "Did you just say what I thought you said? Get rid of the baby?" She said, "Yes" And I replied, "Are you serious? You want to have an abortion, to kill the baby? You must be crazy" I told her. There is no way we can do that, no matter what needs to change in our lives, or in our circumstances, then we will just have to manage and work around it.

There was no way we can get rid of the baby. This was not the way I thought life went. I mean, if you get your girlfriend pregnant then you obviously have to do the right thing, get married and all that stuff and then, make the best of the situation, correct? Well, not for some people, there was huge resistance from my girlfriend's parents who were pushing us to have the baby aborted and to me the thought of that made me sick; it was really a shock to my system. After days of talking, crying, working things out, planning & preparing, we were getting nowhere because pressure was getting the better of us. We were fighting a losing battle as her parents were adamant for her to get rid of the baby. Can you imagine such a predicament to be in? I was trying to stand up as a man, but I was also afraid of her father as he had a very bad temper and was very violent and not to mention over six foot tall and very strong, so nothing I can do there. I was utterly in shock and my parents were behind us both in having the baby but made us aware, that life will change and they will be there to support in any way they can. This was comforting to us, but the biggest problem was not them or us, it was the in-laws to be. I was about to go out of town again for two weeks to work and this situation was not finalized, and they wanted my fiancé to go in while I was away before the fetus became bigger. This became such a burden and we couldn't handle all the pressure so we both sat down and discussed it. I thought of all the negative things that were put in our mind. About our lifestyles changes, finance changes, struggles of being so young, then getting married so quickly, and not being around to help raise the baby and all that stuff. It made us to decide to go ahead and abort the baby. At that time, still being only nineteen years of age, it was not a complete devastation in life losing a baby, meaning we had plenty of time to have other babies in the future and we were not religious at all. So there was no conviction spiritually from us or from anyone else in the family that time. So, we arranged it with the hospital so that my fiancé would have the abortion while I was away working, so when I come back she will just be resting. This was absolutely the worst and most shocking decision I have ever made in my entire life. I '**WILL NOT**' recommend this plan of action to any young woman, or young couple out there, who have found themselves in a similar situation. Even if the potential father is not going to hang around, or has already left you, raise the child on your own, just do it, just have the baby and raise it the best you can, do not, I say do not, abort any living thing that God has made alive inside your womb, because it is completely and truly a blessing from above and a miracle, that such a child can grow and be kept alive inside a woman's womb for nine months and come out a human being, full created in the image of God. Always remember this, that all of us were beautifully and wonderfully created in the image of God.

At this point, I can tell you that my wee fantasy world, my wee American dream was not all going to plan, it was taking a tumble for the worst and I could not get rid of the images of what we had done, in aborting this little child. After I came back from working out of town, I looked at my fiancé and she was pretty exhausted looking and we both just looked at each other not knowing what to say or do. It was a terrible situation to be in. She was released from the hospital and went home and she was resting for a while. Things were not too good between us after that, it was as if something had separated us from where we used to be. It was like a wall was put between us and it was so difficult to get over, or around that wall, and we would start having arguments and lots of disagreements. I was coming up for my second year in college and this was affecting my whole life. I could see my attitude changing and my life was becoming pretty difficult when I was with others. I was becoming very difficult to deal with and to approach, and even my college buddies would tell me that I was out of order the way I was speaking to them. After a few months I gave in to the pressures of everything, the house payments, the car payments, the bills, our relationship, it all took its toll on me, and I fell out of love with my finance because I couldn't handle the relationship. I wasn't completely sure at that point, but I do believe, it had something to do with the baby issue and I truly believe, that I couldn't release the guilt of what we allowed to happen. All I knew was that, I couldn't go on with this anymore, I had to get out of this relationship, I had to get away from it all and start over on my own. I felt as if the weight of the world was on my shoulders, if that was possible. I was just so unhappy with my life and was thinking stupid things in order to get me out of the way I was feeling. You may wonder how could a young man who seemed to have a great run in life with a new house, a new car, a beautiful fiancé, a supportive family, great career opportunity and yet, still be thinking of doing something stupid because a certain situation all went wrong. Well it happens; I can assure you of that. I just thank God above, that I never done anything stupid. There is always a way of out of every situation we face, or comes against us. Do you believe that my friends? Do you believe that every situation has a way out? There is an answer, a remedy, a solution, for all situations in life. It may not be the way out that we wanted, it may not be the remedy we desired, and it may not be the same answer as ours, but it will still allow you a way out or around your present circumstances. Remember, I mentioned the Holy Bible, well I am going to mention it again, as this book of wisdom, warnings and revelations is something you should consider reading, as it has all the answers you will ever need to get through life, and I am not saying the answers are all the ones you will be wanting, or the answers will be for the easy way out of life, definitely not. But, it will be the truth and the practical way of dealing with the trials and temptations of our lives that we may face on a daily basis (If only I knew this before).

The horrible point of me sharing this tragic story and this part of my life is because it brings to light how we can all be so selfish, and will carry out the worse kinds of selfish acts possible in order to keep our life the way we want it to be. That is what selfishness shows in realistic terms. It doesn't just mean that we just keep little things to ourselves without sharing, it doesn't mean not thinking of others and not to offer what you may have, and it doesn't mean not going out your way to help others. What it does mean is, you will do whatever you need to do in order to keep yourself pleased, it means you will act beyond your inner being and not think about the seriousness or consequence of your actions, it means, that no matter what, you will do what you need to do to satisfy your life and your lifestyle. There may be situations in your lives where you just feel so lost, so useless, so weak, so troubled, so guilty that it will drive you to measures of unthinkable decisions, it will drive you to go beyond your normal human instincts and make decisions that you know is wrong, or you shouldn't be doing. But the one thing that it cannot remove once those decisions are made is the memories in your heart and in your mind. You may be able to ignore it and get over it after a while, you may be able to erase it from your life for a while, but it only takes a small incident or something to trigger off that moment of madness, that moment of selfishness that you had when you made those decisions in the past. It only takes a circumstance to bring back that conscience that you thought you never had or can escape from, the guilt may not be there but the memory will. I believe through my experiences in life that, you cannot erase the past wrongs that you have done, I believe they are still logged in our memory banks because it was the person that we were at that time and that was the attitude that we created within us and was allowed to develop through us. But, what I also believe very passionately is that, even though these memories are logged within us there is also a Great Healer that allows us to be forgiven for making those wrongful decisions, and One who is willing to give us the strength and wisdom to work through those issues and allow us to be free of that un-peaceful conscience, that consuming guilt within that you think is not there, that unthinkable thought of what we have done.

Chapter 7

SETTLING IN

So here I am, stuck in the wilderness of a distraught situation of wanting to be out of a relationship that had great potential, a great future, a great road of development for both parties, but the pressures of life can sometimes be too overwhelming and especially at a young age. So I addressed my feelings with my fiancé and just let it all out that I wanted to finish the relationship. Of course, this was not news that she was going to take lightly, it was not something she would be looking forward to hear, but it had to be done. To me at this point in my life, and at such a young age, there was no point in living a life that was just making me unhappy, that was making me resent every day. It was like a noose (like a knot) around your neck and every move you made seemed to tighten that rope a little more. My fiancé really couldn't understand what I was telling her and could not believe, what she was hearing coming out of my mouth. She would question everything I would say, she would deny any issues we were having or going through. I believe it may have been a defense mechanism on her part, but whatever it was she was doing, it was not making me feel any less than I was. It was as if my mind was made up and I was determined to see this through no matter what she was saying, asking or whatever justification she was looking for. You know when you get something in your heart and mind and you are not willing to budge from that decision? That was me. I was sticking to my guns on this one, no matter what the consequences; I believe you could call it 'stubborn-ness', or 'selfishness'.

After days of conversations relating to this split up, my fiancé would cry so hard and it would make me feel sorry for her. But I had made up my mind for my own sanity and I had to push through with it. I believe she thought that it would eventually work its way out of me and I would change my mind, but it never did. I was so adamant in making this happen that I even told her that I would call her parents and tell them the situation. Knowing that her parents wouldn't be too happy about this, she told me that it was not a very good thing to do as they will be so annoyed and angry with me. It didn't seem to make any difference to me and I was not really bothered about what they would say as this was my life, that I was thinking about. Can you see that? Can you see what this was all about and yes it was all about me. How I was feeling, how I was thinking, how I was dealing with the pressures of such debt and responsibility at a young age, how I was dealing with the loss of our potential child, how I wanted out of all this mess. Nowhere in the equation was my fiancé, it was all about me. This is where our true characteristics start showing and this is where our own emotions and feelings kick in, and drive us to get what we want in life. This is where we really don't have, or show, compassion towards others and espe-cially those who are closest to you. I think at this point as you have already got this far in the book that you are aware of my selfishness and that I was 'all about me' and whatever I needed to do in order to get my way, then I would not hesitate in doing it.

Well after several discussions and heated arguments I decided to call her parents and I wanted her beside me when I spoke with them so she would know that this is it, that this is the end of our relationship, and that I was walking out from all the responsibili-ties. Let me tell you, you may think it is easy to walk away from your responsibilities but your conscience can play a major part of all your decision makings. We never had a cell phone in those days or a house phone as we only had the house for a short time and we tried to keep all our costs to a minimum, remember we were only young adults. So in order to call my fiancés' parents, we had to find a local telephone near the house. So when we found one and she dialed her parents' house number and her Mum answered. Well, you can imagine what happened next, the tears were just pouring down my fiancé' face as she was trying to tell her Mum what was happening to us, she was really struggling to speak as her emotions really kicked in, she realized that this was the real deal. I could hear her Mum getting annoyed and anxious with her daughter because she could hardly understand what she was saying, so her Mum gave the phone to the husband to try and understand why their daughter was in such a state, why was she crying her heart out.

Her Dad then came on the phone and I could hear him telling her to calm down, to speak slowly, and he was really panicking trying to understand why she is crying so much. He even asked her "Did I abuse her? Was it something to do with me? She tried to calm down a little and started to speak a little calmer and he eventually heard the point of her conversation, and she mentioned that I wanted to leave her. Immediately, he asked if I was with her and he wanted to speak to me. I took the phone and he asked me what is going on. So I explained to him that I couldn't go on with all the responsibilities that we had, and that I just wanted to break free from it all. He was so angry with me and was getting really abusive on the phone and at that time I thought, I am in big trouble here. I really thought he was going to drive up to our house and knock my head off, even though it is probably what I needed, due to the terrible decision I was just about to make. The conversation seemed to last forever, I just wanted to end it quickly and get it over with and start to get on with my life.

After we finished talking, things really went bad. I got all my stuff together and left the house and went back to live with my parents, just basic clothes. I still needed to work out with my fiancé how we were going to work things out between us. After all, we had a brand new house that we just bought, a brand new car, and other certain items that needed to be agreed upon. As you are probably aware, splitting up with a partner is not easy especially when you have property to deal with on a joint basis then it normally doesn't work out very economically and comforting. We were no different in those days, we had a really hard time splitting the personal belongings and dealing with the new house and car. Once we worked out that I was just going to leave, we decided that my fiancé could keep the house and live in it, as it was only one minute walk from the house to her work, and I would keep the car as she didn't want it as she can't drive. The furniture was a little more complicating as we couldn't agree on who gets what and how to split it, so I just left it all to her thinking that, at least she deserves something right? After all, I had probably just ruined her whole life and future plans at that time.

Being a young man and wanting what I wanted in my life, seemed to be pretty easy just to make decisions and not really bother about the effects or what consequences may follow afterwards. C'mon at such a young age, do you really think I cared? I just wanted out of that situation and relationship, and just knew that I would be fine on my own. I was a promising young engineer and knew that with my salary I could survive pretty comfortably, and already had in my mind what kind of thing I would be doing. Majority of my plans was to just party and have fun with my friends and have no worries on my shoulders. Well, after the initial conversation with her parents and now that it was all out in the open I made the move. I started packing up my clothes and just thrown them in my little car and was ready to head out. Leaving was pretty emotional for us both I guess. We hugged each other and really cried, I was surprised that even I cried being the one who created all this mess. I truly believe that my fiancé meant what she said before I left the house. She said to me, "I know you will come back to me, so I will be here waiting. If you just need time to think about things or be on your own then it is ok with me. I will be here waiting for you Sean". Making my decision in leaving her and then make the move out the house was already enough to build a guilt feeling. And she had to say something like that to make me feel even more guilty and ashamed. I wish I could have just walked out at that very moment without opening my big mouth, but I couldn't. I just had to make a comment, I replied to her, "Listen, I will not be coming back to you, this is it. I have made up my mind, I am moving on and out of this relationship". Well, she just looked at me and cried even more but she was still sure I would come back so she repeated what she just said before.

I must admit that when I walked out that door and into the car and started driving away from our house, I had a tremendous amount of guilt on my shoulders and could not bring myself to understand what I just done. I felt as if someone from above was watching me from the moment I got in that car to the moment I got to my parents house and I was so overwhelmed by shame. There was so much to think about while driving away from her and my first house. I was really wondering, have I made the right decision? Am I being so selfish, am I being unreasonable, am I being stupid? And probably the right answer for all of those questions is, "Yes". But you see, here is a perfect example of human selfishness at its best. I mean, here is a perfect situation where two young people who were together for a few years and built up a nice little career for themselves, and started to establish a nice way of life of having what is called the 'American Dream'. Having a nice home, and not to mention a brand new home at that point, with a brand new car and brand new furniture and all the trimmings that go along with a new place. The house was situated in a very nice neighborhood and it was back to back from her work. C'mon, does it get any better at the age of nineteen? But still I was still not satisfied and could not hold on to the dream, could not live with the success of making a fresh new start and could not handle the responsibilities of what comes along with the dream. I wanted something else; I like freedom to do what I wanted. I didn't want the pressure of having the dream. I didn't care about the other person's life or what effect the decisions I made could be. It was all about....Myself!

Friends when 'I' becomes your number one priority in life then, you will go all out in order to get what you want at the cost of others, at the cost of family, at the cost of friends, at the cost of losing your integrity as human being. If you look at the life of Jesus Christ, what do you think was in His mind when He was called by God to go into the world baptizing them in the name of the Father, and of the Son and of the Holy Spirit? He didn't think about Himself, what He gets in return, what benefit He gets, or what His reward for doing such a task. All He thought about was you and me, and the rest of the whole world. And you may wonder why He would think about others over himself, well it is called 'LOVE'. Yes, I know what you might be saying now, "Oh no, it's the old love word and Sean is going to get sentimental with us now and start going all soft and smoochy". Well, I have plenty of time to get all soft and smooch with you during the remaining chapters but I will give you an insight of what to expect on this topic. If it wasn't for the love of God, if it wasn't for His love for each ones of us, He will not give up His one and only begotten Son, Jesus Christ so that we could all have an opportunity to receive eternal life. Because if not, then we would all be perishing in hell. If it wasn't for the love of God, and the sacrifice He made for us by giving his Son on that cross of Calvary, He could have just wiped us all off the face of the earth as He did in the Old Testament times by allowing the flood to wipe out almost all that existed. But even then, He allowed two of each species to continue and go forth to multiply and that was the world's second chance. Do you think you deserve a second chance? In our own eyes probably not, right? But in Gods eyes, He knew that He was going to make a sacrifice that would allow us to come to know Him in a very special way, which would allow us to turn away from our selfishness, our hatred, our bitterness, unforgiving heart, our sinfulness and our lack of love for others. So He allowed us the second chance and that was through the death of Jesus on that cross in order for you and me, to come to Him and be born again. So you see, even if we are so selfish right now and have done so many selfish and unthinkable things to others, God is willing to forgive us and give us that second chance with no strings attached. He is waiting to accept you, as you are, for who you are, for what you have done, why? Because He knows that through a personal relationship with Jesus Christ, He can transform our hearts into loving and compassionate hearts. At this point, if you are struggling with similar circumstances in your life, if you're tired of continually seeking what is best for you at the expense of others, if you're tired of trying to please others, if you're tired living your life the way you want to live it, if you're looking for a way out of the sinful, lustful, deceitful desires of your heart, then take this opportunity by praying this prayer; *"Jesus, I come before you a sinner, I acknowledge that I have strayed so far in my life and I know that I have done things wrong and I repent right now. Forgive me and let me come to know you in a special way. I confess with my mouth that Jesus, you are the son of God, that you died and rose again, and was crucified on the cross and you bore the sins of man, and that by your stripes we are healed. Jesus, I accept you into my heart as my Lord and Savior. Change me, oh God and make me a new creation. In Jesus name, I pray, Amen".* If you have prayed this prayer with a true and honest heart then, Praise God! He has a great plan for your life. God will reveal the ways of loving others in a way you have never experienced before, and in way you may not understand or fathom, but that is why he is God, only He knows the depth of His love for each and every one of us. You might be so confused now on the things I am elaborating here. As my story ends in this book, you will fully understand, and have the picture of my journey towards appreciating the love of God.

So bringing you back to the moment where I left my girlfriend, as I arrived at my parents' home, my Mum opened the door. She was glad to see me and she thought I came down just for a visit, as I always did. She done the usual thing, ask me if I wanted a cup of tea and something to eat. I had tea and a sandwich and sat with her in the kitchen. My Mum and I always sat in the kitchen. That was her favorite place in the house and where she done her crossword puzzles. Once she sat down after making my tea I started to tell her what had happened, what I had just done. She was shocked and didn't understand, she thought we were happy together and that things were going well. She knew we had good jobs and we were pretty well settled, so she asked me what happened. I started to break things down for Mum in the simplest way I could, just explaining that I basically didn't want the responsibilities anymore. I just told her we are too young to go through all this major commitment and we should not be tying ourselves down at such a young stage of our life. My mum was pretty angry with me knowing the situation we both created and that I was just going to walk away from it all. Mum was really concerned about my fiancé and how she was feeling, and how she was taking this decision.

I spent hours talking to Mum about everything and at the end she was all quiet. I believe, I really shocked her this time because she did not say anything for few minutes. My dad was out at the time and I got to sleep before he came in, but in the morning I had a chat with him as well. He was already filled in with the situation by Mum, so I never had to tell him the whole story. Dad was shocked as well but at the end of the day, I was their wee baby. I was the spoiled child so no matter what I was going through, they were always one hundred percent behind me. That is one thing I can honestly say about my parents, no matter what you do in life, or things that you have to go through, they back you up the best they can and always give their support. So, after that talk was over, it was a case of settling back home again, back to basics. But, it was not going to be that easy I soon found out. Just after a few weeks we were suddenly faced with a dilemma, my fiancé's father came to our house and he was very angry and let me know how he felt about me leaving his daughter in such a mess. There were a few words that come out of his mouth that I will not share with you and a few gestures that would not be nice for you to read about, so I will just leave it as it is. However, I will tell you what he has done. He actually had a van and he went to get furniture from our house that I just left and he brought some that belonged to us and thrown it down on the ground in front of my parents' house and he was screaming at the top of his voice. It was very embarrassing for me for the things he was saying but they were so true. He was shouting out that I can keep the sofa set because I already destroyed it by urinating over it when I was drunk. You see, when I got drunk and believe me I got really drunk, I would sometimes wet the bed and it just happened that one night I came in late and instead of walking up my fiancé I just slept down on the sofa. Unfortunately, the amount of alcohol I consumed must have made me need the toilet and for whatever reason, I must have thought I was in the bathroom and just wet the sofa. So I got the shock of my life when this was dumped in front of my eyes and the reality of the shameful act I committed. My parents were so mad at him that they would be shouting back at him and told him to get away from our house or they would call the police. He eventually left, and we were left with a sofa and some other items in our front garden totally destroyed. So here is a perfect example and outcome, of a certain action that you make or do. You really have to face the embarrassment and deal with it. Think about your actions and the consequences that you might face. There are always options for you to take in your life, there are always different ways for you to go, and these will determine the possible outcome and direction that your life will start to go in. It's not all about the goodness, or satisfaction, but it's all about the outcome of such action, that matters.

That was really the end of our relationship, there was no more communication with my fiancé or any other member of her family, it was like the curtain coming down. So from then on, I started to get on with my life. I really focused on my college work and my career, as I knew this was my only chance of making something in my life and potentially creating a future. At just nineteen, I really went through a very tough and emotional situation that I had to lift myself out of and try to stay positive, no matter how things were. At work, as you know, news travels very fast and most people got to know your business in a very short time span and they all seem to have their two pennies worth of advice, or opinions that they want you to hear. As you experience your own situations in life, you will certainly come to know and realize that this is the way things are. People just seem to think that they know why and how you mess up in your decisions and actions, and try to give answers to solve your problems. Believe me, you will take part when someone else goes through a similar circumstance and you will think that you know where they went wrong and how you can fix their life or situation.

I carried on with my young adult life going to parties with friends, drinking excessively as usual and just enjoying going to clubs and bars. I like the feeling of being free and being able to do what I wanted, when I wanted, how I wanted and with whom I wanted, without having to answer to anyone. At that time, I thought that's what my life should have been from the start and I should not have been in any serious relationship and in a bottle neck of having huge amounts of debt and bills to come home to. My friends were all behind me in my decision and so happy that I was going out with them and living it up, having many crazy boozy nights. When we are at that age, we are fearless of any consequences that may come from our actions. We just don't care as we think were untouchable. When I look back at those nights of partying and clubbing till the wee hours in the morning, I am shocked when I think of how much alcohol we used to consume. I tell you this, we could drink around six to eight bottles of beer in the house before we even step outside, and then once we're in the bar, we would down the same amount before hitting the disco house. And on the dance floor, you burn some of the alcohol away, leaving you room for more. But the funny thing was, when we went outside the disco or club and fresh air hit us, man, we would fall to the ground as we would then realize that we were so drunk. And we start staggering and stumbling around.

College time was great. I thought I would have hated going back to school to learn subjects and yet I truly believe I enjoyed every day of my college throughout the whole four years. We had no real pressure put on us to study for projects or have to concentrate for finals, or major exams. We had to simply complete our modules each month in order to progress on the course. Modules were short applications of learning to carry out a special skill related to our focused subject, so the first two years of our college training was related to pipe fitting and plumbing. This was basically learning about the different kinds of pipes and how to fabricate and install them in various applications. You would come across this type of application with installing your central heating pipes for your house or plumbing pipe-work in your bathrooms or kitchen. Also you would find applications in warehouses, factories, offices or industrial buildings for the supply of water, heating, air conditioning etc. At the end of each month in college, your teacher would assess your work and give you a grade from A to F. You were allowed to get a grade of 'D' but it was not too good. It showed that you never really understood that part of the course, or there was something that you struggled with.

The great thing about our teachers was, they would allow you another chance to get a higher grade and most often we would do that if we got a 'D'. But if you got an 'F', then you had no choice to try again, as this was not acceptable to them. This was two-fold due to the fact that it showed; you really struggled with that topic and it made them look bad also. I believe there were only a few instances where some students got an 'F' grade and that was because they were not paying attention at that specific time. I thank God even though I carried on a lot, and continued to be a distraction to my other student friends; I never got a bad grade on any modules at college. There was only one thing that I thought was wrong with the college that we attended, there were not many girls for us to look at or try to chat with. Well, you know when we are that age, girls are a main part of our thinking and daily activities. Well, I guess that was just the way God had planned it so that we could all graduate from our course (no girls). Could you imagine what may have happened if we were distracted with loads of beautiful girls around? I am very sure that our results and graduation could have been way different from what we actually achieved. If I can just tell to any young adults at this time reading this book who are in high school or college; focus on your studies and don't be distracted by the other party, being it male or female. Let me tell you this, the boyfriend/girlfriend time in your life will come and you will be better prepared to deal with it, you will be more mature in your decisions and actions, and you will prioritize what is more important in your life at that specific time. Of course you are facing the reality of life and being surrounded by both sexes and that you will be drawn close to one or even a few. But trust me, when I share this with you that all it does is slow you down and steer you on the wrong path at that age. Before you know it, they will start being your main priority in your thinking and doing, and no doubt, will eventually lead you into carrying out the unlawful act of sexual activity.

Going back to our modules that we completed during the month at college, these modules were also required to be completed outside of college at our workplace. You see, our college was a trade school; it was an engineering college that was more a 'hands on' practical college. So, when we spent one month there at a time then the following month would be spent actually applying what you learned at college out on the field. If I learned how to measure pipe runs and install supports and fabricate them together, then I would be carrying this out in reality on a specific project site. This was what college was all about on my chosen field. It was about applying in reality, what you were learning. At the same time of carrying out these functions, we also carried with us, our module book that we were completing while at college class. At the end of the month when we were on project sites we were graded on our work. This was very different to being in college class because if you make a mistake in theory you can easily adjust and fix the error and then it won't be a bad mark against you. But if you're in the field, hands-on project, it's so different. This is real time events. Whatever projects you work on are for a specific company who employed the company to carry out a designated contract.

Each contract would be different in nature and application and there was always a time limit to complete. So instead of just messing around and just being in a trial and error environment in college, this was a case of, you must carry out installations at specific sites as specified by our client, and they must be completed in a certain time frame. It was crucial that you carried out your work diligently and successfully as errors cost your company time and money. Believe me, when I say this, although you are only learning your profession as a young apprentice, you don't get too many chances of making mistakes. I can honestly say that the qualified engineers that I worked with in Hillhead Filtration & Engineering were first class. They were so professional at their work and their attitude was fantastic with me, and the customers they were working for. It really helped me in my young life to deal with discipline, mannerism and respect towards others. It also helps develop your character in a positive way that you may never even know is happening, just because you are following other individuals and it actually becomes a natural part of your attitude.

There is nothing more truthful in life than the influence that you will receive from others, when you work with individuals, or being part of, a class or group. Then whatever you watch them do, or hear them say, or how they react and deal with situations, it will definitely make an impact in your life one way or the other. I used to love working with the men as they would spoil me like crazy, they would always buy me lunch and really protect me from any harm and at the same time, teach me all the tricks of the trade. Meaning, mentor me in all the ways to accomplish the tasks in front of me. Due to vast experiences they all possessed and they all had their own talents and skills in carrying things out, I learned a lot of different ways. They were so wise and knowledgeable in their work and life in general, as most of them were almost double my age, so I guess in a way they treated me like a son. It was kind of funny as it felt like I had twenty fathers all imparting me their skills within the work place and their experiences in life. You see, all our lives are such an amazing gift from God as He created us all in His image, but because we join the world, and do things on our own and in our own way, that makes us all different. Being different is not a bad thing at all, when I think about it and how magnificent we all are in our own weird way, it blows me away. Just think about this, almost six billion individuals in this world are making their own mark on history on whatever they do. It doesn't matter that we all don't become as successful as others like Bill Gates, Warren Buffett, Oprah Winfrey, Michael Jordan, Kobe Bryant, Tiger Woods, Brad Pitt, Angelina Jolie and all other millions of other famous people. Were not all cut out to be rocket scientists, but we are still unique in the way we carry out our lives and being that we are, because God is our Creator.

I think it is so amazing that God has created us and allows us to be who we are and that He is willing to accept us for who we are. Why? Because He loves us all just the same, and there is only one thing that matters in the world and that is, that we are called to be 'the children of God'. That is why it is important that you receive Jesus Christ as your Savior and as you go on in your life, that no matter where you find yourself, and with whatever company you decide to be amongst, you must strive to make a positive impact in their lives, at all times. That's what these men were doing to me every day; they were making a positive impact in my life, in my work environment wherein I can still apply the principles today in the manner of discipline, respect, honor and having a right attitude towards others. Of course we are only guided by men in the skills of life applications, but our true direction and wisdom in carrying out our decisions and actions should come from God alone.

My first two college years that consisted of pipe-fitting applications were fantastic in such a way that it build up a passion in my heart to learn, and try to understand, what I was being taught for the first time in my educational life. You already know about me being very unproductive in high school and not obtaining any formal qualification or graduation, so this was an 'extreme makeover' for me. I actually loved college and wanted to just stay there every day and not go out on the field. It was a brilliant time and I had great friends there. As our friendship had grown through the months, we enjoyed each others' company even outside college. We would meet on a regular basis and go to the bars and get plastered and have loads of fun. We would just meet in a selected bar either in Paisley or Glasgow town centre. I loved Glasgow as it was always bursting with excitement and had loads of girls and you were never short of choosing girls when we went there.

In my college days, that is what life was all about, making sure I get drunk and landing a girlfriend at the end of the night. I was not after any long term relationship at this point. I just wanted freedom to enjoy and do the things I wanted to do. So most times I got a girl for one purpose. Take a guess what that is! Yes you're right, SEX. Alcohol and sex was what always at the back of my mind and I made it a point to try and achieve both on a regular basis. However, the girlfriend part was becoming kind of difficult as I was not very successful in chatting with a girl up front. I was not a charmer as I never really had the gift of the gab, as they say. I would never know what to say to a girl when the situation would arise for us to talk. So most opportunities that came my way I had blown it and they ended up with some other bloke. But life was still great; it was the excitement of the chase, the challenge that makes a man strive to catch a girl. I guess it is the animal hunting instinct that is in us. Men love to chase and the ultimate reward is at the end when they are successful in catching the prey, the woman, and once they get their way, sex. Then they feel as if they have conquered the world.

Well, young adult life was such a learning experience for me that it began to shape me up for the real world of becoming an adult, that's what I thought. I never really wanted to be an adult as the thought scared me, of what I saw older ones go through in their lives. I became a very good listener and observer when I am around people. I always listen to what they have to say during situations whether good or bad. I would watch their attitude towards others so that I know how I should probably deal with similar situations that I, may come across. There were many times I would listen to them talk to each other about work issues and other colleagues, then family issues, financial issues and attitude problems, and it was enough for me to learn exactly what not to be doing when I get into my more adult life situations. There was sometimes I would drive up to Glasgow on the weekends on my own and going looking around the famous Glasgow barrow-lands. This was a covered shopping area that was a bunch of, at least one hundred stalls that all sold different items from clothing, electrical, hardware, software, gardening, foods, household and many more things that were normally cheaper than you would find them in any other shopping outlet. But most of them were second hand items but in very good condition.

Considering, that I was not from Glasgow and unfamiliar with the surroundings, I would get lost a few times and would be kind of shy in talking to any of the stall owners because I don't know how to strike a conversation with them. I wouldn't buy anything as I really didn't have much money to spend anyway but I just wanted to visit the place that everybody is talking about and always said that you get great bargains. It was only another fifteen minutes drive from where I went to college, so I knew how to get there. Once I got familiar with the place I really like just wandering around and looking at all the stalls and different things people were selling, I would see quite a few things that I liked and wanted to buy but money was an issue.

Sometimes when the stall owner notices you hanging around for a while and not buying anything they can get a little concerned and start watching you closer, as there is a lot of theft going around up there. The barrow-land is notorious for thieves who are normally drug addicts or alcoholics looking to steal just to finance their habit. This is a great opportunity for them as there are so many stalls and normally the stall worker gets busy or distracted so then they see a chance to move in and take what they can. As I was kind of shy and not the most talkative person, I would be embarrassed sometimes when the stall holders would ask how I am doing and is there anything I was looking for, being sales people they would always try to convince you to buy something. The Glaswegians as they were called were very open and straight forward with their talking and they are not shy people at all. I believe one of their gifts from God was to talk and they are so good at it that they would never really run out of words to say. Well, I was just enjoying myself roaming around the place and looking at the different items and then all of a sudden my eyes came across a girl working behind a stall and for me, she looked absolutely stunning.

Once I saw this girl, I knew that I had to have a closer look at her to see if she is really beautiful in a close up aspect. As you know, looks afar can be deceiving. Once I got a few stalls away from her stall I would glance over at her and have a look. I must have looked at her like ten times already and then she caught me. I was so embarrassed that I just quickly looked away and put my head down. I asked the owner of the stall opposite her stall how much it was for some candy. I had to just do something to get out of the fact I was just caught staring at her. As I was being dealt with on the stall, I would again take a quick look at this girl and again I got caught, so I couldn't just ignore her and look away. So I just stared for a second or two and then gave her a smile, what harm is there in a smile right? After I smiled at her, she immediately smiled back at me to my amazement, so I felt really good after that, and I didn't feel so bad. After I paid for my candy, I walked off towards the direction of her stall by passing it by and I looked over at her again and our eyes caught again and we both smiled at the same time. And you know that is when you kind of lip read and you just say, "Hi" under your breath but move your lips. Well that is what we done. I said "hi" to her and she replied, "hi", and it was so corny. I was like asking myself, what was that Sean? What are you playing at smiling at her and you don't even know her? So once the child like attitude was done with, I just walked away and thinking I am going to see that face again as once a girl gives me a smile I automatically think I am in with a shout. In other words, I think that they want to go out with me and we can hit it off.

As it was still early in the afternoon I decided to hang around and then just continued to walk around the barras and check out the other stalls. But to be honest with you, my intensions were already clear and that was to make my rounds again and go back to see the girl whom, I thought liked me because she smiled at me. My mind was racing a hundred miles an hour trying to come up with a reason to go back to her stall and see her. I didn't really pay any attention to her stall because I was just looking at her, so I had no idea of what she was selling. So I devised a plan to walk around to the stalls around her so I can make it closer to her area and then, make my move to check out what she had. I had to be cautious as I didn't want to make a fool of myself and do something that would make me foolish. So I slowly walked closer and closer to her stall so I can have a peek at her stuffs. Well, once I got there I became face to face with her and we both smiled at each other and said, "Hi". We exchanged a few words like, how you doing? And then I would ask a very stupid question without even thinking. I blurted out to her, "Do you sell men's boxer shorts?" And she replied, "Does it look like I sell men's boxer shorts? This is a kid's stall and I only sell kids clothing". Well you could have opened up the ground and swallowed me under, I felt so stupid. Why couldn't I have just looked at her stall first before opening my mouth and making a complete fool out of myself? So I can honestly say, that never went the way I wanted it to go.

That was a very bad start for me and it made it ten times as hard to make a comeback from such a poor chat up line, but I was not going to give up, after all, she did smile at me so that was all the opening I needed in order to think I had a chance of dating this girl. Let me tell you that one of the reasons I thought she looked so beautiful was that I was into listening to Michael Jackson in those days and there was a girl in one of his videos that was beautiful and had long curly or perm hair and this girl reminded me of her. I know it's pretty lame but it was what got me to notice her. Anyway, I just stayed at her stall for a few more seconds just looking at what she was selling trying to come up with a better line than the miserable one I just tried. She was looking at me and was probably wondering, 'What on earth does this guy want?' hoping that I would go away maybe. So here I go, effort number two, I simply started chatting to her and asked her, "Is this your stall?" She replied, "No, I just work here, it belongs to my Dad". And I said, "Nice stall you have. So how often do you work here?" She replied, "I work most weekends to help my Dad out and sometimes he comes down to give me a break". I said, "That is cool, family business. So how long have you been doing this?" She replied, "Almost six years". This took me by surprise as she was still young looking. So this line of questions really started opening up the opportunity for me to keep talking and to get to know a little about her.

After a few more cheap talk asking similar questions, I had a feeling that we were becoming friendly, so I got bolder with my questions and asked her where she lived and she told me it's in Baillieston, of which I had no idea where it was. It could have been in China for all I knew. I didn't know Glasgow cities at all, except where my college was and the town center. She also asked me where I lived and a few questions about what I did and was I working. I was very proud in telling her that I was in college and was studying engineering. I truly believed that she never fell for any of the stuff that I was telling her and she probably thought that everything I was saying was a lie just to impress her. I wasn't really bothered, I was enjoying chatting with her and as the minutes were going by I was thinking that we were possibly onto something. I was on a roll and I was going for the biggie and ask the million dollar question! I took a chance and asked her if I could take her out one night for a meal and some drinks. She continued to ask a few more questions like, do I have a car? Do I know my way around Glasgow? Do I know many places to eat or drink? After I answered these questions I felt pretty useless. So I thought I had blown my chance, until she said that I could come to her house and pick her up and then we could go somewhere in the town. Well, I was stunned that this beauty of a girl would agree to my request to take her out and I got really nervous at that point and kind of froze on the spot. Can you believe my luck, just met an extremely attractive girl who runs a small business among people a lot older than her and she agreed to come out with me? At this point, she gave me her phone number and address of her parent's house where she lived. Once I got the address I said I would pick her up around seven thirty that night. Man I was so excited, I felt like I can break-dance all over the barras.

I immediately left that area and drove home to my wee town full of excitement and confusion as I didn't have a clue what to wear.

Remember, I wasn't the smartest dresser in town, far from it. I had no idea how to handle a date like this as normally when I chat up a girl, or ask a girl out, it would be in a bar or club and I would be half drunk so I wouldn't really care what I was saying, the outcome, and what I was wearing. You know what it's like, once you have a few beers in your system, shyness disappears and the animal comes out with no fear. Well, this was very opposite. I was going to be sober the whole night as I was the one who would be driving, after all, I asked her out, so I can't ask her to drive and I certainly wasn't going to drink and drive. It was going to be a very strange experience for me in a way that I was not used to. I was always getting drunk and being very stupid and funny, but tonight, it was like I would have to be on my best behavior. Once I left my house in Greenock and traveled the 30 miles to Baillieston, Glasgow, I arrived at their house. My first thoughts were, wow, what a house! It looked massive compared to our little humble community house in Greenock. I was actually very intimidated at this point and pretty embarrassed due to the difference in the communities, the size and splendor of the houses, I could tell that this was a very posh area. Once I drove past the house a few times just to make sure I had the correct address and to get another look at the sub-division and other houses, I then pulled up to their house. I got their at seven thirty in the evening exactly as I promised and I was told to just wait outside and not come in, because she was afraid her Dad would be asking me so many questions and testing me out. When you think about it, isn't that what fathers normally do? Isn't that their job to protect their children and make sure they know who is taking their sons or daughters out? I believe, in this generation that is not happening due to the fact that the youth of today are a very different generation, a generation of intelligent independent individuals who have been given a free ticket to do what they please with their lives. To no avail, this will bring ultimate consequences that both children and parents may regret at a later day. I am not saying that the parents don't care about their kids or that they allow them to do what they want and not care about the potential or actual consequences. But rather, the children of today feel that they have their own rights to do what they want and their parents have no say in their decisions or actions, and that they can just direct the course of their life how they want it to go. In most instances this may be a good way of allowing the children to experience the reality of life and what is lying out there for them, but for me, as an adult, who has experienced quite a lot of lives' ups and downs, with many bad or wrong choices, differ otherwise. In other words, I don't believe in giving your children a free hand to run or ruin their own young lives, I believe the parents or guardians of children need to pay the utmost attention to what is going on in their kids' lives at all times.

You see, a major part of this generation in failing to make a difference in the lives of others is because they are not seeing that difference being made by their parents, their elders, their family members or other young ones. It is so obvious that they are following a pattern that they see very often, a pattern of a lack of compassion and change. As followers of Jesus Christ and being born again of spirit means that, we should not be doing the same old things as we used to do, we should not be doing the same things as others, who do not know Jesus. We need to stand out and be accountable for what we profess or believe in, we need to be the ones who stand in the gap and make that difference, to make that noticeable effect, that love of God that will no doubt touch the hearts of those who are searching for peace, searching for contentment in their lives, work places, families, relationships or just in general to live a simple and peaceful lifestyle. Once I arrived outside and was waiting for a few minutes, I would look at the door to see if she was coming out but all I could notice were a few people standing at the window staring out at me. Of course I was being checked out and they were probably trying to get a look at me and what I looked like. I think once they saw my little Fiat Panda car they must have thought that I was a weirdo or some poor little pathetic guy. Normally the guys have a nice car when they try to take a girl out like a BMW, Audi, Mustang, or a little sports car, but here I come with probably the smallest and cheapest car in the world that can barely fit two people in it, and it can run around sixty five miles per hour max speed, and that is when the wind is behind you pushing the car. At this point there was nothing I could do, I was outside her house in this car and my nerves were running sky high wondering what they would all think about me? Once the door opened and she walked out, I was so glad. I felt an extreme pressure being lifted off immediately. And when she was walking out I was saying into myself, "Is this real? Am I really going out for a date with this girl?" I mean look at her, she was stunning and I was a little wimp. But I soon picked the game up and realized that this was it, it was real and I had to make the best impression I could or it would be all over very quickly. Once she entered the car all I could do was smile at her and we just said hi to each other and she told me to start driving quickly before her Dad comes out and captures me. So I did. We drove off and we headed down town to a restaurant bar type of place. On the way we were pretty nervous and just made some small talk and all that and when we got inside the place we just relaxed a wee bit and chatted about normal things that she enjoys and that I enjoy and it went from there.

We only stayed there for a couple of hours and she only had a couple of drinks of which I was shocked, I thought she would have been downing them like there was no tomorrow, so that showed a little respect on her behalf. So we finished in the bar and then got to her house and expected her to ask me in for a cup of tea or something as that is what normally happens right? And then that's when the fun usually starts, if you know what I mean guys! But she didn't, and her reason was that her parents would be up waiting for her and me to go in so they can fire about hundred questions at me to get to know me. So she didn't want that to happen as she thought it may have frightened me off right away. So I asked her if I could call her again and maybe we could meet up for another date. I was expecting a straight forward answer of "No" due to the fact I didn't really light up her night with passion, romance or laughter. I was surprised when she said "Yes" that I could give her a call but that could have meant a number of things. Like, 'yes, call me but there is no way I will answer your call, you loser'. Or, 'yes, call me, but I will let it go to my answering machine' and a lot more of things ran to my mind. But I just had to take it at arm's length and believe she meant it. You won't believe how I was feeling driving back those thirty miles to home, I mean I was ecstatic and so excited that I was rapping in my car, I put my music up so loud just because I was so happy that I met her and we went out. C'mon, who wouldn't be over the moon at an opportunity like that? Listen, whether you have been in that situation or not, I was in it, and I was going to enjoy every moment. The whole night I couldn't sleep as I was thinking about the night, I was constantly going over what I could remember saying to her to convince myself that I never made a fool of myself, that what I said was cool and thinking back to see, if she laughed at anything I said. You see this is the crazy situations you get yourself into when you start chasing girls, and I am specifically talking to you young men out there. I have been there and know how it feels to be with a beautiful girl and chase numerous others, and as this story unfolds you can see what could lie ahead of anyone of you. Oh, and girls don't think you're getting away free, your turn will be coming soon I have a few wee comments for you girls that I want you to know about.

I went back to college that week and I was on such a high. I was super hyper and in such a great mood and I couldn't hold back from telling my class mates what had happened, and that I had a date with this beautiful Glasgow girl. They all thought I was mad, after all, it was just one night and they were all making jokes telling me she will probably dump me and not see me again. It was funny as they used my wee car as an excuse, for her not to see me, because a high caliber girl would not want to be seen being driven around in a Fiat Panda. I mean, it was probably the smallest and cheapest car in the world at that time, but it got me around and up and down from college so I wasn't caring what they said or their pitiful excuses. I said to them that they were just jealous because I got a stunning girl and they don't, right? For some reason I left it until late in the week to call her back, I believe it was around the Thursday night I called and to my amazement she was in her house. Her mother answered the phone and she shouted upstairs for her daughter to come down. When she answered, her voice sounded like she was glad to hear from me, you know that way, when you can hear if someone is pleased to hear from you or wants to talk to you. It's not like, she was saying what is it, what do you want or something negative, it was a case of 'hey, how you doing? She even said that she thought I would not call her, so at that point I was like hey, this girl is serious here so I must be in with a chance of another date. So after chatting for a few minutes with all the basics, I again asked her out and she accepted. Wow, were in, it's going down, we on for a second date, so I must have done something right eh? So she asked me to pick her up on Saturday night for us to go out on the town, that was cool with me, her reason was that she had to work on the same area on the Saturday for her Dad. I thought it was fantastic what she was doing in helping her father out with his business, it was a family business that they all had been working so hard to build up and maintain, and I just was so amazed that I could just watch them work together as a family to bring success and prosperity.

This is a similar story for us to realize about how we should be working together as a family, not just in a household, but also in the church. After all, aren't we all just one big family under one roof? Yes indeed, we are all children of God and under his umbrella of leadership. And it is in my beginning a relationship of this girl I met at the stall, I remember God's purpose for man and woman to be together. Remember what He done in the beginning for Adam? The Lord God said, "It is not good for the man to be alone. I will make a helper suitable for him" (Genesis 2:18, NIV translation). So the Lord God caused the man to fall into a deep sleep; and while he was sleeping, he took one of the man's ribs and closed up the place with flesh (Genesis 2:21, NIV Translation). Then the Lord God made a woman from the rib he had taken out of the man, and he brought her to the man (Genesis 2:22, NIV Translation). Disobedience on the direction God has given Adam & Eve resulted in a sad way. If I can take you for a little journey on the book of Genesis 2:9, and the Lord God made all kinds of trees grow out of the ground-trees that were pleasing to the eye and good for food. In the middle of the garden were the tree of life and the tree of the knowledge of good and evil. On the same chapter, verse 16 says, and the Lord God commanded the man, "You are free to eat from any tree in the garden; verse 17, but you must not eat from the tree of the knowledge of good and evil, for when you eat of it you will surely die" (NIV Translation). Here, you can see that God had provided for their needs. He created plenty of trees and also gave a clear instruction of what was right and what was wrong, but what happened? Genesis 3:6, when the woman saw that the fruit of the tree was good for food and pleasing to the eye, and also desirable for gaining wisdom, she took some and ate it. She also gave some to her husband, who was with her and he ate it (NIV Translation). She thought it look so good and it would be fine just to have a bite and was persuaded by the serpent that it would be alright to taste it. Eve listened to the serpent saying, "You will not surely die...,for God knows that when you eat of it your eyes will be opened, and you will be like God, knowing good and evil" (Genesis 3:4-5). Yes, he put the temptation to her in a very convincing way that she was influenced by him and therefore decided to take a bite and bang, the human race would now be changed forever. The reason I am sharing this story of Adam and Eve is that this was the beginning of mankind and due to the deception of the ears; deception of the eyes or the persuasion and influence of another, can lead us into making very wrong decisions that could have short or long term consequences.

To relate this story in the book of Genesis to what I was sharing with the beginning of my love for a girl of what I saw was beautiful in my eyes, was leading the way to becoming overpowered by beauty, was now going to be a force much stronger than me that I was not prepared for. I will get to the point here, after a few months of us dating and going out on a regular basis I felt the need to impress her more and more in order to keep her. So instead of maintaining my little Fiat Panda car I thought it would be great to upgrade to a better car that would be more stylish and flashy and would please her and keep me and her together. All the youth out there, I am sure you know what I mean here with trying to impress the girlfriend or the one you're trying to impress, we have all been there so don't think you are alone in the field, some of us adults even still do it to this day. Anyway, I looked around to see what car I could find and to trade in my little panda, it never took me long at all, after like one week of looking, I came across this beautiful white Austin Maestro sports edition and it was fully loaded with the works. Man, if you could have seen this machine in those days you would have thought I was a 'rock star' or 'pro-soccer player' or someone famous and loaded with cash. Yeh right, I was a second year apprentice still in college. But I made my mind up and that was the car I was having as I knew it would please her and help me along with keeping her. Well, all went well for the first six months until, I couldn't make the payments and then the fun started. I am sure we all know what happens when you fall behind with your payments whether it is on a car, house, and bank loans. Yes, loan companies come chasing after you and try to get their money back, correct? Well, the scariest thing happened to me in this area, after receiving numerous letters telling me to pay my monthly payments or I would be taken to court. I ignored them thinking they would go away. I never paid this car for months on end thinking the company would get fed up chasing me and I would be free, well think again Sean.

There eventually came a time where men came to my parents' house to issue a court summons for me to appear in court for missing payment on my car, and I still paid no attention and never showed up on the day. So the inevitable happened, they got a court order against me to arrest my salary and take out the money required to pay these monthly payments. This was one of the most embarrassing moments of my life, having Betty, you remember Betty from the earlier story? Well she called me into the office one day and told me the bad news that forty percent of my salary had being arrested due to this lack of payment. You can do many things to a man and he may get by, or make provisions to adjust, but when you take away money from his hard earned salary and not just a few pounds but forty percent of his take home pay? Then you are going to have one unhappy chap.

I soon realized what it was like to have money taken away from you at a very early age and believe me, it is not a pleasant feeling at all. I couldn't believe it, I was devastated at this news and was so angry I wanted to hit someone, anyone. You see, this is down to our own decisions that we make in conjunction to the situations we put ourselves in. I had the choice to keep my wee panda car of which, I could afford no problem and was giving me no issue's at all, but because we lose our focus on what is right and stick with it, we lay ourselves wide open to the schemes of the enemy and his fancy tactics of making us feel that we always need to have the better things in front of us. This was surely a case of living above your means and putting yourself into a serious situation that will no doubt turn out bad. Well, this was a serious problem as I still was driving the car and now had to pay a lot more than I normally did every month and was stuck with it because if I returned the car to the dealer, I would have to pay huge penalty fees. I had to try to explain this to my girlfriend now and was thinking if she would still hang around or boot me out. But by this time we were going strong and seeing each other mostly every night. I would still drive the thirty miles each way to see her and then go home very late in the evening, and get up for work or college the next day. I guess that is what they call young love, or foolish love.

Now, I was in my third year in college and my salary was increasing and was working overtime, so my pay was getting better so we were managing, and plus my girlfriend was earning good money in her full time job and earning extra working for her father in the family business. So we were still good in our finances. I would even go and pick her up at her house and then bring her down to see my family and after we were finished, would drive her back up home and then come back down again. That would be a total round trip of one hundred twenty miles. Man, I was really tired after those nights. But I believe it was worth it to me being with my girlfriend and letting her spend time with my parents, although we were mostly at her parents' house rather than mine. You may recall from previous encounters with my Dad that he was not the easy person in the world to please and was so strict, so that is why we rarely visited our house. Anyway as time was moving on and we were just being boyfriend and girlfriend, I got shock news from Betty in the office. I was called in again and Betty told me that another warrant was served against my salary and she had to take away another thirty percent of my take home pay due to me not paying a loan that I had taken out with my previous girlfriend when we had the house. The loan was to buy furniture and decorate the house and buy appliances and all that. So it was quite a large loan that I borrowed. There was nothing I could do in this instance as I made the same mistake as the car payments, I ignored the let-ters and the court summons thinking it would go away, you would think I would learn from my first mistake right? So here I am having seventy percent of my total take home pay being swiped away, leaving me only thirty percent of my salary, so, about fifty pound per week, which was not a lot considering I had to pay my car loan, insurance and gasoline. So I was going crazy and was so angry with myself for letting these things happen to me, and my Mum knew everything that was going on and was trying to help my by paying something towards my car payment. Once my sister found out she went nuts with me. Pauline is always adamant that you must pay your bills before anything else and don't put yourself into trouble over money or material possessions. Anyway, after her moaning at me, she stopped and agreed to help Mum pay a little towards my car payments also, that is what family is for right? To pull you out of a hole in times of need. Although this was not the ideal condition for me to be getting help from my family and after-all, my Mum wasn't even working that time and Pauline wasn't really earning huge amounts of money and, they had their own bills to pay. I think that is why Mum, Pauline and me were always close as we would talk about things and try to work things out between us. Those were the good old days. We would always keep in touch and chat whenever possible and they would love it when I never went up to see my girlfriend because then, we could sit in the house and talk for hours. The thing is, although they knew that I was putting myself into all this trouble just to be with my girlfriend, they still loved me the same and done whatever they could to help me out. I think I was the one who always made the wrong decisions between the three of us siblings. Drew never had any debt because he just spent his money when he got it and when it ran out, he didn't care. He just got on with his life and always told me to take one day at a time and don't worry about tomorrow. Man, how true is that statement and I ignored it every time. Pauline was like Dad, she was a worrier. She worried about everything and that is the same as I was. I think we inherited that from my Dad. Even today, when my Dad is sixty six years old, he still worries about every little detail of your life and that is for the three of us. He has always been the same, worrying about me, Pauline and Drew since we were kids. My Mum is quite different she may also worry about us just the same, but she can hide it very well and it doesn't come out in her nature. She is always quiet and allows things to take their toll and see what works out in the end. To be honest, I love them all the same and love them for who they are, maybe I don't agree with some of the things that they do, or their decisions on certain situations, but none of us are perfect, right?

So, here I am in my fourth year of college and almost graduating as an engineer and it was becoming so scary but great at the same time. I was in our Welding class now as the last two years was to do with pipe fabrication and welding using different techniques. It was very interesting and I loved every day. We had so much fun as we were really good friends now and we were maturing as young adults. We still hit the bars on some weekends and had lots of fun together. We all kept asking each other what we thought it would be like when we graduated and started to work on our own, doing projects and having the responsibility of completing tasks by ourselves. We were all pretty scared I think, as we knew the responsibility that our peers had on their shoulders and when things went wrong, they got the blame and even some engineers got fired due to making mistakes that cost the company money and ruined their reputation. When I think of it, our reputation is very important to us, or it should be, do you know why? Let me share why I think it is so important. When you are given specific tasks to accomplish or be involved with, it means that the person or people who entrusted those tasks to you believe that you are capable and trustworthy of completing the tasks, and have the faith in you to carry them out according to their requests. So this is to say, that you are now being held accountable for the end result of whatever it is you have to do, and the responsibility for reaching this achievement could solely rely on you. This will be down to a combination of a few things like, your attitude, your character, your personality, your enthusiasm, your abilities, your mannerism, your respect and various other characteristics within you. Others may see something in you that you don't, or that you are not aware you have it, but that is why they give you a task, or trust you to carry out a specific function in the first place. That is a very good sign that you are entrusted to be held responsible or accountable to carry out such tasks. But the outcome completely depends on you and how you go about dealing with the task in hand. You see, this is what makes up your DNA of who you are and what people see in you. So in short, if you have a terrible attitude towards people you work with, your friends, or who you are in contact with, or your mannerism towards them sucks, or you have little patience in dealing with your situations or responsibilities, then this shows others what type of person you are. And in most cases, will normally work against you in many ways. People don't want to be around trouble makers, or people with bad attitudes, or those who show no respect to others, they want to be around people who are joyful, pleasant, caring, considerate, thoughtful, bubbly personalities, friendly, easy to get along with. This also applies within our Christian walk with God as fellow brothers and sisters in Christ. They observe the same qualities of those who surround them, and the same feelings are felt within the church environment as well. You will notice that, if there are any fellow believers that make life hard for others, or are very difficult to approach, or get along with, or they seem to have a less friendly attitude or mannerism, then people tend to stay clear of them and find people who inspire them or encourage them or ones who are just full of love that comes from the Lord. Why? Because your attitude is contagious, your personality is contagious, your mannerism and respect is contagious, meaning that, what you do either rubs off on people in a positive or a negative way.

Me personally, I want to be around fellow Christians who are full of life and love of the Lord, because I know that their love for Jesus will rub off on me and it will show me that I need to get on the same atmosphere and have that same desire to love God the way I am supposed to. It doesn't mean I will ignore, whom I feel don't show the same attitude, but we need to be careful that any negative attitude does not rub off on you. Influence plays a major role in our lives today and can either be good for us or bad for us. That is why God is so good that He gives us the wisdom to discern. So what can we take away from this? No matter where you are, what you say, what you do, how you do it, or why you do it, others are watching your every move, and will either judge you if they are not a believer, or make a picture of who you really are, and if we are professing to be Christians, then our attitude and all that we do, should reflect this. Because let me tell you friends, if you don't meet up to the standards that you are portraying, then ones who do not believe in Jesus Christ and have not given their life to Him, will be the first ones to come and shove it in your face, and it will give them all the evidence they need to say that Christians are fake, and that Christianity is fake and doesn't work. So, whether we are at work, or in the church, or in the shopping malls or restaurant, always show others the true love that comes from God and this will be a way of how to witness to the world that the love of Christ is true, and is in your life. Because remember, non-believers will not believe until they see, but for believer's, it tells you in Hebrews 11:1, Now faith is being sure of what we hope for and certain of what we do not see (NIV Translation).

In this faith statement, this allows us not to depend on the visible effects of our actions or our beliefs, but total and complete trust in God and his grace. We are all aware that we always don't get what we want and when we want it, and sometimes we wonder why things even happen when we don't expect them, or not ready to deal with them? And again, that is why we must be so focused and so dependent on God and acknowledge, that His ways are not our ways and He definitely know the plans He has for us. This may be pretty easy to say and easy to ask you to believe, that this is how God works, but to be honest with you, I cannot say to you that I understand everything that happens to me and in my life, certainly not. I often wonder why on earth the things I go through, or experience happened, when they can be completely the opposite of what I am working towards or even planning or even in my dreams or desires. But the one thing I can tell you that I am sure of is that, no matter what I face, no matter what challenges comes my way, no matter how difficult a situation I am in or facing, or even when things go desperately against my plans and strategy, then I know God, is allowing it to happen for a reason. A reason that I may never find out or understand or know why, but that is why I know that my faith in God is real, it is no joke or type of game, and it is not part of a special group of people who are trying to convince others in to a trap. I will tell you right now, that if I truly thought that God was not real, or that Jesus Christ cannot change a heart if you receive Him, or if the Holy Spirit is not real when it moves in your life and allows you to experience, and be a part of great revelations and actions from God, then I would not be wasting my life following after God and portraying to be someone I am not. I certainly wouldn't be going to church, bible study groups, prayer meetings, and leading the younger generation into a false hope or false lifestyle. I would be the one on the street shouting against this kind of spiritual relationship. All these experiences will be revealed on the last chapter of this book and how I came to know Jesus Christ and how He became so real for me.

So you see, when we are given any type of responsibility whether it is from your parents, school teacher, class mate, friends, family or even church leaders, you should carry it out with excellence and integrity. You are entrusted with tasks because you have either displayed a specific attitude in carrying it out, or you have the potential to do better than you have already done, or you are ready to take another step of development as a person. To me, this is critical for all of us, to continue to grow and develop as individuals and that it would allow us to be able to be a part of a larger group of which, we all can learn and teach each other in different parts of our lives. That is why I believe Christianity and our relationship with Jesus Christ is so exciting, because it is not just what God can do in using me, but also on what I am going to learn on how God uses others to reach out to me and help me become closer to Him every day. We are all called to go and make disciples, that is what the great commission is and the ultimate goal for each Christian to focus on, and attain. Everything else that we learn, experience, or do in the ministry of God is a plus and a blessing to us, but if we do not have the compassion and vision that we are called to show others and the love of God that can bring them to a personal relationship with Him, then we are missing the whole point. Although it takes time, training, passion, commitment, love and many other characteristics that could enable us to bring others to Christ, and if without the moving of the Holy Spirit, then it will not be possible for others to believe in God, Why? Because they won't see that true love of God in you and also, we cannot do anything on our own accord, it is all by the Grace of God. When you are in tune with God and His will, He will surely guide and direct your paths in order for you to have the wisdom to make the right decisions. When you go back a few pages, when I was in the mess with my car payments and having a huge percentage cut back on my salary to pay for my debts, then it was obvious I was not in a relationship with God. It was obvious that I was not being guided or directed by God, it was obvious I did not have the wisdom to make the right decisions at that time because I was blinded by the attitude, and I had to please another person. You see, I was starting to pay the price for my poor decisions and lack of focus on the right thing in life, and it is not nice at all having to pay for mistakes. When you think you are making the right choices and decisions and when it could possibly have an impact on others, then seriously think about the reasons why you want to make that decision or choice. My mistake was not just putting myself into serious debt and embarrassment, but also because I was in a long relationship and we were getting stronger in love and all that stuffs. My girlfriend was not involved in my troubles whether she liked it or not.

Be careful my friends of wanting to get into a quick relationship and wanting things to develop your feelings very fast, because the tendency is that, you are now both locked into each of your decisions and actions and inevitably, both start working things out together and are now responsible for each other's liabilities, and therefore accountable for each other. Don't get me wrong, we all will be going through this eventually and it is great when you work together as a couple and have God in the center of all your decisions and actions, but when you see your partner becoming irritated, stressed out and very annoyed, because they are now a partner in your mess that you made with your finances or your life, then it seems to bring a different light into your relationship and makes it much more difficult to enjoy those loving moments that we are all searching for. My financial situation didn't help our relationship at all; although my girlfriend accepted this problem, it did put a strain on our relationship. Let me remind you that we were still very young I was now 21 years old and my girlfriend was 20 and we were going through financial issue's that you think you should only be going through when you're married and much older, but that's what happens when you jump in and make decisions without really thinking or planning the potential outcome or consequences. Well, my college graduation was coming up; yep I was going to graduate from college with a certification to prove that I made it, that I actually passed my exams and will earn the title 'engineer'.

This was an amazing accomplishment for me and my family. I wasn't the most clever kid on the block and I always believed my brother and sister had more brains than me, because they finished school and both were working full time positions and they always seemed to know more about life in general, and how to handle situations. I always looked up to them for guidance and watch how they lived their life. Drew my older brother was very easy going, he would just enjoy life to the fullest and he was a very kind guy, although he will probably not admit that in case we all think he is a big softy and his pals will give him dogs abuse. He always acted like he was a tough guy and his words always came across as if he didn't care and was just out for himself, but I knew deep down he was a caring guy and I have seen this through his life. Yes, he was selfish at times and just took care of himself, but who hasn't, we all go through this and even sometimes to this day we have the same attitude. Drew has had his fair share of troubles and trials in life along with disappointments, but he now has his own family with his fiancé Francis and is a father raising three amazing kids Natalie, Dylan & Cameron, my wonderful wee niece and nephews. Then there was my sister Pauline, she had a tough time, especially while she was a young woman. Pauline started out at a very young age in a relationship and got married at the age of twenty two. I didn't really know what marriage was all about as I was only fourteen when she got married and was only interested in myself, as you would have read in the earlier chapters. So I didn't pay any attention to what was going on in her life. Until it wasn't successful for her on that part until later on she met and married Arnott, my buddy brother in-law. Isn't it so that we as a family, we should be caring and thinking about each other, and showing an interest in what each other are doing, or going through? Not for me. Anyway, Pauline looked like she was very level headed being married and all that, and a professional worker in an electronics factory so I thought we were all doing great now; I was an addition to the success of all three kids of Andy and Mary. We're all working and earning our own pay and looking after ourselves and our own families.

So, once I graduated from college I was very excited as I was now an engineer, and could start making the big bucks that I knew other engineers were making, and I couldn't wait. I also thought that this would help my financial situation a lot better because I was struggling so bad and if it wasn't for the help and support from my girlfriend then, I would have never been able to manage to get through those college years. You see friends, even when you do make mistakes and pay the consequences of those actions, there is always a way out. There was no God for me, there was no relationship with Jesus Christ there for me, there was no depending on the Holy Spirit to move and guide me through my troubles, there were no other brothers or sisters in Christ there to help me through because, I made the choice of not wanting to know Jesus and I made the choice that I didn't need to know God, or if there even was a God on those moments. After all, I was far too young and clever to need God or acknowledge, if there was a God. We can all conquer the world on our own right? Well, after graduation, I was sent out to the field now as a fully qualified engineer, responsible for my work and services to my company. I was so nervous in the event I made mistakes and it would cost the company money and I would probably get fired, isn't that our worse fear, not doing our job right and getting fired? I started to build confidence in my work and really focused so hard in what my duties were. So much that I would always look over my tasks very diligently before carrying them out and then double check once I was finished. I was being noticed for my work due to the fact I did it very quickly and very professionally and my colleague and manager would recognize it and say "Well done" all the time. Word soon spread within the company, and I was being sent to more jobs on my own and giving more responsibility to handle and, I was making much more money. I was working extra hours every night and some weekends and I loved it. My girlfriend was also working extra hours in her job so she was earning great money at the same time. We really focused hard to pay off our debts that I caused, to clear our heads and get this behind us as quick as possible.

We were now in our fifth year of our relationship and we made a big decision to get engaged, yep we made the move towards getting married and committing to each other. We were excited and our families were happy for us. I was 24 years old and thought it was perfect timing and we were getting mature, so we knew what we were doing and what we were aiming for. We were very faithful to each other and made a commitment to each other to say, 'if we ever wanted to be with another person', as in, want to quit our relationship then we would tell each other immediately before we made a mistake of sleeping with someone else or in other words, having a sexual relationship with somebody else. So this was quite clear and this is the way I wanted our relationship to be, very open and honest. We had a great relationship and lifestyle together, we would go abroad on holidays once or twice a year and we would go out to the bars and clubs on weekends, and go to parties and have fun and get drunk, on all occasions. We eventually cleared all our debts and we started to see our bank balance grow quite nicely and it was a great feeling to actually have money in the bank. We would then start thinking about finding our own place to live and I was a little apprehensive about this because of my previous relationship where I walked out from my fiancé and left her with the house and all the bills. But for some reason, because we were engaged and had a great understanding of each other and after what we had just faced and overcome, then I thought this was the right thing to do, in order to move on with our relationship and grow together as man and woman, eventually we would be getting married and have to get our own place anyway. Well we had a great opportunity, my fiancé's father had his own business and he had a two storey house where it was converted, his business was conducted from down stairs and the top half was a self contained apartment. It was a win-win situation for us and her father because we would have our own flat and paying a very cheap rent, and it was nice and secure and he would have his business secure, because we were in the house so nobody would break in. So we did it, we moved in and started to live together, and in those days it was called 'living in sin'. Why, because you were living together out of wedlock, in other words, we're sleeping together without marriage yet. It was a 'thing' in those days. A lot of young people were doing it, so we just joined the club. Well that was us for a couple of years and it was great. I was always working away from home and my fiancé would work as much as possible for her Dad at nights and weekends doing clothes parties, and working the barrow-lands. Remember this was the place where we first met? So yes, she still worked there for her Dad and she loved it. She was a brilliant sales woman and had the confidence to go with it.

We had made plans with her father to buy his house from him as we loved it and we had great ideas on how we can convert it into our perfect entertainment home with gym, fitness area, entertainment room and all sorts of fantastic furniture and materials inside. We sat down with her Dad and worked out a finance plan where we would have saved enough money to give him a pretty good cash down-payment and then mortgage the rest. So this was now our goal, and we worked it out to reach this goal in twelve months. When you set yourself goals, it means you make a commitment to change your attention from a selfish attitude to a more mature outlook to reach something better for your life whether it is on a financial aspect, physical aspect, or even spiritual aspect. Ours was more on financial and pleasure aspect, where we wanted to make more money to save for a house and for the pleasure of owning one and having our own freedom to do as we please. We were so focused and excited about this that we never went any holidays and we never really went out to the bars much. We just worked and saved as much as possible to reach our goals. We were on target and we only had like two more months to go and to reach our goal of having our down-payment and cash left over to furnish some parts of the house and make alterations as we needed. But then, we got thrown a curve ball. We were sitting in her father's house watching television and chatting and then he asked us how are we with our down-payment. And we replied that, we will have the ten thousand pounds on time as agreed and then we can arrange to move in on the date we agreed. Well, he turned to us and said, "You mean the fifteen thousand pounds?" We both looked at each other with shock and both answered, "You mean ten thousand?" He got up off his seat and faced us both and said, "What are you talking about? You know it's fifteen thousand. Where are you getting ten thousand from?" We both started to get really nervous and told him we agreed on ten thousand pounds and that is why we worked it out that we could have it in twelve months and agreed the dates to move in. Well, the whole house went into a sudden roar, he would start to laugh at us and said we were off our heads thinking we could get the house at this price, and that he wanted more money upfront. We both were in a state of shock and amazement, that he would start saying this to us and that he was lying to us about this down-payment. Our whole situation just turned upside down and we didn't know what to do at this moment.

This was a huge turning point in our relationship with my fiancé's father and it was so bad that we would not speak to each other for over a year. Let me tell you, this was the worst scenario I ever faced with not speaking to someone, this was horrible. We would not go and see her father or mother, and it was very bad indeed. It was a mess and you could not stop thinking about it every day as this was family, and we would get to the point of hating her Dad for what he had done to us. So, our plans was up in the air for that house and we had saved all our money and spent our time working so hard and it was all for nothing. Well, after that, we decided we needed a break and went on a three week holiday to the Caribbean just to relax and let the pressure get away from us and focus again on what we should do next. Things got even worse as time went on, since her father was still working his business out of the bottom of the house and we were still living in the top half, we would see them and still not talk, then we would argue and make things worse and tempers really got heated up. It was becoming unbearable to live there because of this situation and the funny thing was, we were still working for her Dad doing the business because we were used to earning the money and the greed of money was starting to kick in for us, the more we had, the more we wanted.

It happened, after a major argument, her father told us to get out of his apartment and not to work with him anymore. You need to know something here; both my fiancé and her father had the same personality and character. They were so outgoing and very powerful in their words and actions and they always clashed with each other. There were certain times were violence actually came into play and we were all fighting with each other and I mean really fighting. It was like we were rival gangs instead of family. So I think, it was only a matter of time before the situation was going to have a major explosion, and this was the time. So from here, we moved down to stay with my family in Greenock and I thank God that we had room in our house and that my parents would allow us to come and stay with them. My parents we over the moon at the fact that we were moving in with them, it meant they could keep an eye on us and really look after us. Let me tell all of you young ones out there, if you think your parents give you a hard time asking you to do some chores like, cleaning your room, or washing the dishes, or cleaning the bathroom, or picking up your dirty clothes and putting them in the washing, or helping with any chore in the house or the garden then you better show them the respect that they deserve and do, as they ask. The reason I am urging you to do this is because I have been there where I did nothing to help my parents around the house. I wouldn't do a thing in the house, I would laugh at them and then run out and play with my friends, or go play with my computer games or find some excuse, not to help out and I am sure you all know what I mean here. I know that you can all be having similar excuses not to help out. We were back in the house and we were grown adults and ready to get married and now facing a dilemma of nowhere really to stay on our own and at the same time, be in the same house as my Dad. As you know by the past chapters that my Dad was very strict in his house, you either had to go with his rules or you're out. And my fiancé was not really the one to live under other peoples rules especially, with my Dad being so stubborn and straight forward in his ways, but he always teach us the right ways.

This was the most trying time of our relationship together as my fiancé hated staying with my parents, and she hated Greenock, as this was a little poor town and boring compared to the big city of Glasgow. And it made things unpleasant for us staying there and my parents would actually start getting annoyed with her as they knew she didn't like being there and she would never want to sit with them or talk to them. We were there for quite a while until we started looking for a house up in Glasgow again as my fiancé was going crazy living in Greenock and living in my parent's house. I was ok, as I was with my parents and I could handle it no problem, except with sometimes my Dad would annoy me with his rules and regulations, but it is his house and he is my father, so I should be obedient and respect him, correct? It took a lot of work but we needed to respect my Dad as it was his house and he deserves the respect. I was so unhappy and confused on what to do, so that is why we looked for somewhere to stay to keep my fiancé happy. So we started visiting lots of houses in the Glasgow area and we searched and searched for months and months until we eventually found a wee house in a town called, Gartcosh. It was a great little area and the house we found was a double storey with two bedrooms, it had huge potential and pretty cheap in price, so we went for it and we got it. It was fantastic once we got in there and we got back to living our own lives together and getting on with it. We were still not speaking to my fiancé's parents. Unfortunately, her mother got dragged into the fight as she would stand by her husband so she got treated the same and she never deserved it as she was a wonderful, caring, gentle woman. I am not sure if we were wrong about the down payment or not, but we never gave in.

Once we got settled into our house and we made all the alterations and decoration changes that we wanted, we sat down and finally made a date to get married. This was a very scary moment as we were now going to be husband and wife. We never really knew what would that actually mean but we thought there was no turning back now and changing partners after all we had been through and we had a great relationship and worked well. Even though my fiancé was very overpowering to me, and I would just agree to anything she said so that it would not cause an argument, I hated arguments. I had grown up in my life always hearing people and at the same time my fiancé's family arguing and fighting and I didn't want my life to be going in the same direction, so it was always better not to argue or disagree. I played the simple card of peace at all times. We had been with each other for nine years now, five years as boyfriend and girlfriend and four years her being my fiancé and now we would be married after our fifth year engagement. So it was not as if we just jumped into this without thinking, we gave it as much time as we thought was needed, in order to make sure we were right for each other and we both knew and made sure that we were ready to commit the rest of our lives to each other, no matter what the world throws at us. I was twenty eight years old and getting on, the younger years were quickly disappearing.

Our careers were still going very strong; I was still working in the same industry within the water engineering industry but with a different company. I left Hillhead Filtration and started work with the second biggest company in the United Kingdom called Barr & Wray. This was like a promotion for me to join a bigger organization even though I was doing the same work except on a larger scale, it was still the same. But much more exciting with a lot more responsibilities, with extra compensation off course. My fiancé was still working in her machine factory and was one of the best performers there and would earn extra bonuses every pay check for her performance. She was super fast in what she does and the quality of her work was remarkable, so they rewarded people who performed very well. We were still going on our annual holidays twice a year but then put it on hold to save for the wedding and go for a very nice honeymoon at the end. But to be honest, we had put aside our savings over the years, and were not short of a few pounds so we were in very good shape. I want to share something to you before I move on with this story of the wedding plans. I was pretty good in the finance part now and we had quite a healthy bank balance with no debts except, a mortgage. We had paid our car in cash and the rest of our savings was just building up and up. There were certain times where my parents would be struggling with money and being overwhelmed with bills and never had much at all, because they used what they had in raising their three kids, me, Drew and Pauline the best they could. I knew of their struggles and when my Dad would sometimes ask if I could lend him some money, I would refuse. I would make excuses that we never really had much and we had too many bills to pay. Wow, what a lie, isn't that the worse case of disrespect ever, lying to your own parents that you had no money to give them when on those times, you have much more than you need and you refuse to help them? The same would be with my Mum and Pauline, they would face some difficult times where the bills would come in and they would be struggling to pay and it would leave them really short. Again, they would mention this to me and ask for a little help for a while and that they would pay me back as quick as possible. Again, I would make some weak story of we never had much and were struggling and completely lie to their face. Don't get me wrong, I felt a little guilty, but not that much, to give them any of my money, let me just tell you here that it would have been easier getting 'blood out of a stone' than it would have been getting money out of me. I know that it was a bad thing to do, but let me explain to you why I wouldn't give. It was not because I never had it to give, it was not because I never realized they had a need and I was able to help out, no it was because I had the love of money in my heart, I had the greed of loving money.

Let me share this fact with you my friends, we hear often that the love of money is a sin, and we think of all those people that are loaded, that are stinking rich above means, that don't ever have to work again in their lives, so they must be sinful people because they are storing it up for themselves right? Well, if that is the case with any of these super rich people, then I was no better than them. Even though I only had thousands in my savings, I still had the disease of the greed of it, and to have more and more of it and not share it. When you have more than what you need and you know people in need and you can give a little to help and you don't, you may convince yourself that you need your money for a rainy day, that you need your money to look after your family, that you need your money for your needs, then you might be correct in a way. Let's not get out of reality here and not to forget that we need to plan for our family's daily needs. We cannot just throw it all away and then say, 'what will we do?' of course you have to acquire some wisdom with your money and how to use it. But what we need to look at is, if what you have is not being used and is just sitting in your store-house, meaning bank account and there is no immediate need for it, but you know there is a brother or sister who needs help, then what is the right thing you should do with what is stored? You see, this is where I failed, I knew what I had in my storehouse but failed to put it to use in a proper way, yes you might say, 'it is understandable for you not to give as you were planning for a wedding and you just purchased a new home, so you have bills and all that'. But even before the house, even before the marriage plans, even before the engagement, I would still not give my family anything and I don't understand why I was so overpowered by the greed of money, until later in my life I understood and I will share that with you in the next coming pages. So you see, we cannot just use a situation to justify why we won't give when the need arises. There is no excuse or lie that we can fabricate that is more important or better, than the need. For when there is a need there is a purpose, there is a special reason for a need to be met and the great thing about our God is, that when a need arises and He touches a person's heart in order to act, that determines our true calling as a Christian, and child of God. And it allows God to truly see how much you love Him on how you respond to that need. We cannot change the whole world by giving everything that we have, no matter how little or big it may be, but what we can do is potentially change the life of another person who has a need at a specific time, and our contribution can go a long way in determining the outcome in that specific situation that God has placed in our way, to act upon. You see friends, the same goes for our giving in tithes and offering, and don't get all tight on me here, I am not going to preach to you a sermon on why we should tithe and/or give our offerings to God, but I will share with you what God is looking for from you. It is not your money. This short illustration is for all to know and be aware of, whether you are a Christian and follower of Jesus Christ, whether you are not interested in a relationship with Jesus Christ, whether you are of another denomination that knows about tithes and offerings and the purpose of giving and the benefits, or if you are wanting to know what it all means, then I am going to share with you my revelation and understanding of it all.

God Almighty, Creator of heaven and earth, Ruler of the universe and Father to all, owns everything. He created everything and He owns everything, and He allows us to borrow and use what He has created within His kingdom. God is not in need, or desperate to get our pitiful amount of money that we offer back to Him. He is not in need of the thousands or millions that others may be able to give. He is not in need of the billions that others may have and are not giving to Him. God does not force us to give anything back to Him; He is a gracious and compassionate God. The greatness of our God, the compassion of our God, the loving-kindness of our God to all of His creation is so much that, He is just concerned about our obedience on His commands. So in this instance, I think about how I react towards an all powerful, all wonderful God who has put me in a position of great responsibility of the financial part of my life of which, He has truly been so faithful to me in providing all my needs according to His riches and Glory. That's how I look at this situation of giving back something to God, I look at it as an open door for me to show just how much I appreciate the blessings that I have been getting, the blessings that I continue to get, and the blessings that are stored up for me. But on those times, I didn't know all these by heart. It is just now that I came to know that God has stored up an abundant supply of blessings and is just waiting to release them on us. It is just now that I learned the value of God's promise when we entrust Him our finances. As it says, in Malachi Chapter 3 verse 10, "Bring the whole tithe into the storehouse, that there may be food in my house. Test me in this", says the Lord Almighty, "and see if I will not throw open the floodgates of heaven and pour out so much blessing that you will not have enough room for it"(NIV Translation).

Well the first part is that God gives us a little at a time in order to see how we react with what He has given, he waits patiently to see our attitude and how we go about making decisions and what kind of actions come out of our lives. We may not realize that God watches our every move and that is where we may be failing in order to see the blessing from heaven flooding in our lives. Why, because we only think about ourselves. This is where I went wrong, where I went off the wall chart in receiving what God has stored up for me as I only thought about me, what I want, what I need, what I deserve and what I like. When you have a 'what I' attitude it usually means, you are not working in the realms of Gods plans and directions. It usually means, you are not following the true paths of what God has put in front of you, it usually means you are starving yourself of the gifts from God that He has promised you; so much, that you will not have enough room for it. It blows my mind to imagine what can be poured down onto my life, my wife to be, my family, my relatives, my friends, my neighbors, my co-workers. Anyone I know or even come in contact with, but I took it for granted because I didn't know it yet. For me, this step took a very long time for me to comprehend and accept, it took me years and I am going to share it with you. I continued on being selfish, neglected what effect it could make to me and my family. This is the part where I separated myself from the purpose of which I was supposed to receive, and how I used it. This is when I put a hold on the floodgates of heaven pouring out on my life and potentially the lives of others in my circle of society, meaning anyone I knew. How can this be you may say? Well, due to my selfishness and uncompassionate heart for others by thinking about myself, then I was robbing God of what is right-fully His in the first place. God blessed us in order for us to give to others. He wants us to share that of which we have received, He doesn't just shower us with His blessings for us to go and enjoy if there are others in need that He allowed into our lives. God doesn't put you in a place with another person without a cause, without a purpose. Have you read the Purpose Driven Life book? If not, you should because the name of that book says it all. Every aspect of your life has a purpose, every situation or circumstance has a pur-pose, every outcome has a purpose, so for me, I never found that out because I had my own purpose, and that was to enjoy my store-house for myself in the most selfish manner I could. I never wanted to share anything with anyone. So for me, it was like what I had was mine and mine only and I was giving nothing away. My family can attest to my attitude and they will tell you exactly how I was with money and material items. Friends, I want to tell you how you can avoid the mistakes I made. This is what this book is all about, to let you see my journey of life that has so many doors opened in order to bring a life of fulfillment and joy. In the last chapter you will see the turnaround that will bring more detail in what you will read in these last few pages of this chapter, and will give light to what I am sharing with you but for now, here is a quick version.

God blessed me continuously on a regular basis and I never knew it, or realized it. He gave me a fantastic opportunity when I was going through high school to listen, learn and develop my knowledge and He gave it a little at a time. Why do you think school is broken up into subjects, classes and times? So we can learn a little at a time and give our attention to that situation. God opened a door and gave me a fantastic opportunity when I left school to work as a trainee for two years to develop my skills once again, and even rewarded me with a salary because of my obedience and commitment. God opened a door and gave me a fantastic opportunity immediately after my training course was complete, with a full time job and again, giving me a little more salary for my obedience and commitment. God opened a door and gave me an amazing opportunity to get a college diploma and graduate after four years as an engineer, and along the way, gave me more salary each year for my obedience and commitment. After the graduation, God opened a door and gave me a full time position as an engineer of which, I carried out for eight years and He gave me more salary every year for my obedience and commitment. God opened a door and gave me a life changing event of which you will read in the next chapter and you will see what He done for me. I am allowing you to understand where I am coming from on this topic of giving back to God, and how I failed. It was due to the fact that I never acknowledged or recognized who supplied all my needs, and why. I thought all along the way that I was the one who directed my own life, I was the one who made what had happen, that I was the one who was working so hard and put in so many hours to get the salary, the houses, the cars, the holidays and the material items. I thought I was the one who worked so hard and continued to work so many hours and days in order to pay the bills and keep the roof over my head to avoid many sleepless and stressful nights worrying. When all along, all I was doing was missing the point. I never got the big picture. I never understood the mighty plan and I never recognized there was another dimension in my life that was missing. You see, in all of these things that I was working hard for, I was always complaining about why we had to pay taxes and the tax man was taking so much of my salary every week, and it wasn't fair. That greed for money that had kicked in was still there, controlling my attitude, for supplying my desire for making and storing up my money.

So here's the crusher that took me years to understand and finally accept. We are allowed to work as long as we want and when we want in order to earn more money, right? Well the tax man loves it when we do that because he knows that he will get more money from us every time. We will always try to find ways from paying him more than we have to, and we will try to persuade our accounts people to put in expenses or costs under the non-taxable bracket to avoid tax being taken out of our salary. But even after all these hard working hours, days, weeks, months and years that we are putting in to enlarge our wealth, or sustain our lifestyles or better our circumstances, we always have to face the truth of paying the taxman. We will always try to find ways to rob him of what he is duly owed. We will always try to work the system in order to avoid his reduction from our salaries, and the reason I hit hard on the money side is that, the majority of our life is really controlled and directed by money, of which can be because we know of no other method or practice to that which can draw us into another direction. Every aspect of our lives whether it be relationships with friends, family, co-workers, schoolmates or others, there is a promise from God that He will open the gates of heaven and pour out His blessings so much that we will not have enough room for it. Well, does that not sound like a pretty good offer? You see, I never knew of that offer when I was going through this part of my journey in life, I never knew there was a God who would give this all to me, I never knew that there was any other way. And this is where the promise of God, that you just read, comes in; this was the turning point for me when I learned it later on. I now know, that this is to be a true statement and indeed a promise that God carries out according to His plan. When I've learned about God's promise in the book of Malachi, Chapter 3, verse 7-9, "Ever since the time of your forefathers you have turned away from my decrees and have not kept them. Return to me, and I will return to you," says the Lord Almighty. "But you ask, 'how are we to return?' "Will a man rob God? Yet you rob me. "But you ask, 'How do we rob you?'" In tithes and offerings". You are under a curse – the whole nation of you – because you are robbing me (NIV Translation). Can you see it? Can you feel it? When God has supplied us with everything we have no matter how much it is, and when He supplied it, and we don't return something back to Him, we are robbing Him. I tell you the truth friends, when this got a hold of my heart, my mind, my inner-self, and my spirit, I cried out to God and asked for His mercy upon me for being so selfish and irresponsible for my actions of not knowing what the purpose of His giving to me. How can I, a child of the Creator of the universe, the Maker of heaven and earth, the Supplier of my needs simply not want to give back a little of what I have received? But I didn't know then, I really just didn't know.

This really took me to a new level of my understanding to why I should give back to God what He has asked when I learned about it. He is only asking a tenth of what we make, He is not asking for it all. When we give that tenth what does God tell us that it is for? It is not for something useless or for Him to deposit it into a Bank of America savings account or into a Chase checking account. No, it is so that there is food in His storehouse, meaning that it will be used to cater for the needs of others. Do you get it? Everything that we give back to God He will turn it around and give it out to others so that not only me and you are blessed, but for the ones whom He will then bless through giving the tenth of what we earn. Praise God from whom all blessings flow. Remember that song. So the short version is to understand, that God is the supplier of all our needs according to His riches and Glory and we are to give back to Him a portion of what He is asking in order for His love to be displayed in us, by our obedience in His word. Almost all the latter part of this chapter about God was no doubt not into account yet during those times of my experiences. As we go to the last chapter of this book, you will see how gracious, forgiving, merciful and loving God is and how did I experience His grace and how I received, the free gift of salvation.

Chapter 8

THE ENCOUNTER

Before I came to the understanding of what I just shared in knowing God, as the Supplier of all our needs and that we are only asked to give a little in return, we obviously never gave anything into the Kingdom of God, as we never had a relationship with Jesus Christ that allows us, the access to come before the throne of God, and to acknowledge Him. I never knew about giving before, so I guess, you can use that against us as a reason that we were pretty comfortable in our savings account along with another reason that, we never gave to our families anything either. Now we are taking the next step towards our long term relationship and that is planning, to get married. I knew from the 'get go' that I would not really be much of a help in preparing the whole marriage planning thing as I was not the type for all that stuff because, my patience was not the best and I had no sense of taste for anything, whether for clothes, venues, picture taking, choosing cars, reception halls, flowers, catering, music or bands and all the other million things associated with a wedding. We were pretty excited because this was the next chapter of our life together and this would be the tenth year of our relationship, after the first five being boyfriend and girlfriend, then the five year engagement so it was like solid of our intentions and our commitment to each other.

All of who have had the pleasure of arranging your own wedding plans will share with me the excitement, stress, pressure and time constraints that took place to put it all together. When we first announced the big date, it was, all systems go from that moment on. I mean, our heads were down and it was as if they were never back up until it was all over. We thought that one year planning was plenty of time and because I knew that my fiancé was so clever in arranging things and that I was confident that she knew exactly what she wanted, would make it all be a piece of cake. I must admit, at this point, I was so comfortable allowing my fiancé to plan everything her way as after all, it is the woman's big day isn't it? Things got running that moment. First thing we had to do was, writing down all the names of both family members and then see what kind of numbers we came up with. Did you go through the same arguments and disagreements that we went through, deciding who should and who shouldn't go to our wedding? I couldn't believe it. We had just started our planning and we were fighting already, we were debating who was not entitled to come and who didn't deserve to come because of something they may have done in the past, or they had an attitude towards us in a separate incident, which we would never forgive or forget. Families are funny sometimes and when you have a celebration or an event of some kind it usually comes to a head when people are to be invited. This is exactly what happened here with us, all sorts of excuses came to light how some of my relatives should not be invited, and I could not get the courage to face my parents and tell them a jacked up reason why we won't be inviting either their brother or sister or very close cousin or relative. So then I started to question why all my fiancé's family and cousins and relatives were invited and some of mine weren't. You would think that planning such a fantastic event, a life changing event that will unite both of you together for the rest of your life would be such an awesome and friendly and respectful activity, not for us. It took about two weeks to gather all the information and go through the regime of who will be attending and who won't be and you know, it got to the point that we argued so much and each of us would not give in to the other ones requests that we said, "Forget the wedding". Yes you heard me, we actually got so angry with each other that we said that there will be no wedding and we threw the names away. We could not compromise with each other and we nearly broke up our relationship over it. It is so childish I know, but it was one of the most serious issue's I ever had to plan and one that I completely lost my patience over. We would not speak to each other for a few weeks and it was my fiancé parents that would eventually have to sit both of us down and talk to us. They were the mediators as we again, got all the names gathered and discussed the same agenda of who should be going to our wedding. They had a great way of helping us work out this situation but first they made us apologize to each other and make up with a great big hug and kiss, which was nice. Then we got down to business and started working out who's who, and where they will fit into the plans. Once we came to the point again of who was to be taken off the list, was where the help of her parents came in, as we would go down the list and say, "Right they can't come". Then they asked for reasons. We explained why, so then, they took their name off the list and we did it each family at a time. So then, I would remove one name from my family, and then my fiancé would remove one name from her family and then we would go down the list of names like that, just accepting one and removing one from each family and you won't believe that we actually managed to finalize our numbers that night and with no arguing and we just shouted a big loud hooray, and that we were glad that it was over. Sometimes things happen for a reason that we don't know, think about, or even understand, but there is always a purpose for everything, right? On this occasion we had to have the intervention of parents in order for us to look at this situation in a different manner, so that we can come to a solution and move on. Now that the numbers are in, we were now good to go and find a suitable venue that could cater for the number of guests and a location that would suit both families. We were thirty miles apart from each other and both families were spread all over the place so the logistics of arranging a venue was going to be very difficult. Always remember, that both families always want events close to where they live so we were always going to have a struggle in coming up with a venue that will please both parents and our siblings. We searched down in Greenock in my neck of the woods, and there was nothing really that we like and thought was suitable for us, and then we searched many places in Glasgow but found them too expensive or wrong locations. This was becoming a very tiring task and time was against us. We came across a beautiful location in a place called Rutherglen and it could cater for the number of guests that we had planned and the best thing was, it was free of charge if you take their catering. You might be thinking that it is a con. Well that is how places like these make their money by you having to take their catering package of which they can charge a fortune, but this package was very reasonable. We obviously had choices and the price was determined by your food choice and the number of guests.

I believe we had a total of around two hundred guests on our wedding and we tried to accommodate as many from each family as we could, and with that number we got a very good price per head on the catering from the establishment that was offering us their place. The only thing was that, this hall was actually fully booked in advance for another one and half years so there was no space for us to have our wedding and especially the date we wanted to get married. Anyway, all we could do is leave it with them to see if there would be any cancellations and to give us a call and let us know. In the meantime, we would continue to search for more locations. After a few weeks we received a call from the management of the hall and they said they got a cancellation and would we be interested? We immediately said yes and we would take the date but we had to drive to them as soon as we could put down our deposit to secure the date or they would have to let it open to others. We jumped in our car and went down and booked our hall. Yippee, we were on our way now, to plan the rest of the wedding.

We still had like eight months till the date we planned with the hall and we just got our heads down in saving more money and planning the other details. I will not take you through the whole wedding planning thing but will just fast forward to the days leading up to the wedding. As like many family events, there was always going to be disagreements in some decisions that we make and we were continuously being remembered that the place we choose is very far away and it's not fair for my family to travel away up there and even though we were hiring a bus to pick up each family and drop them home, there was still some complaining. I was getting a headache with trying to please everybody and at the same time, trying to budget our finances to pay all the bills and make sure we were getting the best prices we could for the services we were asking for. It was not like we didn't have enough money or we were pretty tight, it was just that I didn't want to go overboard on something if we didn't have too, but my fiancé wanted the best wedding, so that's what mattered. I must be honest to say that what she had arranged was pretty amazing and she got really good prices as well, so we were not too bad I think, although others may not quite agree. We spent around fifteen thousand pounds equivalent to around thirty thousand dollars in 1997 which I think, was quite a lot of money at that time. Well, the lead up to the wedding was getting pretty stressful making sure everything was all in place and everybody was all taking care of. It was quite an amazing thing, to orchestrate your own wedding; you don't really seem to realize how many things have to all come together at the same time for a successful wedding. I was getting so nervous in case I messed anything up, not for the fact that I was getting married, but so fearful if I messed any of the wedding up for my fiancé, as I knew, what she would be like, after all her planning and preparation and especially, it is her big wedding day.

I just thank God as I look back and everything went as planned, and it was such a great day, I saw the joy in both families as they mingled together and celebrated the wedding of one of the children, and it brought together two different families from two very diverse backgrounds. It was now official; we were Mr. and Mrs. Mc Fadyen and heading towards a new life as a married couple on the next journey of life together. We thought that we were going to now settle down, buy a big fancy house, get a couple of wee sports cars, go a couple of holidays every year like we have been doing, continue the partying and going to bars and clubs and leading our selfish lifestyles. That was one thing that we were consistent on in our relationship and that was, the partying part. We loved to go out and get drunk at every opportunity we could. We never thought about having kids as this would have totally spoiled our selfish lifestyle, all we wanted was to have more and more money to feed our materialistic wants. However, there was going to be a dramatic change of event for us in the next few months that we could never had planned or wanted. We loved going our holidays, sometimes twice a year and all our friends knew exactly how we enjoyed them, they knew that our holidays meant so much to us as it was our time to get away from work, families and all the other things in life that annoy us. So one time our friends told us to go to a place called Dubai, it is a city in the United Arab Emirates which is part of the Arabian Gulf. When you think of an Arab country you automatically think of sand and rules. Places like Saudi Arabia are known for its strict Muslim rules and laws and even punishments, so it is not a very appealing place to think about going on holiday is it? Well, we thought the same thing when we heard where Dubai was, we had no interest in going there at all, as we thought that we couldn't drink or party as it was against their religion. Our friends came back from spending two weeks in Dubai and said it was absolutely amazing and it was one of the best holidays they had ever been. We thought they were crazy, how could you possibly enjoy a holiday in the desert and among people who are so strict and don't let you drink or party? Well, we couldn't have been so wrong, after looking up Dubai on the internet and going into to various travel agencies to get proper information about the place, we were convinced that it wasn't what we thought. But still, we weren't too sure if it would suit our party lifestyle and allow us to be crazy with alcohol the way we used to be when we're on vacation.

We took a chance and we booked up for two weeks and gave it a shot. We were pretty scared in the event that it might turn out rubbish and we would have wasted all of our money and time off work, but what could we do, we booked it and paid the money so, there was no turning back now. We went their expecting the worse and we were totally amazed at how westernized it was. I mean, it had everything you could ever want. I counted over one hundred bars and clubs with so many choices of restaurants, and with fantastic beaches and not to mention the weather was absolutely fantastic. We loved the sun so much as this is what our holidays were all about, partying like a rock star and coming back with a great sun tan to show off to everyone that you were on holiday. As we were party goers it wasn't that difficult to meet other British or expats, as were are called, because all the expats went out and partied the nights away. It is our hobby. So we met up with many people and built so many friends very quickly, and that is what makes our holidays enjoyable. There was a great expat community over in Dubai and they were always out at the clubs, so we could always tag along with some of them and just make the night enjoyable, we would stay out to like three or four in the morning unless, we went back to somebody's house to have a party and then wake up bright and early to hit the pool or the beach, for our daily dose of sun burn. We were having a ball and we loved every single minute of being in Dubai. I even played soccer on the beach with some friends we met and it was amazing, it just felt like you were in Scotland except with loads of sunshine and beaches. Well, after two weeks of heavy drinking and getting sun burn it was time to head back home, head back to bonnie Scotland and get on with our new life as husband and wife. We always hated going back to the cold and the rain and the thought of work, but it was our life, we had no choice.

Here comes the bang! One day we were so fed up with the normal routine life in Scotland and just doing the same old same old, my wife came up with an absolutely crazy and ridiculous idea; she asked me what do I think about going to Dubai? I said, "We are just back, and you want to go again? Plus we have used up all our holidays and we have no more to take, it would mean losing another two weeks' salary if we done that". She laughed and said, "Not on holiday, but to live and work there". Well my heart stopped a few beats and my mouth was opened wide and just stared at her with shock. At that moment, I couldn't say what I was feeling except for sheer amazement, at such an idea, obviously when I took it in after a few minutes, I immediately went on the defense and completely shouldered it to the side lines with ridiculous examples of how we would struggle and fail and end up with nothing. I would start running through all the negative aspects of leaving our home town and our great jobs for a move to a place where we don't know, and with people we don't know and with no knowledge of the working environment over there. There were so many reasons for me not to do such a thing plus I didn't want to think about leaving my family and I just used any excuse under the sun to get this idea out of her head. It worked for a short time and then she came back at me again with the positive sides of the idea like, we would be living in the sunshine all year round, we would be partying when we wanted and would be hanging around in shorts and tee-shirts most times. We already made some great friends to mix with and they would help us get settled and all that. I would counteract again with negatives and the most important aspect of both of us not having a job to go to, so we would soon run out of money. She would still try to convince me that those friends we met would get us something to start with and we can progress from there. This conversation would go on and on and on and the more it went on, the more she was convincing me or winning the battle of positive against negative. I would again use our house and cars and job security as weapons for us not to leave Scotland, to go to an Arab country where our rights are like next to zero, but she was determined and she kept pushing it. Well, like always, I gave in at the end, I decided to agree with her idea and take a chance and give up everything we had in order to go abroad. Indeed, everyone thought we were crazy to give up great jobs and our great lifestyle and not to mention our families, for a life in a place we hardly know, except the bars in which we spent most of our time in. My family was absolutely against it, and they made it quiet clear to me their thoughts on the subject. My Mum and Dad were so afraid for us to go there as they always hear bad things about the Middle East and that it wasn't the place for us to go. They would try to negotiate and advise us to go to Australia, Canada or even the United States, but we had made our decision and that was it. This was ultimately, the biggest decision we were making in our whole life after the decision to get married of course. But this was a risk and a very dangerous risk as we were giving up our livelihood for something that we were not sure was there, or we can even make happen, but we were determined to go and give it a try. We had plenty of money to get us through for about a year, pretty comfortably and then we would assess the situation after that, if it wasn't working out. We knew we could always come back to my parent's house and live with them in the worst case scenario and they even made it clear if we want to come back we are more than welcome to stay with them. That was my parents' idea to have us back home so that they could keep an eye on us. It was pretty funny and nice of them, but I knew exactly what their tactics were. Well, we went into action immediately and started planning the whole departure process and looked into how long we can visit as tourists, and how we go about getting jobs and what happens with our tax in the UK, and all those things you need to be aware of.

We started with a goal, and the goal was to leave the UK around a certain date in August. I can't remember the exact date but we were very specific and just gave ourselves a deadline. Without a goal and plan, we would probably get cold feet and back out, as that is normally what happens when we get ideas and don't put specific tasks assigned to it with a certain time frame. So we made ours and we were so determined that we went to the travel agent and booked our tickets in order for us to make it a reality. We did this because, once we spend money on tickets then there is no way we will lose that money, so we knew at that point, this was really happening. So, the 'heat is on' as they say and time is moving, so we had many things to do and accomplish, so we can go away pretty much stress free and not carrying too much baggage with us. In other words, not worrying about too many things we are leaving behind. We only had about two months to conduct all of our business in order to leave in a pretty organized manner, we started working out our finances, how much we have, how much we are willing to spend on a daily basis, what our budget was, what is our limitations, what duration can we withstand the constant spending without revenue coming back in. These are just simple methods of working your budget as we do here on a daily, weekly or monthly basis, whether it be for grocery shopping, clothes shopping, entertainment, hobbies etc. etc.

We spent only about a week working out our finances and we thought we were pretty solid and ready on that side. So next, we looked at our house and furniture's and materials that we gathered up over the years and both of us agreed to sell everything. We did a fantastic job of selling all our stuffs, our friends bought a lot of things from us and then we went to the barrow-lands to sell stuffs on the weekends. Remember what happened in the barrow-land? It was in that place where I met my wife. So this was very familiar territory for us and I knew in my mind that my wife would do brilliant, as she could sell ice to the Eskimos and sand to the Arabs. So after a few weekend stunts at the markets and selling to our friends and neighbors we got rid of all the smaller items and the main electrical like televisions, music system, DVD players and all those type of items. The biggest concern for us was the house and the car, as this was the biggest commodities we had that could possible hinder us. But we remained focus with the objective of leaving on the date we bought the tickets. We were very lucky at that time, as a young couple who just had a baby was looking for a small 2 bedroom house to start their new life together as a family, and our house fitted them perfectly. Our house was in fantastic shape, it was immaculate and we done some internal remodeling like, I fitted a complete shower system inside a closet (obviously, clothes are not there anymore) and it was tiles throughout, it was a showpiece. We installed new central heating system, brand new fitted kitchen, brand new bathroom suite upstairs, redecorated the whole house and put in double glazing windows, so all that couple had to do, was walk in and they would be settling immediately and would have no major works needing done. I mean, this wee house was fantastic for them. So it happened, we sold the house within three weeks and then it was just our car. Things were moving on so well and we were starting to now realize that this is it, we are actually going to leave our home, our families, and our country and go abroad and search for greener pastures.

Only two things left to do, the first one was to sell our car of which was easy, as we had no debt to pay so what we sell it for cash in our pocket, so we knew if it came to the crunch we can sell it very cheap for a quick sale. The second one was to tell our company that we were going to resign and that was going to be the hard part. The thing about resigning was that, if we do it too early, then the company may decide to let us go immediately and then, we would lose potential salary. So we had to plan it carefully like give them a couple of weeks notice only. We both gave two week's notice period, as legally we only need to give one week, but we thought we would be nice to them as we both liked our company a lot. Our companies were shocked, but at the same time very happy for us that we were still young and making a very brave decision to walk away from a good environment that we had created for ourselves. So first thing was the car, we advertised in the magazines and newspapers and even in the grocery malls, and low and behold we got it sold within one week. So to us, everything was falling into place and we believe that this was clarification to us that it was meant to happen because, all things were falling into place as we needed them to. We did make one stipulation to the new owner that we cannot sell it to him before a certain date to enable us to still drive around and do our business, and they agreed. Next was the jobs, this was scary as I never told an employer that I was leaving to go abroad, it was very difficult but still had to be done. So I did it and so did my wife and we were so relieved when it was over. Now it is really kicking in, the reality of what we planned is coming to light and that were heading off to sunny Dubai. It was only two weeks to go before we were heading off into the sands of the Middle East, and we were getting nervous and excited at the same time, our nerves were starting to kick in and we kept saying to each other, "Are we doing the right thing? What if it doesn't work? What if we can't get jobs then everyone will laugh at us". All sorts of negative things start coming into your mind and it's the same with our Christian walk with God. On occasions, you will be faced with decisions that will put you right in the spotlight, and you will have your doubts and your fears of failure, or disappointment, of what others may think of you, if you mess things up, or if you don't reach certain expectations. That is why we know that we can trust our God, as 'He knows the plans He has for us, plans to prosper us and not to harm us, plans to give us a hope and a future'. But not having God in our lives made us depend only on our own strengths and our own works. Sometimes God is so gracious and considerate that He allows us to do things our way, as there is a purpose behind everything we do. There is a reason for all our actions, our decisions, our desires that He watches us make or plan. God already knows what the outcome is going to be, but just wants us to experience the aspect of us trying so hard to make things work that suit us, that is tailored for us and only us, because that is what we want for our wee selfish life and then He comes in, and makes it much more easier and sensible, if we let Him. God knew exactly our intension of going to Dubai, He knew that we wanted greener pastures, more money, great lifestyle in the sun, party as much as we like and have great cars and all that material stuff and live a 'show off' lifestyle. He also knew what would be lying ahead for us over there and that we would eventually fall into the trap of our selfishness, greed, ignorance, prideful and other sinful and shameful attributes. This is not to ridicule Dubai or any people living and working there, not at all, this is just to let you know how God already knows me and my wife and what would become of us before we even set foot in the place. I still have many friends there and I love the place to this day and would embrace the opportunity of going back there to live, but within a different environment and attitude. You will find that as we journey on, through this chapter. So when God puts you in a situation where you must make a decision of which can make a huge difference in your life or make an impact on you and/or your family, or in the lives of others then always ask for His wisdom and read the word of God, and then, He will direct your paths. Whatever God sets you up for, and then be assured that He is not doing it so you can fail. He knows exactly why He wants you, and puts you there. But in our own case, we made our own decisions that were focused on us and us alone, what we wanted, what we liked, what we, what we and what we. 'What we' is not a very good way of making an impact in the life of others, unless it is completely directed with the best intentions and motives that would be beneficial not for you, but for them. Even though we were asked many times by our family and friends not to give up this settled life that 'we' had, this already established career, this pretty good status that 'we' had, 'we' only thought of 'we'. 'We' still did what 'we' wanted to do, 'we' still went ahead with the plans that 'we' made and the rest, well, we couldn't really care what happens because we were going to do what we wanted and that was final.

The time had come, we were down to the last days of packing and preparing our stuffs, getting our bank details all together and working out all our personal things we had to change, or close out, or deal with. It was really getting exciting as we continually focused on the bright side of the decision, the positive side being in the beaches, sunshine, partying, friends we already met, no more cold winter rains, or fierce winds blowing in your face every day. This was keeping us focused more and more as we were dealing with the negative side coming from the family and some friends at this end. I will seriously miss my family and friends. I always loved to just be able to visit my family when I needed or wanted to. I will definitely miss my best friend, Billy and his family. I worked with Billy for so long, and I was very close to his family, Joan, Michelle, Nicola and Stephanie. I never met a family who cared so much to each other, who went out their way to help others, going extra mile to help others in need. The compassion, kindness and generosity of these guys' hearts were remarkable. I had known and watched Billy and Joan's girls grow since they were babies. And they are such loving and respectful girls now. I see them all grown up and living their lives. I will forever be thankful for their wonderful friend-ship and support. So we did it, we were on the plane and heading to the Middle East to build a new life for ourselves. The trip was amazing and the flight attendants were absolutely fantastic, they were so friendly, helpful, courteous and pleasant and met every need that we had, so we were off to a great start. We still asked each other, "Are we really doing the right thing?" I guess we were getting really nervous, but we just had to stay positive and make it happen. It was a very strange feeling once we were going through immigration knowing that we only had three months to get a job or we had to leave again. We already booked our apartment so we knew we would be getting picked up at the airport and once we got to the hotel we just jumped up and down with excitement, we unpacked our stuff and right away went out to party. We set-tled very quickly and the first couple of weeks we just partied and enjoying ourselves, making the most of our time going to beaches, water parks, going for BBQ's that people would invite us too, and just meet loads of people at restaurants and bars. Although we were spending money and not making any, we weren't thinking of that part, yet. Our money was getting a little low with the apart-ment costs and all the partying that we were doing we still didn't panic as we knew, we could just send some more money from our bank account in Scotland. Things got working for us very quickly, I joined a local soccer club called 'The Patriots' and it was a mixture of Scottish, English, European guys whom we got to know pretty well and some of them became our very close friends. One of the guys worked as a 'recruitment consultant' and he tried to get me a job then after the third week we were there, he told me that he got another job and that his job was vacant and asked if I wanted to try being a 'recruitment consultant'. I never knew how to interview people for positions or even have a clue how to advertise and all that stuff so, I said not really. But he persuaded me to because, when I have knowledge of the market and companies out there looking for people, then I might find a better job for myself. That was a really a nice and positive way of putting it across to me, so I said why not, it will also give us a salary which would be helpful. So I went for the interview and the boss liked me and offered me the job immediately. So that was it for me, this was the beginning, and now we knew that all we need now is for my wife to get a job. I was completely shocked and amazed for in Dubai, it is really not what you know, but who you know. We were just down at the soccer field playing and chatting and having beers with the boys and then I met another Scottish guy who played with our team but he wasn't a regular as he lived in Jeddah, Saudi Arabia so he just played when he came to Dubai. So one of the guys on our team was a close friend of his so he introduced me to him and we got on well immediately, being Scottish and both of us liked Glasgow Celtic so we hit it off. So we got chatting about work and what we both do and why are we in Dubai and all that stuff. To my amazement he was a director for a company in Jeddah which had the franchise for a huge company and he was planning to open a store in Dubai and needed a store manager to set it up and manage it. Well, my ears popped up and did not hesitate in telling him about my wife. He was very interested in her and had us arrange to meet him the next day for a coffee so he would speak to my wife and see if she could be considered for the position.

My wife was so excited and couldn't wait to meet him even if she never had management experience of setting up and managing a proper shop. She had the passion, desire and confidence in herself that if she put her mind and talents to a thing, then she will be successful. This is so true even when we are going through this journey of life with God, that even though you may think you are not qualified to be in a ministry, or qualified to be a part of a leadership group, or even be a bible study leader, you always have to remember that our strength, our courage, our confidence comes from the Lord and that He won't give us something we can't handle. Yes, it may be a rather difficult task and we are not really prepared for it, or even wanting to do or be a part of, but His grace is sufficient, and His plans are not our plans. One thing we will know for sure is that whatever He puts in our way, or allows us to go through an experience; He has a special purpose for us to excel through that situation. Although we were on our own path in those days and just got through life by our own abilities and desires, God is still allowing us to experience areas in our life, and allows us to go down those paths that we feel we need and want, so we can eventually learn our lesson. The coffee meeting went great and this director was pleased with my wife so much, that he gave her a proper interview a couple of days later and she walked away with the position. Wow, what a start, both us got jobs within a month and we were on the road to living abroad and experiencing life as an 'expat'. So from there on, things were great. We got settled quickly and moved into a small apartment and then just partied more and more and met more friends and really enjoyed our lifestyle. My wife started in her job after a few weeks and then started all the preparation for the store set up and big opening day, so she was so excited and she would work like crazy because this was her little baby, she had to prove herself to this director to assure him, he never made a mistake employing her over more qualified candidates.

One thing my wife does well is selling, with a great ability for display, so she was in her element when the shop was being set up as she was doing all the window displays and arranging where all things should be in the shop. After a few months I found another job with a rental company doing what my friend said. I was trying to find people to fill positions and then I was the one who got offered this position due to there was no suitable candidates in the market. So here I go, jumping ship to work for this company and the great thing was that, they gave me more salary, housing allowance, fully expensed car, and other benefits and I was amazed, so I jumped at the offer and started within two weeks of my interview. We were so excited that both of us were now working and we were earning good money, more than what we were getting back home. My wife was earning more than me so she was happy and always rubbed it in my face. Didn't bother me at all as I said to her to keep earning the big money and I can just retire. We really loved Dubai and the fact that we settled very quickly allowed us not to get home sick, it kept our attention away from thinking about our families because on most occasions that is what normally affects people and they end up going back home. We had no intention of going back to the cold wet Scotland and would do what we could to make things work out in Dubai. After about two years working with this rental company and meeting lots of new people and getting myself around with networking and business functions, I was offered another position with a bigger company. I was starting to make a mark in the market place and people were noticing my performance and how I conducted myself around the business arena. This offer was a fantastic opportunity for me to grow in my career and at the same time earn even more money and get better benefits. My wife was still going strong in her store, she was beating all sorts of budget and revenues that were set for her to achieve so she was in good standing with her boss. But at the same time she was spending a lot more time at her work and then going for drinks after work with her boss of which, was not an issue to me as you need to stick in with the boss, right? Well I was really naïve in my relationship with my wife and basically allowed her to do whatever she wanted as I hated fighting or arguing, so I would take the peaceful way out and agree to everything she wanted. Sometimes it may be the right way and sometimes it may be the wrong way, it seemed to work out the wrong way for me. When she went out drinking with her boss, she would come home very early in the morning but to me, it was ok, as I knew it was strictly work related and I trusted her with my whole life. As I mentioned in the earlier chapters, I could trust my wife with my life, there was no reason for me to ever doubt she would do anything that would hurt me or damage our marriage, as I knew she was always a very straight forward girl and hates lying.

There was some of my friends that would come to me and tell me that they saw my wife out with her boss and they were very friendly and really looking as if they were close to each other, meaning that people would think that they were a couple, like boyfriend and girlfriend. I never paid any attention to them and just said that she is enjoying herself and it is her boss, she has to entertain him and keep things good. Although, I was starting to wonder what if, but then I just shrugged it off and assured myself that she would never be so stupid and do anything with him, she knows the consequences of messing around in her marriage. But there was something inside me telling me to ask her if everything was ok and was there anything I should know or be worried about. But I knew, if I asked her this then she would go crazy with me and it would cause a big argument, but still, I had to ask, so I did. Man, I was so right, she flew of the handle at me and started shouting and cursing and really losing her head, she actually walked out the house and never came back for a few hours as she was really upset with me, asking her such a thing. Once I saw her reaction and her disgust in me by doubting her trust, I knew I made a mistake and was really kicking myself for asking and causing this argument. Once she came back in I apologized so many times and said I was really sorry, but I was just concerned and missed being with her during these times she is with her boss and that I was getting a bit jealous. She really was so hurt and told me that she would never do that to me, and hurt me or ruin our marriage. She said that she loved me so much but sometimes she needs to be with her boss to keep on the good side with him and keep their working relationship strong so she can get better benefits and all that stuff. Well after that, I never questioned her again and she continued to be out with her boss on every occasion he visited Dubai, so I let it go and let her do what she needed to do.

Well things took a turn for the worse for me as when I joined this new company, it was a competitor of the company I was previously working for. So in Dubai and most Arab countries the rule is that, you don't go and work for the competitor as your old boss will not be too happy and they can insist on you receiving a punishment. This punishment is by putting a ban on your passport so that you cannot work in the country for at least six months, by allowing this to happen it gives your previous company time to get a replacement for you and to recover from what business you may take away from them and give to your new employer. Makes sense really, but can be unfair to individuals who are just trying to better themselves and go up the ladder in the business world. In my situation, it turned out nasty, my previous employer took my resignation really bad and once he knew I was going to a competitor, he made my life rather difficult and made sure that I would get a ban on my passport so that I needed to leave Dubai. He really done it good style as he managed to get a one year ban on my passport explaining to the labor department and authorities that it would take him one full year to recover for the business that I would be taking away from his company, and giving to his competitor.

Well for me, it was a terrible result of me trying to better myself but at the same time the greed for money and recognition got the better of me. I solely done this for the money and benefits that I would be receiving and I didn't; really put any thought into what would be the outcome or damage, done to my previous employer, after all, we are all in business for the money right? So with my selfishness and lack of compassion and understanding for my previous boss I look back, now and say that I deserved this punishment although I never thought that, at the time of getting it. The end result for me was that I had to leave Dubai for one full year before I could return and work there, that was a pretty shocking position to be in, considering that my wife would still be there working and could mean she has to give up her job and follow me wherever I may have to go. I tried to push my new employer in getting this ban on my passport lifted as they had ensured me that they can do this and I wouldn't have to leave the country. Sorry to say, that this was not the case, once you have a ban on your passport there is nothing an employer can do unless, your company is owned by a very high up local businessman or high up official in the government, or royal family member, and I was not a part of any of those areas. So here comes the painful part, after I completed my ninety day notice period I would then be escorted to the airport by the company public relations officer and he made sure that a red stamp was put on my passport detailing, that I was not allowed back in to Dubai for a one year period. During my ninety days notice period, my wife and I were very worried as to what our plans were going to be, now that this had happened. We never had many options except for her to follow me, wait for me to return, or we go back to the UK. The UK was really the very last option as we would be going back to no jobs, no house, no cars, nothing, and back to the miserable weather conditions. So we decided that I would go ahead to Bahrain, another area in the Arabian Gulf where I was tasked of setting up a new business there for my new employer and manage it. Well, if it wasn't hard enough to give up my life in Dubai and leave my wife behind, they also asked me to start a new business of which, I had no idea about or how to start. But I guess I had no choice to go there and do what I had to do. After all, they did promise me that I can come back after my one year ban was lifted on my passport, so it shouldn't be that difficult and my wife was going to follow me after I got settled and all that. It was such devastation for us, to be in this situation after everything was going so well for us and we were really settled in Dubai. This is a reminder for all of us that God can bless you with a job, or places you in a certain company in a certain area where He obviously has plans for you and you should just go with the flow. But, in many cases and especially in my case, we always want the better things in life, we always want bigger things, we always want more money, more salary, more benefits for ourselves and our family, correct? You may ask, what is wrong with that? Is that not what we are supposed to do in life, progress further in our career and get as much as we possibly can? I would say I believe that could be our idea, but is that Gods idea? Is that Gods plan for us to move around and look for better jobs that pay better money without looking into the consequences or circumstances that you will be putting yourself or your family through? I know we work for money and to get looked after, but I found out later in life that maybe I am not supposed to be that director that I so badly want to be, maybe I am not supposed to be in that high leadership position, maybe I am not supposed to receive that six figure salary, maybe God has something bigger and better for me further down the road and He is just waiting to see how I handle the small trials that he is throwing my way first, before He reveals His true plans for me. I never thought of what effect it would have on my old boss by me leaving and going to a competitor, but I soon found out the hard way. At the same time, I wasn't really caring as all I was thinking about was my benefits and what a difference it would make in our lives, it would bring me up to the level of my wife which I was very happy about. I was now at her level with the salary range, although I got more benefits than her as she only got a salary, a car allowance, and a small housing allowance that went straight into her pocket, as my new company would be paying for our house.

I went off to Bahrain and got on with my task ahead and started knocking doors to build up our business and get things in motion. Again, the best thing for me was to get involved in the local expat community. So I joined the 'British Business Group' and got net-working in there to meet people and find out who does what and what is happening in the market place. It wasn't too long before I built up friendships with people who were living there for a very long time and they would update me with what was going on, and who I should be speaking to, for potential business. I was doing the usual business stuff by taking people out to the bars and enter-taining them in order to build a relationship and get to know who will be giving me business, and at the same time, getting drunk with them and enjoying my time there, as I normally did in Dubai. My wife was ok with staying in Dubai for the meantime and then, it was after about six months she decided that we needed to be together and wanted to join me, so she did. She packed up her job and came over and stayed in Bahrain. It was great, we had a great time there but it ended after the year as planned. We came back to Dubai and I got settled with my company as agreed and we got a new apartment and got settled again, the biggest pain for us was the packing and unpacking that becomes so stressful and you get annoyed and frustrated as some of your personal items always got broken or damaged, and you have to then put in a claim and wait for the insurance company to pay out. But the issue was not the money, but your personal items being destroyed. I guess that is the price you must pay for moving around so many times and not being settled in one place.

So back to Dubai we come and we're just as excited as we were when we first got there from Scotland, and it was as if we had never left the place. We got settled very quickly and my wife got another job and we were all set. This time we were not leaving, we planned to stay and live there as long as we can. I started to travel locally around Dubai, building the business and getting to network with other expats who were either my friends from before I went to Bahrain, or I met them through soccer, or by other friends introducing them, as this is how business is done, not what you know, but who you know. Things were great, business was fantastic and we were growing and all was going as planned. My wife was settled and loving her job and we were so happy. I loved the soccer scene in Dubai, it was so competitive and really challenging and it really got you into shape. Although we were out drinking all the time, somehow we managed to still run around a couple of times a week for ninety minutes, but we felt like dying after the game. So what we always did after the game was have a few beers just to keep hydrated, water was not an option, we needed the beer. Anyway, this was now our fourth year in the Middle East and third year in Dubai, we covered a lot of ground in Dubai in relation to night life, entertainment, social scene and all that, we went on desert safari in the sand dunes, sand boarding, dune bugging, BBQ's, hit the beaches every weekend, traveled around the seven emirates and just lived a life of luxury while my family were back in Scotland and not receiving anything from their beloved son and daughter in law. The more we were enjoying the life abroad and living a very comfortable life, the more we seemed to forget about what we left behind, 'our families'. Time seemed to pass by so quickly and before you knew it, you were years away from home and you missed out of so many aspects of being with your family, missing all the Christmas and birthday celebrations, anniversaries etc.

During one of the games of soccer, I was introduced to another new friend of who was in a similar business as us, they were just starting their business in Dubai and they were being funded and directed by their head office in Aberdeen, Scotland. This manager that I met at the game asked me to meet him for lunch during the week to see if we can do business together. Obviously I responded and made a time and place where we could meet. Once we agreed, he also mentioned that his boss is in town from Scotland and maybe he would like to come to the meeting also, I said, "No problem". The higher the better as I could maybe get a decision out of the big boss there and then to secure any potential opportunity that I could create with them. I was looking forward to it and already had my sales pitch lined up for them both. This was a young company and they were only in the market around six months in Dubai but were going strong in Scotland for around eight years or so and had a good reputation back there. I had no issue in dealing with them as I knew they would have the financial backing to pay their bills if we do business together. I was looking forward to the meeting, I met them in one of the top hotels in Dubai at the time, the Burj Al Arab, the fancy hotel that looks like a sail from a boat, the one that is out on the water and that was very famous as Tiger Woods arrived there in a helicopter and actually hit a golf ball of the roof of the hotel. I was as excited, as it was the first time I was in the hotel and I was amazed at the splendor of this world class venue. Anyway, I met these two businessmen and we got talking about what I do, and what they do, and then to my complete surprise instead of asking me to supply our services for their projects, they offered me a job. Well, I was stunned with this offer, and it took me by complete surprise and I was pretty shocked, as I never expected such a thing to happen during a business meeting. After a few minutes, I began to wonder if it really was a business meeting I was attending or maybe I was being set up. After I got over my shock I started asking a few questions of why they offered me a job when they don't really know me and how I work. They had covered their ground work by asking around in the market about me and the company I was working for, and got their information that way. I could understand this, as I was always very professional in doing business and very respectful in all aspects of my attitude to work and towards people in the market place, but to offer me a position without an in-depth knowledge of me and what my aspirations were was pretty courageous in my books. I got digging a little deeper and started to enquire more about this offer they put on the table and to my amazement they offered me a huge package to come and work for them, but the only issue was that it was, back in Scotland and not Dubai. Man, I was confused now as we had just started to build up our life in Dubai when this happens and I get offered a deal of a lifetime, and to even go back to my home land to live and work. I was really mixed up at this point as I had just met this managing director of what looks like a pretty successful and growing company who are looking to expand into the international business arena and they are offering a little sales guy like me a pot of gold to come and work for them. You know, I believe that our lives are really planned out for us and everything that happens to us, or is put in front of us, is for a reason and has a special purpose. I am convinced that meeting this manager at our soccer game was no accident, and I meeting the managing director of the company was no accident, and I believe that the offer that I had received before my very eyes was no accident and I believe me being offered a position to go back to my home land and work was no accident and I believe that the next part of this story happened, for a reason. I was going to have to do one of the hardest sales pitches in my short term as a sales man and that was pitch this idea of going back to Scotland to my wife, yes you got it, this was going to be a loser from the minute I said, "I was offered a job", because I knew that the first thing that would come out of her mouth is going to be, "Where?" And I was right she automatically asked me, where do they want me to work?

Once I explained to her it was in Scotland she was not interested one little bit due to the fact that we gave up everything we had in Scotland to come to Dubai in the first place, and now, we are thinking of going back to nothing and starting all over again, she was not pleased at all. As I was saying, all these situations that come before us, or we are faced with, are definite trial periods to see what we do, or how we handle them, or what out motives or intentions are. My first priority was always money, and how I can earn more and get more and this seemed to be falling right into my plan of progressing forward in the money part. After some long discussions and some serious arguments we both decided that we would give it a try and understood that if the worst came to the worse we can always jump on a plane and head back out to Dubai and find work as we have established a great reputation for ourselves and we would always walk away in a positive manner with our companies and were not a problem to them. I always believed in treating companies with respect since this is a small world we live in and you never know when you will meet the same people further down the road. This was certainly a challenging time for us in deciding to take a chance and go back home, it was also a step of courage knowing that we would be facing our families and friends and they would be kind of rubbing it in our face and maybe laughing at us because we were back to where we started from. So here we go with our new plans, another new direction on our journey, another new episode to add to the drama of our unsettled lives. Having only four years experience in sales, I was climbing up the ladder in my field and having accepted the position of 'National Sales Manager' for Scotland, I was heading in the right tracks for my career to sky rocket and meet my desired dream and goal of becoming a director by the age of forty years old. I was only thirty three and things seemed to be working towards me achieving this dream. When I told my family that I was returning to Scotland they were so excited, especially my parents, they were so overjoyed that they were preparing our room for us to stay with them. Here was going to be another drama point in where we would be staying as my parents were determined to have us stay with them, but my wife was not interested in this and wanted to stay with her parents. Here I was again, stuck in the middle of having to try and please my wife and at the same time hurt the feeling of my own parents and tell them that we won't be living with them. This was really tearing me apart and I was so hurt and annoyed at this and tried to persuade my wife to stay with my folks, but she was not having it, she really hated staying with my parents. So here I go, try to explain to my Mum and Dad why we are not going to be living with them and that we were going to live with my in-laws.

My Mum and Dad really were so upset at this decision and took it to heart, they felt really bad and were asking me what they had done to us that were so bad that we wouldn't come and live with them. I had no idea how to explain this except just to say that my wife wants to be with her parents, because she will work in Glasgow and to save her traveling every day up and down, and that it would save us money every week. Also the fact that I would be traveling all over Scotland and wouldn't be home much, she wants to be with her family to keep her company. I don't believe this was accepted by them and that they fell for these stories. They are not stupid, and they know when they are not being appreciated. I had to live with this and it was hurting me so bad that I couldn't stop thinking about how I wasn't telling them the truth just to fix a temporary situation. It is similar to our walk with God, we often find ourselves in situations where there will be a temporary fix in order for you to get through at that time, or to put the issue on the back burner for that moment, but it is not the right way to do it, or the right answer to solve the issue. We tend to go for the easy way out and not think about the long term effect that it may have, or effect it may have on others. You see friends, God always gives us a way out of every situation that He allows in our lives, God always allows a remedy to be used in order for a solution to be provided, and worked on for the better of all concerned, but it is always down to our choice and decision. I had the decision here, to tell the truth and face the facts that my wife hated living in Greenock and hated living with my parents and that she had no intention of being around them. I, as the man of the relationship had all the right to stand my ground and tell it as it was, and then make a decision as a man, but I never, I chickened out and opted for the easy method of telling lies and burying the truth under the carpet hoping, it never comes to light.

It happened, we started living with my in-laws up in Glasgow and I truly upset and broke the hearts of my parents, and I couldn't forgive myself for doing that to them. I regretted every single moment that I was not with them. I tell you the truth friends, my parents went out their way to raise the three of us and they raised us, on what they had at that time and yet, we can easily walk away from them in a single moment to live our selfish little lives. I tried to get down to see them as often as I could when I got back from traveling, but my wife always remained up in Glasgow and I always covered for her with some type of excuse as to why she is not with me. It was difficult at the beginning trying to get back to the way of life in Scotland, back to the weather, the people, the area, the working, but after a few weeks I loved it and it was great to be back with old friends and family. My wife landed a fantastic job in Glasgow city centre as a store manager for the same company that she worked for before in Dubai, so she was over the moon as we say, and she really got off to a great start. She got great benefits and was very highly thought of, by her boss because of her previous experience and success in Dubai. She got a really good reference from her old boss, the Scottish man who worked in Saudi Arabia, so that helped her a lot in getting her this job. We were back again earning great money and we soon settled back into saving up as much as we could and giving others nothing. Even though I had missed my family for all those years when I was in Dubai and I had earned good money there and saved a nice little amount, I was still the same old Sean, selfish and stingy with my money.

I noticed my attitude changing towards my family and I wasn't as respectful as I should have been, I wasn't really as caring as I used to be, or was brought up to be, and I believe it was because I was being spoiled by our lifestyle that we were used to in Dubai. Probably, the fact that we had a good savings account and that we were not going without anything, in other words, we could really buy what we wanted, when we wanted. It made our attitudes change. You see, once you get to a level where you feel that you are above others, or that you can do more than they can financially, it seems to give you a sense of power over them, or it lets you think, that you can rise above them in any situation. That is why in the book of James 4:6, but he gives us more grace. That is why scripture says: "God opposes the proud, but gives grace to the humble" (NIV Translation). Meaning, don't be so proud of yourself that it makes you believe you are better than others, always have and show humility, then you will always remain in a relationship with your Heavenly Father. God allows us to face these challenges of being more successful and not thinking about others but there may be a price to pay at a later day when He shows us the lesson to be learned. Oh, don't worry; my life lesson is coming very shortly as you will read in the next few pages. Once I arrived at the head office in Aberdeen, I was introduced to everybody by one of the sales managers of the firm who was told to show me around and make me feel comfortable with the surroundings. The people were great, very friendly and helpful and made me feel welcome, I guess that is what they were told to do, right? Anyway, I was staying there for the week in a hotel until they got me settled in and fixed up with my usual cell phone, laptop, business cards and the car. Man, when I was taken out to my car that I was given, I thought I was a partner in the company. The MD was the one who picked it up for me and took me out to show me. I could not believe the car he gave me, it was an Audi A6, fully loaded and it was brand new, straight out the wrapper. I felt as if I was the most important person in the company and it went straight to my head, I could feel the pride running through my veins, I could feel the importance within myself, meaning I believed I was the best salesman that ever walked into Aberdeen. Once you get to this status of feeling important and believing that you are much higher than others just because of the material possession you have, or have been given to use, then it is the start of your downfall. There was nothing that anyone could have said to me that would have made any difference to my life, I was on my own planet at this point, I was on cloud nine as they say, I was away with the stars, I couldn't wait to get out of this office and drive around and show off my new car. I wanted people to recognize me and acknowledge that I must be successful in order to drive around in a top of the range Audi. As I said, when pride kicks in, so does a lot of others things with it, and it begins with jealously, and it usually starts at home, or with the ones you work with, and it certainly was in my case. I started to feel the resentment from some of the colleagues in Aberdeen, and I could feel them talking about me and being spiteful towards me. I guess, this is normal in business as others don't like to see people better themselves or even, do better in their career or personal life. It wasn't too long before I started noticing the other co-workers in the office not really going out their way anymore to assist me or even try to make me feel welcome, and I knew why.

Jealousy is a very nasty and dangerous tool and most often gets used against innocent people just for the revenge or pleasure of others. I began to see the jealousy in certain people I was working with and it wasn't very nice at all. I decided to move down to the Glasgow office and use that as my base just to get away from the workers in Aberdeen. I informed my boss of this decision and he didn't mind at all, he basically gave me the freedom to do what I thought was right and would work for me and the company. My main responsibility was to build the business around Scotland but with international interest, meaning, get into the markets abroad within the oil & gas, petroleum and manufacturing industries and use my contacts to secure business deals. This was not a problem for me, as I had confidence in the service that I provide to my clients and the products or solutions that I sell. I never had a problem with people feeling this way about me, at the beginning, as I was on a mission to prove myself, and to become a hero within the organization, and the MD has stressed to me that he is looking for someone to really run with this business and make it grow, and that there was fantastic opportunities for the right people who are willing and able to make it happen, so I said to him, you are talking to the right guy, I am your man. I got off and running hitting the road and getting around all the companies that I knew, and did research on, trying to make new contacts and get to know the players. It was difficult as it wasn't like Dubai or Bahrain, where you can just walk in and talk to people, you always had to make appointments unless you really had a great relationship with them. The first month was hard and the second even harder, as I was again coming up against resistance from the workers in the Glasgow office. I couldn't believe the attitude of these people as I was here to help the business grow as a whole, and to be more profitable, which would be beneficial for all. After the second month, I had to have a talk with the local manager and ask for his assistance so I can help build the local business. I asked for a list of their clients and potential clients that they have worked with in the past two years, this was so I can look at their history and where I can add value, or see any potential opportunities to push on. Well, he would not give it to me and insisted that I get my own contacts. I mean c'mon, if someone is willing to help would you not want to give them some rope to see what they can produce? He wouldn't and made it quite clear to me that I was on my own and he was not willing to help me at all.

I did my own thing and built my own database of potential clientele and went around knocking on doors all around Scotland. Then, I managed to get an enquiry from a company whom I knew from Dubai but their head office was in Aberdeen so I drove up there to meet them and then we talked business. We got speaking with their people in Dubai and we came to a solution for their needs, and we needed to ship two of our large pumping units from Aberdeen to Dubai ASAP. I was very excited as this is exactly what I was employed to do, and we would be making a very nice profit margin on this project, as it would last for two years. I got a hold of my boss and told him the great news and I sat down and discussed this with the finance manager, and he was all for it and then for some reason my regional manager whom I reported to, pulled the plug on the project. I couldn't believe what I was seeing, I was doing what they employed me to do and then they stopped me from carrying out the order. They simply gave an excuse that they were not ready to service the international market and just wanted to stay local for the time being. I couldn't understand this, and sat with them and asked them exactly what they expected of me from this point, onwards. They just wanted me to be a local sales manager and to develop the business around Scotland and not to focus on international projects. I was completely shocked at this news and was not happy at all and from this, wondered what on earth my purpose in this company is? From here in, it was all downhill, my motivation level sank into the ground and my desire to succeed disappeared with my motivation, I was grounded, basically into nothing. I went home and for those next few days I was so unhappy and my wife was getting a little stressed and began to think about what I was going to do, she never saw me so disgusted like this and she knew I was not going to last much longer in this company. We spoke on several occasions about what was the best thing for me to do and what options did I have. I told her that I cannot stay in the company and I need to start looking for another job, and she was one hundred percent behind me. She was doing very well in her job and everything was going nice and smooth for her. My first thoughts was, to give my old boss a call in Dubai and chance my leg to see if he would take me back, although, I never held much hope for this after leaving him for another company. I tell you now, God is so great and His mercies are new every morning, because when I called my boss and told him my story and that I had made a big mistake in leaving, he immediately told me to get on a plane and come back to Dubai as my job was still open, can you believe that after three months my job was still vacant?

I lasted two more weeks before I went to the boss and handed in my resignation and told him that this is not what was explained to me and I didn't feel that I would be able to bring any value to the company, due to the fact that, they don't want to look for work internationally and also the fact that I believe, I wasn't welcome within the company and I don't want to be a problem to any of his other employees, so we both agreed it is best to go on my way. That was very sad news to me, my wife, and especially to my family as now, they would be worrying about us going back abroad. I know that they were going to miss us very much and wanted us to stay with them forever, parents are just like that, they want you to be around them, it brings joy to their hearts unless, you're a wee trouble maker like me, then they may be thankful that you're on your way out. Here we go again packing the bags and running off to greener pastures and the sunshine. It didn't take us long to make up our mind after me getting my old job back, it was like as soon as my boss put the phone down we booked a flight, no wasting time in the event he changed his mind and gave the job to someone else. My boss Ian was a fantastic guy and excellent leader of people who had a great vision to drive the business forward and continue to generate revenue. He was in sales for a long time and knew his stuff. I really enjoyed working under him and he took me under his wings to teach me the ropes. I believe Ian was glad to see me back in the company and let me get straight back into things, or I guess he would have not have offered me the job back, right? It was so cool as my first morning back to work I heard of a large construction project going on, so I paid a visit to the companies involved with the project and I walked out with a contract in my hand, and Ian was so happy as it made him look good in his choice to bring me back.

During the first few months back in Dubai I noticed something different about my wife. Her attitude changed from being a hot headed person who got easily angry if things never went her own way, to more of a calm person. She was not that excited if things were not going her way, or as she planned, or wanted them too. And she was more into listening to people and what they had to say, instead of telling them what they should know. I observed her attitude more than normal as I was shocked to see why she seemed to be a different person. After a few months, I had to ask her why her attitude has changed to be more relaxed and settled, and she said that she was tired of all the fighting and arguing and struggling to please people all the time and that she is just changing her ways. I know that this is not normal and definitely not her talking and I was still not convinced of why or how she can change like this. I was wondering maybe she got a fright one night and she realized that life is too short to keep having an aggressive attitude and that's why she changed, I mean, what else could it be? I asked her again what made her change, how did she change, or what is the reason for her change and she said, that she became a Christian...... Well, I will tell you exactly what I did when I heard those words, I laughed my head off. I really burst out laughing at her as I thought she was playing a game with me. I said to her that there is no way she is a Christian and it's impossible because of her attitude, bad temper and constant aggressiveness towards others, she assured me that she has changed for the better and that she is more in control of her actions and outbursts and she is more considerate to others feelings, and again, I just laughed and didn't believe her. I was shocked to hear this from her after all we had been through with listening to her father preach to us day after day, and we hated it so much. So there was no way I could believe that she would turn into the same as him, no way on this earth is that possible, as we loved our lives too much for her to turn away from the drinking, the partying, the materialism, the selfishness and the money, although, I did notice the changes in her attitude, I was still not convinced.

I watched her for weeks and weeks and never saw her getting angry once at anyone and never saw her getting excited when things didn't go as she planned or as we wanted them to, and I know what she would do normally, when things like that happened to us, believe me, it was a nightmare to deal with. But now, there is a change, there is something definite going on in her life that I was not convinced off, but the evidence was there, I was witnessing it with my own eyes and my own ears. If there was one thing that I thought was impossible to happen to my wife was her change of heart, her change of attitude in a more positive way because of our lifestyle and upbringing, but here it is right in front of me. So after a few months I started to see a consistency in her behavior and actions and I was so amazed at this that I actually liked it very much, it brought such a peace to our house and we got on a lot better as I had no reason to be concerned of her coming home from work angry or upset or wanting to have a go at me for no reason. During these months she would arrange to have what Christians call a 'bible study' night at our apartment and invited people from her work mostly and they would all gather together and do their activities. I would always make sure I was out of the apartment before they would arrive as I wanted nothing to do with these people and their Christianity. It was not for me, as I loved my selfish lifestyle and was not changing for no one, and I believed I wasn't a bad person anyway so, I didn't need to change. This went on for months and I would always question what they were doing and what they were up to during these gatherings. For some reason the longer she was meeting with them doing this 'bible study' thing, then the more I saw the continuous changed in her attitude and it was actually pretty cool to watch and experience. Then, there was times that she would ask me to go to church with them and I would point blank refuse, as I was not going anywhere near a church. I never was interested when I was a catholic in Scotland and I am surely not going to be interested when I am having a great life in Dubai, so I would constantly say no and tell her not to ask me again. For me to say no to my wife and have her not reply in an aggressive manner was absolutely fantastic to watch and be a part of, it was just peaceful and so relaxing to be amongst.

After months of constant observation of my wife's attitude and behavior, I would still be amazed at her change of attitude towards me and others and it was just a miracle that this could happen.

Although I didn't believe in God and all that spiritual stuff, I knew there must have been something that changed my wife from the person she was, to the person she was becoming, and that can't be through normal human experience. After many months of persuasion she eventually got me to attend church with her and her friends and I went along for the sake of just seeing what this church and Christianity thing was all about, although I had no intentions of being a part of their wee group things. So I went along with them to their church and I had the most stubbornness attitude you can ever imagine, I mean, I had my whole body armor and ready for a fight against this church thing, and I was determined not to even like any part of this God thing that they do. I was dressed in shorts and tee-shirt because the weather was fantastic and really hot and there was no reason for me to wear anything else, I was not interested in what they were all wearing or expected me to wear. I just went along for the curiosity and because she asked me to go with her. Once I was inside the church, I saw a lot of people setting up instruments and preparing chairs for people to sit, there were others getting different things all ready and they seemed to be very busy. I was really observing these people at this time and to be sure of what I was seeing in my wife, was actually true inside this church. Church service started and all I noticed was people singing, clapping their hands, raising their hands to honor their God and I was shocked to witness this kind of actions inside a church, as I thought a church was supposed to be all proper with singing hymns and making not making much noise, and be in control of the sound of their music and all that. These guys were very different as they were shouting, dancing, jumping up and down and raising their hands and swinging them in the air and then there was smiles and joy coming from their faces and the interesting thing was, that they looked as if they were really enjoying what they were doing. I must admit that I felt so welcomed inside the church and the church people were so friendly when they made conversation with me, it was like they really wanted to know me and chat with me. I still was skeptical about the whole Christian and church thing so I never paid much attention to the service or what the pastor guy was talking about, and quite frankly, I couldn't understand all that he was saying anyway. The church service lasted for two hours and I was pretty glad it was over, two hours in a church service was far too long for me as I was wasting valuable sunshine time inside there. I couldn't wait to get out in the sun and then get some food and hit the bar for a few beers with some friends. The funny thing was that my wife would always join me in having some beers so there was still something that wasn't right in my eyes. I remember back in Scotland when some of my friends were church goers they would also still go to the bars and drink and talk about naughty things to me, it was just the same scenario as I was witnessing with my wife.

A month or so went by, and then I was invited to church again by my wife and I was like, what's the point of going, I am not interested one little bit in this church thing and I could be down the beach having BBQ and beers with friends enjoying myself. Although the going to the bars things was still going on with my wife I was still noticing her attitude was remaining the same. She was peaceful, controlled and looked like her stress was reducing, so at least that part was consistent. I decided to join her again at church for the second time and as the first visit, I went dressed in my shorts and tee shirt with my Nike shoes. I was a simple guy who didn't like to over dress at the best of times, during the working week I had to wear a shirt and tie, so at nights and weekends I like to relax in my sports clothes or chill out clothes. I was the only one in the whole church who was wearing this kind of clothes as all the other church goers were very nicely dressed in their Sunday clothes even though church was on a Friday in Dubai, as Friday and Saturday was our days off. In church, the same stuff was going on with the singing, dancing, clapping of hands and sometimes a wee dance up and down the aisle by some of the people which I thought, was a little too much and over the top, but who am I to say it was wrong? I was still observing the actions of these church people and how they were truly worshiping their God of whom I never knew or had any intentions of knowing. I still couldn't wait to get out and get on with my life, get out and enjoy myself with my friends in the pub. This was the same old routine for me, I couldn't wait to get out of the church and carry on with my selfish lifestyle but what else was I supposed to do, this was my life, this was our choice to live in Dubai and do the things we wanted to do, to live the 'expat' lifestyle and enjoy life to the full. I was doing very well at work and enjoying working for the company as there was so much for me to learn in the business and from my colleagues. They were so experienced and knowledgeable in what they were doing and it just encouraged me all the more to learn from them. One of the most enjoyable aspects of my work was the people, I mean the people were so focused and committed to the vision that was put in front of them and they embraced it and bought into it with a passion. I had been working from the age of eighteen in companies and I was with great men and woman who loved what they were doing and it showed. But there was something special about this company I was working with. The excitement and enthusiasm among the people was one of the key indicators to me that these people really take joy and pride in their work and they are extremely focused on being successful. One of the other aspects of seeing the company grow and expand at an extremely fast pace was the willingness of them to work together as a team and achieve not only the company goals but their own individual goals. It was remarkable to witness and be a part of, such an amazing effort of a bunch of different nationalities, different cultures, different expertise, but with the same vision. I was doing quite well in my role as a 'Senior Sales Engineer' looking after existing customers, and at the same time, building new customers within all industries in the marketplace and the benefits were fantastic, so that helps right?

Another month past and I was invited again to church by my wife and let me tell you she was inviting me to go every week, but I told her to stop asking me all the time as it was annoying me and getting me angry. So she was very careful when to ask me to go with her, I believe it was all about timing for her. She knew when I was in a good mood and that was when she made her move it was very clever and sneaky I must say, but it worked. I agreed to go again for the third time and guess what I was wearing? Correct! Shorts, tee shirt and Nike shoes, my wife tried to convince me to wear pants and a nice shirt but there was no way I was into that and she knew not to push me too far or I would have just turned around and told her I won't be going. The people in the church must have been wondering why my wife couldn't get me to wear something nice like them, but now I know when I think about it and look back, they were not interested in my clothes, they were interested in me. There was no change from the last two times I went in regards to the singing, clapping, dancing and shouting out songs. I was always intrigued about the last part of the service as the pastor man would be talking and all the people would close their eyes and bow their heads as he spoke, and he would be talking and offering people a chance to come to the front of the altar. I had no idea what that was all about and found it pretty weird, but people were going down and as the pastor would put his hands on them and pray for them, some of the people would be crying so hard and people in the audience would also be crying, I was wondering what on earth is happening here? Why are all these adults crying because someone is praying for them? I really didn't have a clue what it was all about but something was happening and I felt pretty uncomfortable to be honest, but there was also something telling me that it was ok and not to be afraid, don't ask me what it was cause I have no idea, but there was something there allowing me to enjoy what was going on, although I didn't understand it.

It was summer time in 2001, and we decided to pay a visit home to Scotland just for a week for a little break. It was just a time to get away from Dubai and take a rest to see the family and chill out. Nothing much had changed back home and everything seemed ok except, for my father-in-law as he suffered from a muscle disease called 'Myasthenia Gravis' which is a muscle weakness and practically cripples you when it kicks in. He had it for a number of years but we didn't really care about him due to our focus on ourselves remember? It was all about us. When we went back, my in-laws were so excited about my wife turning Christian and they couldn't believe the change around in her attitude, as I mentioned before, she and her Dad could not get on at the best of times and would constantly argue and fight. So for them to see her in this new life changing event, it really brought joy to their hearts, and to have peace around the house was just amazing. That week, home was the most joyful experience we ever had with my in-laws and my wife even decided to visit my parents on a few occasions and they were absolutely shocked to see her come down so much in one week. There was a sign of a change in my wife that was so evident to others and they would always ask, "She has changed? Did something happen to her? She seems different". I would not admit what she had done to my parents that she became a 'born again Christian' as I didn't know how they would respond; I was kind of embarrassed, so I kept it a secret. I was really ashamed to mention it to anyone that my wife became a Christian as I was afraid of their response and actions. Anyway, after our week was up, we came back to Dubai and the funny thing happened to us. As we were heading up the stairs inside the terminal to go to customs clearance and you walk up the stairs and over to the immigration, you can see the whole of the Duty Free area where you buy all the gifts before you leave Dubai on your outward journey. And some of the workers that my wife knew were on duty. They had noticed us walking up the stairs and they ran to the window to greet us and during that short period they asked us to come to the church anniversary on a Friday, which was June 27th 2001.

Here we go again, I was immediately asked by my wife if I wanted to join them in their annual celebration. Wow, you could not imagine my response, I was like a raging bull, I just saw red. I don't know what happened to me at that point as I got so angry and upset with her and really said a lot of things that shouldn't have been said. My wife was so shocked at my words and attitude that she actually just said politely that it was ok if I don't go, and that she was sorry that she asked me. Let me tell you something that I experienced in my life, that when I was wanting to argue or fight with someone and they didn't retaliate or answer back or give you any more reason to continue the argument, then you simply stop what you're doing as it seems like there is no reason to fight carry it on. This is exactly what happened here in this situation, just because my wife wouldn't get into the argument then I ran out of things to say, not really like me to run out of things to say, but it happened. The moment we left the airport till we reached home and even as we went to sleep, I was in an awful mood and kept on trying to argue with my wife, and she would not fight back and all she would say is that it was ok, and she would just go by herself. This was fine with me and was working out to as I wanted, so I was happy but we went to sleep in a bad way as I never spoke to her and went to sleep in an angry mood. When we woke in the morning my wife would just get up and then start her preparation to get ready and go to the church celebration and you know what happened, when I woke up I had the strangest feeling in my heart and I was shocked to say to my wife that I will join her at the church celebration, yes, I actually told her that I wanted to go with her. Don't ask me what happened or what made me change my mind, because I don't have an answer, all I know is that, I couldn't refuse.

If you could see the expression on my wife then it would have painted a picture of a thousand words, she couldn't believe it and she would tell me not to joke about this as it is a serious event. I assured her that I was serious and that I was going with her. I explained to her that I have no idea why I want to go, but I just know I am going. She wouldn't believe me until I actually got ready and arrived at the hotel where the event was being held. I was pretty nervous going into the event and as usual had every intention of just sitting and not talking to anyone and just be an observer like I did on the previous Sundays at the church. Have a guess what I was wearing? You got it. Shorts, a tee shirt and my Nike running shoes were my church gear. Not the most appropriate thing to wear to a church annual celebration but again, I was not there to impress, and not there to really take part, just showing up to support my wife, I think. When we arrived I noticed everyone was very well dressed and it was like a very well organized and planned event. I began to feel a little uncomfortable with my dress wear and started to think that people would start talking about me, so I was just waiting for the first one to say something about what I was wearing and I was out of there like a shot. But it never happened, not one person made any comment towards me as they were just so joyful to see me attend the event. I was actually pretty shy because there was so many people there and the place was huge, it was held inside one of the nice hotel in Dubai as they rented out a special hall for the event. I had never seen so many people in one place ready to worship their God. It all started with a couple of songs and then a prayer was said to open the event like they did in church and then more songs and the people were all getting into the spirit of things as they say, and it became very lively and entertaining. I was starting to clap my hands a little, not swinging them up in the air or anything but just clapping for the sake of clapping and I certainly wasn't jumping up and down like some people were. The funny thing I noticed was that people were acting the exact same as they did during church, the singing, clapping and raising of hands along with the shouting, this made me realize that there was a consistency among this behavior or worship, as it was called. After a long session of singing songs they went into their program of events as there was a few special numbers or skids as they call them, where certain people would go in front and carry out a play or act out a scene of which was very entertaining and well orchestrated. I was really impressed with their program and it really touched my heart, whatever kind of heart I had, but never the less, it made me feel relaxed and allowed me to focus on the rest of the event.

The whole event really was going very fast, so I was happy it was almost over so I can get out and do my normal routine. Little did I know that I was in for a huge ENCOUNTER? As the event was coming to the end, again the band were playing very soft music and the people were all bowing their heads to the certain songs and ones were down on their knees, and I witness people crying again and crying out loud, really loud and I was like, "Oh no, not again, what is this all about". I was just looking around and watching everyone and observing as I normally did, and then the pastor who was at the front of the stage area, his name is Pastor Rene, gave an opportunity for people to come down the front and he would pray for them. This was the most uncomfortable moment for me as I didn't really get what it was all about and never really believed in what was going on. I knew by asking my wife that people were offered to give their lives to God and that was their way of declaring it and receiving him into their hearts. While I was watching people going forward and giving their hearts to God, the music was so powerful that it started to do something in my heart. It started to really hit me and as I was watching these people go in front, I would start to cry. I mean the tears were rolling down my face and my heart was pounding like a drum and it was becoming so unbearable to stand.

I was trying to fight whatever this was that was happening to me, trying to ignore the fact that maybe God was touching my heart and speaking to me, whatever that meant. As the music continued and Pastor would still ask people to come in front, I was not really paying much attention to anything but trying to stop what was happening and then I felt a hand on my back pushing me to go in front. So I looked around to see who was touching me and you won't believe it, there was nobody behind me close enough to touch me and this was amazing. Here I am, standing with tears strolling down my face and my heart ready to burst and with a Hand on my back pushing me forward. I didn't know what was going on except all I knew was that, I am going down there in front to give my heart to Jesus. I was still resisting this, but my heart was just getting heavier and heavier and the tears more and more, and that Hand was still guiding me forward, so I touched my wife and I looked at her and she was crying too. I said to her that I am going forward and she was speechless and couldn't even do anything, she just stood there in amazement. Well I done it, I walked down to that altar and I was crying like a baby and even though I wasn't sure of what was happening, one thing I knew was that, this was real, this was no show or performance to impress people. It was really happening to me. I was just about to give my life over to Jesus Christ and accept that I was a sinner and had fallen short of the glory of God. It sure was. I said the sinner's prayer with those other people beside me and maybe even some that was in the crowd that maybe was too shy to come forward, but it happened. I acknowledged that I was a sinner. I asked for forgiveness for my sins, that Jesus Christ is the son of God and He died on the cross for my sins, was buried, and after the third day He rose again. I couldn't believe what had just happened, I just gave my life over to Jesus Christ and it was an amazing feeling of such freedom and release of my heavily burdened heart. Wow, what a day it was! I was immediately hugged by a Pastor who used to conduct the bible studies in our apartment and we just hugged each other for about five minutes and we both cried. Not the normal thing for men to do and especially, for me to be doing now, is it? But once God gets a hold of you, then you are not you anymore. I was embraced by so many people and I felt the love and warmth

in their embraces and I could see the joy in their smiles. We finished the day having the usual Filipino hospitality with a buffet type
lunch and there was so much food, but to be honest I wasn't very
hungry and the food was a little weird looking. After that, we went
home and I just lay in shock and wondered what just happened. I
attended church and started to get to know what this Christian life
was all about and what it meant to have a relationship with Jesus
Christ. I was always looked after by the men in the church and they
would always invite me for bible studies and other events that took
place. Although I took it very easy at the beginning, as it was all new
to me, and I obviously had to check this all out to see what it all
meant and what I had to do in relation to this change of life.

I attended the various groups for bible study and gatherings
whenever I could and I was beginning to get so excited, although
I never knew anything about God and Jesus and how it all works.
After a few months of attending church and group studies, I was
beginning to enjoy this new life; it didn't mean I stopped everything
I used to do overnight. Oh no, it was going to take time for that all to
be changed. However, I did like what I was experiencing and it was
making me stronger and stronger in my relationship with Jesus. So
my wife and I would now be attending church together and going
to certain group studies and even attending prayer meetings, which
felt pretty scary for me. I never liked the prayer meetings as it was
all too weird and not normal to me. I was building a great friendship
with other brothers and sisters in the church and the men were
great. I never really had much interaction with Filipinos before, so
it was pretty awkward at first, not knowing what to say and how
to treat them. I joined another bible study group called the 'cross
cultural' ministry of which was a mixture of men and woman from
different cultures like Scottish (that's me), English, Welsh, African,
Dutch, Filipino and Italian. So that was very interesting and helpful
for me to get along with people. Things were going great and
we were enjoying this new life changing experience. The biggest
problem for me was my work. I never really knew how to handle
this and tell my friends and co-workers of my change of life. I knew
it was going to be really hard and it would be such a challenge for

me to refrain from my old lifestyle of drinking and partying and talking about woman and stories etc.

I had to start somewhere, so I guess the best place was my work. I tried to find ways to slip it in to conversations and drop wee hints but nobody would pick up on it. It was so difficult until eventually I just had to tell people individually, and at the right time, so that they would not make a scene. That didn't work out very well, as there was one of my colleagues who is known for his comical acts and jokes etc that once I told him he just went around and broadcasted it to everybody. I mean, he told the whole company and from then on, it was not a secret anymore. It was pretty embarrassing for me in those days as I was the only one in the company who was a 'born again' Christian and as my friend called it, a member of the 'happy clappy club'. This was frustrating at the beginning as he would constantly make fun of me and I didn't know how to take it, I would get pretty angry but still couldn't really answer back as he always had an answer for everything. I would have just made the situation worse if I tried to answer him back.

It was around the fifth month of my new life with Christ that we got a serious phone call from Scotland, it was from my mother-in-law. She called to say that her husband was rushed into hospital and that he was struggling to breathe due to his illness. My wife was so upset, and so worried, and cried that she was afraid not to see her Dad again as the situation was critical. So without hesitation, we arranged our tickets and went home to Scotland to be with her father. It was pretty bad to see him just lying there as he couldn't even move a muscle or even speak to us. His muscle weakness deteriorated very badly due to this sickness. We stayed there for a week as that was all the time we could take off work, and in that short time we only noticed a little recovery, so he remained in hospital. Once we got back to Dubai my wife was so worried about her father and after a few weeks of hearing that he was back home, he couldn't do anything by himself. She decided that she wanted to go home and look after her Dad. This was obviously a big sacrifice for her and for us, as she was ready to give up her job and our status here in Dubai would change, but when it comes to family, this time she would put them first. My wife went home to take care of her

Dad as he was sick and in a bad condition. To me, this was a sign of a real Christian person who had changed from the selfishness of her own wants and addictions, to giving it up to take care of someone else, a complete act of humility before my very eyes. This to me was a confirmation that God can really change the hearts of people and that He can work miracles in people's lives, after all, he just managed to get a hold of me and that in itself, was a miracle for me to see and believe. So no one can tell me that God isn't real, and that he can't change a person. Once you experience the Grace of God in your life whether it is in your own personal circumstances, or with a family member, co-worker or even friend, then you will realize that this is not a game we are playing, this is real people, with real lives, living in a real world. God doesn't play games with us, He teaches us, He directs us, He gives us instructions on how to manage our lives and get through the various challenges, the trials, the obstacles and barriers that are in our way. He always provides us a way out; we just have to look for it. How does He do that? By giving us His word, the Holy Bible, the spoken words of God. The bible is an encyclopedia of everything you will ever need in your life, it has all the wisdom, guidance, direction, purpose, the right and the wrong ways, the punishments, the healings and most important the truth. All we have to do is believe, just believe that God is real and that He gave his only begotten Son to die on that cross for you and for me, so that we could have everlasting life.

It was going to be difficult for us having my wife so far away and us giving up our comfortable lives together with no more involvement together in the ministry, but what could we do? Her mother, being the wee magnificent woman that she is, couldn't look after her father on her own, she was such a frail wee woman and her father was rather heavy big chap, so it had to be done. My wife travelled back to Scotland to look after her father and I was left in Dubai. It is never easy for a couple to be away from each other and especially as we were relatively new Christians, so it is very important that we were together so we can help each other with our walk with Jesus. I would always keep in touch by telephone and calling most nights. A few months had past and I started to feel a little strange when I was speaking to my wife on the telephone, it was as if she was distant from me, I mean, it felt like she was not really interested in talking with me or knowing what was going on with me. I would ask her if everything was alright, thinking that she was worried and concerned about her Dad's health, but it wasn't that. I would think it was because she was maybe bored for not working and being stuck in the house everyday but it wasn't that either. There didn't seem to be an answer to her attitude and she would always say everything is ok. Then one time shortly after I called, it was her Mum who answered the phone as my wife was out. I would ask her where she was as she knew I would always call at this time. She was hesitant for a while and then she came out with the truth and told me that my wife went to see her old boyfriend and had been seeing him for a few months. She said that she was sorry for not telling me sooner but she was told by my wife not to mention anything as they were just having coffee together and that she was just visiting his club. Well, can you imagine what was going through my mind and I can't even get a hold of my wife to talk to her, she seems to be off coffee drinking or whatever with her old boyfriend. I couldn't sleep that night and I called her as soon as it was feasible with the time difference between Dubai and Scotland. I got a hold of her on the phone the next day and I asked her what was going on, that her Mum had told me that she was visiting her old boyfriend. Well at first she denied it, but then, once she knew I was not letting her away with it, she admitted she was only having coffee with him and she visited his club. Oh his club! It's a martial arts club, he is a martial arts expert and that is where she met him. She wanted to learn martial arts and after a while they became boyfriend and girlfriend. This was not kicking it with me at all, I asked her why she needed to see him, why she felt the need to have coffee with him or even go to his club. She said it was just a coffee and then he invited her to see his new facility so she went and that was all it was. She assured me that nothing was going on and that she would not go back again to see him, so for me that was good as gold, as I totally trusted my wife with my life as I mentioned previously. After we got that out of our hair we just chatted and everything was fine. We discussed the issue and resolved it, so I thought. We spoke many times that week and we were on good terms but I still felt something wasn't right. I still had in my mind why she needed to see him but I was not going to bring it up again, it was finished. Then, all of a sudden she hit me with the bomb-shell, she told me that she was seeing her old boyfriend and that they were having an affair together. Oh man, if you could only have seen my reaction, I was so angry and I was screaming at her over the phone. I lost the plot altogether, I mean, I went crazy at her and I just couldn't stop giving her abuse over the phone. It was purely disbelief; I could not believe what I was hearing. Here I am listening to my wife of five years, my fiancé of five years, my girlfriend of five years my partner in life for 15 years, telling me over the phone that she is having an affair with her old boyfriend! I wasn't taking this in, I was so in shock that I just thought I was hearing things, I would ask question after question in order to try to comprehend what was going on here, and all she could say is that she loved him.

I was so lost that night after hearing those words, when I couldn't listen anymore I slammed the phone down on her with rage, and I wanted to smash everything in my apartment. I didn't know what to do at this point, I was so in shock and I couldn't really talk to anyone, I wouldn't even know where to start. I couldn't sleep at all, I was crying and crying, and now I understand when people say they cry until there were no tears left to come out, well that was me that night. I never went to work that next day as I could not face anyone with what I just went through and I am not the person that can hide my feelings. I couldn't wait to call my wife again and talk. I called her when I was off that day. I was calm this time, as I needed answers to why this act of adultery, lust or whatever it is best described, I needed to know what was really going on and why. I asked my wife to explain everything to me, the full chain of events, I needed to know. She explained that it really started with them having a coffee and I even questioned, "Why would you need to go for a coffee with him?" After going back and forth with so many questions and trying to figure out her answers, I decided the best thing to do, fly to Scotland to talk face to face and deal with the situation. I was so shocked when she told me not to bother coming home as there is no point, she said that she was in love with him and wanted to be with him. Man, I couldn't believe what

I was hearing I was stuck for words and felt a total loss inside, as if someone had just ripped my heart out. I have never felt such a feeling of complete and utter emptiness. Although she told me not to come home I said, "I would be on a plane and home at the weekend as we needed to talk".

I can't imagine what was going through her mind at this time; there are no words to express how I was feeling in regards to her doing this, I mean, the last person in the world I thought would hurt me would be my wife. I got there a few days later and planned to spend a week there hoping I could turn this situation around and come back with a positive result. I got there to my parents house and I never told them what had happened and I was honestly not planning to tell anyone, I just wanted to get to the bottom of it and get it resolved and save my marriage. I went up to her parent's house the next day and she wasn't there, I spent a few hours with her parents asking them what they knew about this situation and they were devastated. They could hardly look me in the face with embarrassment and they kept apologizing for her actions, but hey, it had nothing to do with them. They couldn't believe that after the way she was raised, she could turn around and do this to me. I got the story from them how it all started with the coffee, and then visits to the club, and then the affair started, and she told them first before me, that she was having an affair with him and she wanted to be with him. Her Mum was the one to call her and ask her to come to the house so we can talk and she refused to come, I mean, she didn't even want to see me or speak to me. She had made her mind up that we were over and was not willing to discuss it. I was feeling so useless, so helpless so ashamed of how I could allow my wife to do this to me. I started to think why I left her behind in the first place? But this was just the rejection setting in and the feeling of not being accepted by my own wife. Her mother persuaded her to come and talk and it was the least she could do so we can work things out, eventually she agreed to come and I waited, and waited. When she came in she wouldn't even come near me, I went to give her a hug and she turned away. I couldn't believe what was happening, she sat down on the sofa opposite me and said so prideful and arrogant, "Well, what you want?" What a start eh? So I kept my calm as I knew I was going to be fighting an uphill battle from the start, so I just asked her to explain what happened and why. She told me the story and then said that she had fallen out of love with me and she realized that she wanted to be with this other man more than me. Of course I tried to reason with her and say, "How can that be possible? After the years we've been together and the times that we have spent with each other and that we are married and spent fifteen years together". But that seemed to mean nothing to her and she just said, "Well, it's now over, so you need to accept it, and move on". This was her decision and she was sticking to it, and I knew that her boyfriend had been telling her what to say to protect her against me.

After about two hours of me begging her to forget him, and realize that what she is doing is wrong and come back to Dubai with me immediately, and we will start over again. I said to her that I forgive her and was willing to move on and put it behind us, I was willing to put it down to a moment of loneliness and vulnerability, and that she was taken advantage of. But she was not interested or listening to any of my reasoning, she had made her mind up and that was it. That meeting with her ended bad as she just got up and walked out of the house and said for me not to bother contacting her again as it was over and she will be filing for a divorce, she said she wants to marry this other guy. Wow, when I heard those words I just crumbled, I just got a spear thrown into my chest and it was being twisted tighter and tighter and it hurt so much. I was in a state of shock and when she went out I just cried in front of my in-laws and they hugged me and there wasn't a lot of words they could say except they couldn't believe this was happening to us and that she has went down this road after all these years together.

After a day or two went passed, I called up her Mum and asked her to call my wife and arrange a meeting again with her. Can you believe I had to use my mother-in-law to call my wife so I can meet and talk to her? It's like she was the CEO of a huge company and I needed an appointment to see her. Again, she refused to meet me as she said there was no point for us to talk. Nope, she never changed her mind and I never got to see my wife again that trip. I still never told my family about this as I thought it could be solved maybe once she had time to think things over and realize the mistake that she is making. One of the things that really got to me was that we were supposed to be Christians and yet, she committed adultery and was willing to give up her marriage and get a divorce. I returned to Dubai a very sad, confused and ashamed young man not knowing what to do with my life and how to deal with this tragedy. I never mentioned anything to anyone as of yet except to my boss, as he would need to know why I would be taking time off work as I planned to visit home as often as I could in the next weeks or months to try to save my marriage.

I went home again after one month, I thought it would be a good idea to let my wife cool down hoping it would allow her time to think things through as we normally did when we are going through a phase where things are not going that well. Sometimes it works, and I was praying that in this occasion, it would work for me. So here I go again for the second time flying back home for another shot at the title of bringing my wife home with me and saving our marriage. I kept thinking about the Christian part of life this time and not the human part. I tried reasoning with my wife on human terms, expressing my love and concern about her, expressing the years we spent together and the challenges we faced and came through as a couple, the barriers we got over in dealing with many situations and trials and yet, we allowed things to come to this. So it was time for God to be brought into the picture, after all, we are born again and we should be trusting on God now for results in our lives, correct? I remember the scripture reading in Mark 10:9, "Therefore what God has joined together, let man not separate" (NIV Translation). I was quoting scripture and believing that this is the truth, and that we must follow it and that it would bring us back together again. It wasn't to be, my wife agreed to meet me again but it was for an even shorter time than the last one and she was consistent in what she wanted and was doing. She stated that, I was wasting my time and she had no intentions of us getting back together, she had made up her mind, she had made her decision and that was to be with this other man. I tried to speak to her from a Christian point of view and was reminding her that she gave her heart to Jesus and was a changed person, and that this was a moment of where she was lonely and was taken advantage off, but that seemed to make her angry and defended her boyfriend. This method seemed to backfire on me as she claimed that she didn't really give her life to Jesus and that it was maybe a mistake. That she was just persuaded into that environment. I quickly defended the faith and Jesus and explained, that God called her and people witnessed the changes in her life and that she was enjoying the fellowships and being in the presence of God. And explained that God was really working in her life, and she might not know it and she might not want to accept it at this time, but it was evident to others. But she cut me off and said that I was just making this up and she wasn't interested in listening to me anymore.

Things got really worse and she told me not to try to contact her again and she told her parents not to contact her either when I was in town, as she wasn't interested. So again I went back to Dubai after spending another week at home and she would only see me that one time. I would come back again the third time and to let you know another part of this tragedy was that, we recently purchased a brand new house in Glasgow, very close to her parent's house and she was living there while I was in Dubai and we had plans to rent it out when she came over. I was sending the majority of my salary to pay for the mortgage and the bills etc and keep the roof over her head. On my next visit, I said I will be spending my time living in our house for the week, I was thinking if we were in the same house it may change her feelings and we can build on our relationship. This must work, as we will be sleeping together as we had no other beds in the house, as it was all we could afford to furnish one room at that time. So here I come back the fourth time with great confidence that this time it will work, as once we make love again our love will be rekindled and the spark will be ignited again.

I arrived at our house and I was so happy to be back there and she was in waiting for me of which I thought was a great sign because before I had to make an appointment and call for her, things were off to a great start I thought. Well, I was about to be in for the biggest shock of my life. I was looking around inside the house just admiring our house and what we accomplished, I tried to work on her through the materialism as I knew that was a very high point for her, as she loved the materialistic side of things. But she was not even interested in anything I had to say about the contents, or the house. Anyway, I started doing my rounds and went upstairs to the bedrooms and when I went into our bedroom I go the most sickening feeling in my stomach, I got a sense of evil being in that room and I felt unclean in it. I noticed that the bed covers were not made, like she just woke up and never corrected the bed covers, and I asked her if she was just sleeping or what? She said she never had time to clean up, but I knew in my heart and soul that what she said was a lie and I had a gut feeling that her boyfriend was in this house and in my bed. I confronted her and I was right, this guy had been sleeping with my wife in my house and even worse in my bed and we were about to share the same bed. But I had to keep my composure as I was there for one thing, and one thing only, to save my marriage at all costs. I had to swallow whatever pride I had in myself to cope up and deal with this situation. I had to turn a blind eye to the circumstances and think positive, think marriage, think family, think restoration. I know for a fact that the only reason that I was there was because God was working in my life. God was giving me the strength and courage to deal with this situation. I knew that God had a plan, what it was? I had no idea, but I just had peace in my heart that I knew He would work out something according to His purpose.

We got down to sleeping that night and I would try to put my arms around my wife and show her love, to try to see if we can spark a little fire again, but she rejected me and told me not to bother, as nothing will happen. I accepted this, as it was only the first night, so I said, "Patience Sean". We have all week and she will come round, still thinking I had it all planned out. She woke up first in the morning and then I followed shortly afterwards, I went down stairs just to see where she was, she was having tee in the kitchen, so I tried to chat and was not really getting anywhere, but still, patience was on my agenda and I had to persevere. I just went up stairs and into the bathroom and to my complete shock I found a pregnancy test stick in the toilet garbage bin and you won't believe what it read. Indeed, it was a positive result, my wife was pregnant, and I guess you don't have to be Albert Einstein to work out that it wasn't by me. This really knocked me of my feet, at this moment I just froze, I was sick inside my stomach that I wanted to vomit, and at the same time I was so angry and hurt and disgusted. I called her up and addressed the issue and asked her to explain, as if it needed explaining, but I needed to hear it from her. She admitted that she was six weeks pregnant and I didn't even have to ask her who was the father, but she took great joy in telling me that it was her boyfriend, that he was the father, and that is why we are over. She even rubbed it in even more by saying that he has been sleeping in my house with her in my bed and that they have been going away for holiday weekends with the money that I sent home from my salary. There are no words to use for how I was feeling at this moment, knowing that all I was doing was feeding their affair with my hard earned money. I just looked at her and expressed my sadness in what she is doing to us and to herself. I couldn't believe my wife has fallen pregnant to another man after all those years of not wanting a baby with me. She was so adamant that she didn't want kids and just wanted to focus on her career and have a great life. That all seemed to change for her and this was what she wanted in her life now and it seemed to tie the knot in the end of our relationship. At this point, I was finished, I couldn't take anymore. I had reached the end of my rope. I couldn't go on any further and I couldn't ask God for help as I was drained, and I wasn't that long in the Lord to deal with this kind of hardship. I was just a baby Christian. So at that very point, I told her that she has broken me and there is nothing left inside me. She has stripped off, all my dignity, all my honor as a man, as a husband, she has taken my heart and destroyed our marriage and life together, and she simply couldn't care, her actions said it all. So I advised her not to let this man back in our house or I will get the police involved. I told her that she will not be living in this house as I will lock it up as soon as she leaves this day. She will not be allowed to enter back into this house unless I am present. I said "We will be selling the house and everything in it, so please take what you want now, or come back later as the rest will be given away".

After this, I went straight to my parent's house and told them the full story, man they were so mad and couldn't believe it, I have never seen them so angry like this before and they started to really go crazy. I managed to calm them down after a while and just console them in such a way to tell them that, I will be ok. I told them that I understand their actions but it won't get us anywhere and we just have to work through it and that I will need them more than ever in order to help me through this. My family was so shocked and never really had goods words to say about the situation, but that is understandable, considering what had just happened to their youngest child. After staying with them for a week, I started the preparation of getting in touch with a lawyer for the house sale and all the personal items. I headed back to Dubai not having a clue how I was going to handle this break up. I had to face a lot of people and obviously explain my wife just had an affair with another man and that she wants to divorce me. There was no training, no preparation, no planning, no skills or talents you can learn, in helping you to deal with such a life changing event. There is only one thing I had left that I could turn to, that I could possibly have a way to allow me to overcome this situation, only one thing that I would need to hold onto and trust, and that is God. Before that, I had to try and convince my wife not to divorce me and I knew as a Christian, and a child of God, that God hates divorce and it is forbidden in the bible, so I was trying to follow this command and instruction to the end because what would happen to me if I divorced.

After a month or so, back in Dubai, I got a call from my Mum saying that the divorce papers had come to the house and that my wife wanted my consent to file for a divorce. So after a while, I contacted a lawyer and expressed my denial of accepting to file for a divorce. This was then related back to my wife and her lawyer, but then she sent another lawyers letter stating that she will take it to the courts without my concern and have it carried out and all will come out in the open. After consulting my lawyer he advised that I should accept, and let it go though, as there was no signs of any possible reconciliation between us and that she is pregnant with another man's child, so she had grounds for herself to force it through and at the same time, am I ready for all this to come out in an open court for her to win the battle in the end to my embarrassment? So I agreed, I signed the papers for the divorce and it went through after two to three months, the divorce was final, it was all over, I was not married to my wife, my partner of fifteen years just like that. I felt that someone had just stripped fifteen years of my life in a split second. Once all my colleagues at work found out, I knew that they were probably making some sort of fun of me, you know how it goes when a wife may cheat on husband, and they automatically think that the husband is not good enough for his wife or not satisfying her needs, and all that stuff. Although it was so hard to face them, I knew that there was someone greater in me, someone much stronger than I was; someone far powerful than man or any situation and that was, my God. The first weeks back in Dubai were horrible, I had never felt so lonely in my whole life, I was devastated and in a very bad shape. I felt sorry for myself and couldn't get over the fact that I was being divorced. I got to the extremes of depression that I even set up my video recorder and started making a video of myself and expressing how much of a loser I was in not even being able to save my marriage. How, I allowed another man to sleep with my wife and now she is having his baby and she never wanted one with me? I was at the edge of doing something really stupid because I felt so hopeless, so useless, so lonely, so ashamed and embarrassed, as disgusted with my failure in life as a married man, as a husband. The video that I recorded was so shameful and degrading, it didn't justify the true me, my positive nature, as it was just so depressing for me to look back and think of how I could have felt this way? But when Satan gets a hold of you and starts his work in your life, then he is out to do as much damage to you as he possibly can and this was the signs for me that he wasn't just satisfied of ruining my marriage, but he wanted me finished off, he wanted complete destruction of my soul, but that wasn't his to take, that belongs to God. I was so concerned on how I continue as a Christian, on how I continue my faith with God, knowing that I broke a huge command by God. I was a young Christian as I shared with you earlier and never really knew anything about the bible or scriptures verses to deal with this kind of circumstance in my life, and I was not the boldest guy in regards to my Christian faith. I was still very shy and reserved; it wasn't easy for me to share things with others and especially a huge thing like a divorce. I decided to lock myself in my apartment in Dubai for as long as it takes in order for God to reveal His true presence to me, in how I was going to get through this and continue my walk, or just walk away and give up, and go back to my old lifestyle, it was just between me and God now.

This is when it all began, this is when I came before God in all honesty, all humility and completely surrendered myself to Him. There was nothing I could do on my own behalf in order to see me through this situation. There was no person who could tell me that this happens for a reason and that I can, or cannot serve God being a divorced man. So I gave God my utmost attention, I took two weeks off work and stayed in my apartment and got down to business with God. I came before God in prayer, crying my eyes out in a way that I never thought was possible for me, being the shy and reserved Christian, being a man who is supposed to be the head of the house, the macho part of a relationship, the tuff as nails symbol, not me. When I asked God for His presence, He was ready and waiting, just to see how much I was willing to allow Him to move, to allow Him to take over, to allow Him to show Himself to be real to me, and boy, He is real! I would be down on my knees and just focusing on Jesus, focusing on what Jesus did on that cross, focusing on the reason why God allowed His only begotten Son to die on that cross for my sins, focusing on God's love for all mankind.

I was constantly communicating with God though my cries, through my broken heart, through my bitterness and anger, through my hatred, through my jealousy and envy of such a man taking away my wife from me. I was coming before God in a way I have never done before, or even thought I was capable of doing, due to my lack of experience as a Christian, but I was not holding back here, this is where the rubber met the road; this is where my faith in Jesus would be put to the test. This is where I would find out if I really accepted Jesus Christ as my Lord and Savior. There was no negotiating on this one, there was no thinking about this one, and this was it. It was all or nothing for me. If He was not real then I would be walking away from this thing called Christianity and all that was associated with it.

I would put my Christian DVD's on and would start worshiping God. I would give my utmost focus on praising the name of Jesus; I would be exalting His name above every other name. I would be magnifying His holy name and rejoicing in the main room of my apartment. This was my breaking point with my relationship with God, in such a way, that I would never be the same in my worship. I would never be the same in how I would praise His name. During my worship with Him I would constantly be on my knees and crying out for His mercy and grace, crying out for His sanctification, His justification and His cleansing of all my iniquities. This was such an awesome experience that I was at times, lost in His presence and lost track of time. I would just praise and worship, praise and worship, praise and worship the name of Jesus to highest point of my whole being. There was no distractions, no disturbances, no obstacles in my way; it was just me and the Holy Spirit working together showing me that my God is true, real and alive. After days and days of worshiping God I would be laying flat on the ground trying to get as low as I could in honoring God, getting on my knees was not low enough for me to show my humility and honor towards God. I knew He was working with me during this time and that He was working on a breakthrough with me in all areas of my relationship with Him. I loved the fact that I was lying on the ground as low as I could asking for God's mercy and grace to be upon me, to forgive me for my sins, to forgive me for my actions, to forgive me for not being able to stop my wife divorcing me. But coming to the point of surrender, that I tried everything I could to reconcile my marriage, to reconcile our relationship, to mend my broken heart and offer forgiveness to her for what she had done, to assure me that I can still follow Him because of a divorce.

I was asking and seeking two things from God to assure me, I had a true relationship with Him. The first one was that, I can continue to remain a child of God and that was through the revelation of His word about divorce, and the second one was a break-through in worship, to be released from this curse of divorce and depression. In the NIV bible version, Jesus says in Matthew 19:9, "I tell you that anyone who divorces his wife, except for marital unfaithfulness, and marries another woman commits adultery". This was an assurance for me that I will not be abandoned by God in agreeing to my wife's request for a divorce. It was for the reason that was mentioned in the bible. Why? Because of the hardness of the heart of my wife, she left the throne of God to commit adultery. You see my friends, when we decide to harden our hearts during any conflict, you are leaving the presence of God, and you are departing yourself from coming before the throne of God and seeking His grace. You are simply allowing Satan to come in and take control of your heart and therefore, allowing him to rule over you. "Above all else, guard your heart, for it is the wellspring of life" (Proverbs 4:23, NIV Translation).

In the worship part, I was really losing myself to God and going all out in order to receive the break-through that I needed in order to be released from the bondage that Satan wanted me to remain in, the bondage of depression, loneliness, rejection, bitterness, anger and all the evil associated with possible revenge. So I was down before God acknowledging who He was, what He has done for me, and what He is going to do for me. He is the God of all creation, the Maker of the heaven and earth, the Creator of the universe, the highest God, our Redeemer, our Savior and the mighty God. I never felt so blessed and so honored to be in the presence of God and felt the moving of the Holy Spirit in this way. And that is why I know now that we truly have a personal relationship with Jesus and we just have to come to that point of surrender to enable Him to show Himself in such a way that you know it can only be by the grace, mercy and love of God that can conquer all aspects of our lives. For me, this was it, this was my moving forward point, I was praising and worshiping God with my DVD's going into my second week in my apartment enclosed, and on my own, when I was worshiping along to a Don Moen DVD and then came my breaking point. I was asking and seeking Gods revelation and on comes the song, 'God will make a way, where there seems to be no way, He works in ways we cannot see, He will make a way for me, He will be my guide, hold me closely to His side, with love and strength for each new day, He will make a way, God will make a way'. Well, let me tell you friends that brought me to my knees, in complete and utter surrender to His Authority over my life. That was my security right there. I felt that God was wrapping His arms around me right there and then, He just confirmed to me that no matter what we will face, no matter what we will go through, no matter how difficult it gets, no matter the struggles and trials, no matter the hardships, no matter the rejections, He will make a way. This is now the turning point in my relationship with God, this is where He met me in my need and now it is my turn to meet Him in being used to reach out and tell the world of His great love, His mercy and His grace that each one of us can share, and will experience if, we truly surrender our lives to Jesus. God didn't just give up His son for me, or for America, or for United Kingdom or Europe, nor for Asia or Africa but for the whole world, so that whoever shall believe, they shall have everlasting life.

As I continue my journey in life, there is no better way for me to share God's love and blessings in my life than to reach out to the world by writing my experiences down and allowing others to see how God works in my life, in my families lives, how He works in the workplace, and in every aspect of me. I cannot get around the world, so I trust God to do it His way, in the form of this book. So I encourage you to take a bold step in your walk with God and put your trust in Him, rely on Him to guide your paths, believe in Him to direct you towards the right decisions and actions that you will make and just stand back in Awe when He does His marvelous works. Join me as I go deeper into my walk with God and as He allows His spirit to work within me in writing my next book that will allow us to experience God in a more supernatural way, in a more powerful way, in how He reveals His plans and purpose for our life. Life is one big journey of which, many challenges will come our way, many pathways to take. I ask you today, take the one path that leads you to your salvation, take the path that will secure your heavenly place that will allow you to enter the gates of heaven and that is, accepting Jesus Christ as your Lord and Savior. If you want a life changing event, if you want to place your life in the hands of the highest power, if you want to conquer your fears and be able to lift yourself above all obstacles and hindrances in your life then I challenge you right now to repeat this prayer. Just say this with an open and honest heart, this is between you and God, not me and not any church, or organization, it's personal.

"Jesus, I come before you a sinner, I acknowledge that I have strayed so far in my life and I know that I have done things wrong and I repent right now. Forgive me and let me come to know you in a special way. I confess with my mouth that Jesus, you are the son of God, that you died and rose again, and was crucified on the cross and you bore the sins of man, and that by your stripes we are healed. Jesus, I accept you into my heart as my Lord and Savior. Change me oh God, and make me a new creation. In Jesus name, I pray, Amen".

Friends if you have just prayed this prayer, get to the nearest bible based church in your area, email a church, email a Christian radio station and ask for a church in your area. Go and share you new relationship with God to others. I praise God for allowing you to join me in this journey. And as He uses me to unfold my remaining stories, on how did I walk hand in hand with God to conquer the different pathways to an ultimate journey, it is my prayer that you will continue to see God's love and mercy in each story.

The Lord blesses you and keeps you. The Lord makes His face to shine upon you and give you peace. The Lord makes His countenance upon you and is gracious unto you, Amen. God willing, I will be joining you again in 'One Journey Different Pathways, A Scotsman's Life Story', book II where you can experience with me God's wonderful and amazing attributes. I humbly say, "Thank You Lord" and may God bless us all!

TO GOD, BE THE GLORY!